THE EDUCATION OF
AN AMERICAN SOCCER PLAYER
IS SOCCER'S *BALL FOUR*

"THE FINEST BOOK YET
ON THE U.S. SOCCER EXPLOSION."
—UPI

"A DANDY BOOK . . .
You don't have to ever have seen a
soccer game to appreciate it."
—NEW YORK POST

"Messing is much like the league in
which he plays . . . young, brash, lucky."
—SPORTS ILLUSTRATED

"Extraordinarily amusing, irreverent,
really more about people than sports."
—NEWSDAY

"IT IS A BOOK FOR EVERYONE . . .
Breezy, thoughtful, humorous, tender
and insightful. Messing pulls no
punches and he has a lot to tell."
—HOWARD COSELL

THE
EDUCATION
OF AN
AMERICAN
SOCCER
PLAYER

SHEP MESSING
with David Hirshey

Illustrated with photographs

BANTAM BOOKS
TORONTO · NEW YORK · LONDON

THE EDUCATION OF AN AMERICAN SOCCER PLAYER
*A Bantam Book / published by arrangement with
Dodd, Mead & Company*

PRINTING HISTORY
*Dodd, Mead edition published June 1978
Bantam edition / April 1979*

*Bantam Books are published by Bantam Books, Inc. Its trade-
mark, consisting of the words "Bantam Books" and the por-
trayal of a bantam is registered in the United States Patent
Office and in other countries. Marca Registrada. Bantam
Books, Inc., 666 Fifth Avenue, New York, New York 10019.*

PRINTED IN THE UNITED STATES OF AMERICA

For Arden with love,
and to the memory of Milt
S.M.

For Gerri, again and always
D.H.

Acknowledgments

A lot of help went into this book. The authors are inestimably grateful to: Alan Richman for his long-suffering friendship and painstaking editing; Jonathan Dodd for his faith in the project; and especially Peter Weed, for his patience and skill in wrestling it all into shape.

For access to background material, special thanks to: Paul Gardner, Lawrie Mifflin, Peter Bodo, and Steven Singer.

For their staunch support throughout, thanks to: Alan and Bailey Biren, Allen Bernstein, Jim Bouton, Hank and Marianne Clay, Mickey Cohen, Roger Director, P.F. Duomo, Bob Gersten, Hank Gola, Alfred Goldman, Rolf and Grange Habermann, Norrie Harrower, Larry Hausner, T. Howard, Jerry Izenberg, Cynthia Kingdon, Ken Korotkin, Kurt Lamm, Dick Lemon, T. Levinson, Mike Lupica, Alain Maca, Seamus Malin, the late Joe Marcus, Tina Marburg, Steve Martin, Jordi Matons, Julie Menendez, Barry Nova, Dick Schaap, Fred Schruers, Dave Sims, Stan Startzell, Bell Stevenson, Paul Szabo, Jim Trecker, Tina Trimble, George Vargas, Hubert Vogelsinger, and Jack Wilkinson.

ACKNOWLEDGMENTS

And, most of all, we would like to thank our families: Eli, Anne, Marc, Albee, Roy and Grandma Messing; Gert, Debbi, Bobby and Robin Rothenberg; Jeanne and Bob Sommer; and Max Hirshey.

Contents

"What did Dr. Thurmer say to you, boy? I understand you had quite a little chat."

"Yes, we did. We really did. I was in his office around two hours, I guess."

"What'd he say to you?"

"Oh . . . well, about Life being a game and all. And how you should play it according to the rules. He was pretty nice about it. I mean he didn't hit the ceiling or anything. He just kept talking about Life being a game, and all. You know."

"Life *is* a game, boy. Life *is* a game that one plays according to the rules."

"Yes, sir. I know it is. I know it."

Game, my ass. Some game. If you get on the side where all the hot-shots are, then it's a game, all right—I'll admit that. But if you get on the *other* side, where there aren't any hot-shots, then what's a game about it? Nothing. No game.

J. D. Salinger, *The Catcher in the Rye*

Prologue

On Lexington Avenue, the Salvation Army Band is in its pre-Christmas campaign, saving shoppers with a scratchy loudspeaker rendition of "O Come, All Ye Faithful." Upstairs, on the second floor of Bloomingdale's department store, an undercover security man is sweating profusely.

"Keeeeristmas, what a day!" he says, climbing over a red velvet rope. "I got four key operatives keeping the gapers away from Christina Onassis in Designer Coats. I got serious breakage in Fine Furnishings. And now you guys got people lined up to Infants Outerwear. Keeeeristmas. Never figured your floor space beyond ten feet."

My teammate Werner Roth and I are standing under a large banner that reads COSMOS: 1977 NASL CHAMPS. We're tucked into a niche, between a Bloomie's Panties display and the Young Gentleman's department, signing 8 × 10 glossies as fast as we can peel them off the piles on the table. The crowd is growing and the heat is rising. Pictures are sticking to our hands, smearing the ink. Voices jab at us from the crowd:

"Won a fin on you guys in the playoffs; thanks a lot."

"Hey, Shep, you're number one, baby."

"Does Pele tape his angles?"

A stout woman in a fur coat pokes my ribs with a silver fountain pen. "Right here, Mr. Messing, make it to Barry, the best center forward on the Gramercy Hornets. That's B-A-R-R-Y-E, please."

We autograph arm casts, T-shirts, shopping bags, knapsacks, comic books, visors, sneakers and grimy little hands. Behind us, a salesclerk is burrowing through the piles of soccer shirts, looking for an extra-small with a green Number 1 on the back, muttering something about how the department manager made sure they'd have shirts with Werner's #4 and my #1 on hand. One kid tells me he already has a light blue goalie shirt with "SHEP" on the front. I slip him two extra pictures.

"Soccer is *HOT*," a sportswear buyer had told me when we were setting up. "We have a whole line of soccer style leisure and playwear and," she punched the air in a victory salute, "it is *moving!*"

This is all happening in the only store Queen Elizabeth visited on her Jubilee trip here; the store that features live models between satin sheets, where cookie czar Famous Amos introduced chocolate chip decadence to the Eastern seaboard at $3.50 a bag. It's the high temple of mass chic, a fast paced atmosphere that reminds me of Andy Warhol's famous prediction that someday everyone will be famous for five minutes. In New York, it means you'll get floor space at Bloomie's.

Now, in addition to the Persian bed jackets and ivory back scratchers, Bloomingdale's carries striped English soccer socks, satin soccer trunks, men's and boys' soccer shirts, soccer key chains, soccer books, soccer balls and, today, soccer players.

"If my mother could see me . . ." Werner is interrupted by a kiss from a soccer mommy. Her son is mortified and darts out of sight. I am being backed against a potted palm as the crowd presses the table in against our legs. There's a log jam on the escalator. Werner and I are laughing, loving it.

Suddenly, a shriek. "Look! Cosmos!" The security man is leaping back over the velvet rope, making his way toward the up escalator where two teenage girls are trying to fight their way down. Above them, a man in a bowling jacket turns around and yells over his shoulder, "Hey Messing, go chew on a glass."

"Keeeeeristmas," I say to Werner, laughing. "So this is success."

1

"FOR YOU, FOR YOU"

Sam would have hated Portland. Sure, the air is clean, the sod is fresh and the water bugs are big and juicy. But the moment I arrive there, it begins to rain. And when it's not raining, the sun looks like a moldy crouton in a pea soup sky. No place for a creature accustomed to lounging on the beaches of Long Island, New York. So after checking the coastal weather reports, I decided to leave Sam with my mother-in-law and fly to Oregon without my iguana.

We loaded up in New York, a chartered plane filled with the strange and exotic cargo sometimes called "the Cosmos family." By ones, twos and threes, we all clambered aboard the plane: secretaries teetering on their Carmen Miranda platforms after an hour in the hospitality lounge; grim-faced trainers toting little black bags full of salt tablets, gauze and painkillers; Lanvin-suited executives trailing the kind of women who get rashes from anything less than silk. And the soccer team itself, twenty-one guys who are going to win the championship of the North American Soccer League.

Just a formality, really. The Cosmos had already

made a considerable downpayment on the trophy, something in the neighborhood of $8 million. That's what it had cost to build the richest, most powerful team in the league. Yessir, this charter jet is carrying $8 million worth of talent in just four pairs of shoes: Pele, the greatest player in the history of the game; Franz Beckenbauer, the greatest player at this moment; Carlos Alberto, captain of the 1970 championship Brazilian World Cup team; and Giorgio Chinaglia, the goal scoring legend from Lazio in Italy. Add the more modest salaries of guys like me—salaries still double the league average—and the total investment probably equaled the military budget of a small Third World country.

The flight to Portland is smooth and, by normal standards, uneventful. I take the 14-year-old son of an executive for a quick $20, trip sevens to his Kings up. Tough luck, kid. In-flight hospitality has put traveling secretary Steve Marshall in his usual position, waiting outside that little bathroom where the "Return to seat" sign flashes just as soon as you get in. Assistant trainer Marty Hamrogue is frantically searching through the trashbin for his upper plate which somehow got discarded with the remains of his vulcanized veal.

In the center aisle, my roommate Bobby Smith is doing his imitation of a kamikaze pilot, synchronizing his spasmodic movements to the crackling coming through his headphones. We are watching *The Eagle Has Landed*. At least some of us are. Pele is sleeping with his head on his wife Rose's lap, like a small child on a long trip.

"I never see anybody sleep like Pele," says Peruvian midfielder Ramon Mifflin. "Once, when we play for Santos, I see him sleep from Brussels to Tokyo. Twenty-six hours, half a world, Pele never open his eyes."

5

After traveling with Pele for two years, I'm not sure he sleeps so much as simply shuts his eyes to close off the rest of the world that wants to touch him, talk to him, or cop an autograph on an airline napkin. "It is sometimes the only way to be alone," he once told me. "Very simple to close the eyes."

If this flight is fairly calm, the season that's led up to it has been one long bitching stretch of turbulence, bumpy enough to shake off a coach and a team president as well as a few bewildered players. By August 28, 1977, the Cosmos had survived corporate wars, star wars, player suspensions, fistfights, trade rumors, treachery, deceit, and personality clashes that left more than a few egos in intensive care. The players were like survivors staggering through one of the grislier combat films turned out by our parent company, Warner Communications. The folks who gave the world the devil in *The Exorcist*, killer bees in *The Swarm*, a record company named Asylum and a magazine called *MAD* had also built the Cosmos, an executive toy that seemed destined to self-destruct. "The Boys of Turmoil" one writer labeled us.

For me, it had been an average season: several hundred dollars in fines, five threats of suspension, a half dozen shouting matches with two different coaches and eighteen inches of new scars and stitches. Fan mail was up. Likewise, TV appearances and press interviews: "Yeah, I like to wear a comfortable pair of boa constrictors when I'm lounging around the house. No, I didn't wear anything when I posed for *Viva* Magazine. And there's nothing to eating glass, once you get past the first mouthful. So what if I roomed with a South American bear at Harvard? What's the matter with you guys, anyhow? Never interviewed a goalkeeper before?"

Actually, most of them hadn't. Many of the writers, pulled off the Yankee pennant race or Jets training camp to examine this thing growing in the New Jersey Meadowlands, entered the Cosmos locker room gaping like Omaha schoolteachers examining a circus geek. It was so *unnatural*, so un-American, this game. Yet soccermania was real enough. Henry Kissinger had it, turning up in the Cosmos locker room just as his former boss had done with the Washington Redskins. Elton John had it, and started a new fad among rock stars by buying a team in L.A. Rolling Stone Mick Jagger chipped in with Peter Frampton and Paul Simon to purchase the Philadelphia franchise. Even fashion designer Oscar de la Renta led a contingent of the Perrier-and-lemon set out to the Meadowlands. The beautiful and the near beautiful dropped out of the sky in corporate helicopters, while down below New Jersey housewives in pink polyester pants suits found themselves in traffic jams getting to the games. So did pin-striped stockbrokers, large Ukrainian families, college students, bored baseball fans, the Governor of New York and the President's son. Worried Little League and Pop Warner coaches call it an epidemic; those of us who were there in the beginning, the mud-caked crazies who played for foodstamps and the sheer fun of it, call it a miracle. And the New Jersey Meadowlands, sunken between oil refineries and the Manhattan skyline, is our Lourdes.

Three years ago, before Pele first stepped from a helicopter onto the pitted field of a decrepit Randall's Island, the Cosmos were drawing less than the skin flicks on Eighth Avenue. In 1977, Pele's last season, 77,691 screaming converts had watched us play the Ft. Lauderdale Strikers in Giant Stadium. We started outdrawing the Yankees. The same seats that used to be given away free with each purchase of a Burger King Double Whopper were being scalped at outrageous prices. Once Warners tossed out those Cracker Jack prizes and came up with Pele, the arithmetic was Malthusian: in three seasons, from average gates of 10,449, to 18,227, to 34,142 in 1977. Nothing stopped the fans from coming out, not the mini-monsoon that dumped torrents on 73,669 diehards at the playoff game against the Rochester Lancers nor even the massive traffic jams that stretched back across the Hudson River to the New York side. They wore soccer shirts emblazoned with a favorite player's name and number, T-shirts carrying such slogans as "Soccer is a kick in the grass" and "Soccer players do it for 90 minutes." They arrived with coolers, plastic ponchos, tailgate picnics, bedsheet signs and kids. Thousands of kids—who discovered the joy and freedom of a sport that required no fancy equipment, no brawn or excessive height, no boring strategies, just the ability to run and kick.

This is all like a dream, still playing itself out as we near the end of our present long trip to Portland. Players are smiling in their sleep, perhaps at being able to quit those other jobs many of us held in amusement parks, delis, airline offices, real estate agencies, high schools and wildlife preserves. The wives are smiling, too, past all those TV dinners stretched with soybean fillers, past all the uncertainties. By the time the nose of our 747 is probing the rain clouds over Oregon, the plane is quiet, and I float off into a reverie of my own.

I have several dreams, some short, some technicolor two-reelers. They're daydreams, really, psychic cassettes I can plug into my consciousness. On nights before a big game, they relax me; on a road trip they can ease the soreness of losing, and the tedium of travel. In the short one, I suddenly acquire this gift, the magical talent to pick up a ball I've saved, dropkick it, and to have it sail like a phosphorescent moon into the opposite net for a score. Goal, Messing.

My other dream lasts the whole year:

I'm playing out of my mind, superhuman, invincible; all season long, I haven't allowed a goal. It's more incredible than pitching a string of no-hitters, and by August TV crews are at every game, hunched, waiting, looking for someone to break Messing's streak. Everybody in the world is offering me bonuses, a hundred thousand, a quarter million. Steve Ross, chairman of Warner Communications, offers me a million dollars if I can go the entire season without being scored against. I ask for more.

Finally, it's down to the last game. The shots are coming like heavy artillery. I stop a penalty kick to the upper left corner, deflect it out, a guy hammers it back. I make a foot save, the ball bounces back to a guy running in for a header. He rams it to the opposite corner and I'm floating, slow motion across the goal just in time to punch it out before it kisses the net. It's 2–0 Cosmos with ten seconds to go as I make one last save. I hold the ball and stare up into the crowd until I find Ross' box. I nod to him and point at the ball before I kick it into the net. Defiant and proud. Only Messing scores on Messing.

Practice hits me like a cold shower. It's a grey, clammy morning and beads of moisture cling to the hair of the attendant who swings open the chain link gate to Civic Stadium in Portland.

"Hut one, hut two, hut . . ." Out on the playing field, a Portland State quarterback is fading back to pass. When he sees us, twenty guys in short shorts running onto the field, he signals an end to practice. His hulking teammates gather their gear, grunting as they shove the tackling sled off the field, to make way for the sport of the future.

Our baggage is simple, just a dozen lightweight balls and an armful of towels. For the first time in months, practice is fun; players are yelling, slipping, rolling happily across the scarred, patched Astroturf. On the sidelines, our assistant coach Julio Mazzei is pointing a finger at his close friend and protégé, Pele.

"When you see Pele start to organize things, you know how much it means to him," Mazzei tells a reporter. "He had this same attitude in the 1970 World Cup in Mexico—happily, laughing, involved."

Mazzei knows Pele better than any of us do. He's seen the spark in those expressive brown eyes many times before. He says it comes when Pele has something to prove, an obligation to fulfill.

"When you assemble a group of class players like we have," Mazzei is saying, "it is expected you win. You should produce, and prove that soccer is a game of creativity, art and improvisation, the game Pele is famous for. This should be the future of NASL soccer. If the Cosmos become champions, it will change a lot here. This is the coronation of a mission—when the era of the 3rd and 4th Division English players will be at an end."

I laugh as a reporter scribbles down his words, that old stuff about the British Connection in American soccer that extends from Welsh NASL Commissioner Phil Woosnam down to the third rate carpetbaggers who leave the lower divisions of the English leagues to pick up a few bucks over here.

"U.S. Player Demands: Boot Out English Mafia" read a London tabloid after one of my early eruptions; and for once it wasn't much of a stretch. I'd

10

actually used the word mafia. What else could one call an organization (the NASL) that has, in addition to its Welsh Commissioner, an Englishman in charge of referees, British coaches in over half the franchises, and a player ratio of 40% English to 40% American to 20% *really* foreign? Too many times I'd seen a good American player shoved aside by an English has-been or never-was who couldn't wait to hightail it back across the Atlantic for the start of his own season.

As it just so happens, perfect specimens of this are our opponents the Seattle Sounders—the same scruffy band of lower division renegades now arriving at the far end of the field.

"Limey cocksuckers!" says Smitty, sweetly. "Those guys have put too many of my American friends on the dole. Can't wait to kick the piss out of them."

Pele signals for us to leave and as we move off the field, our traveling sideshow of writers and photographers withdraw as well. This leaves the Seattle players to themselves, except for a band of kids competing on the sidelines in the "Kick Me" contest, the NASL's version of "Punt, Pass and Kick." I love it.

From the moment we touched down here, the Cosmos have been the darlings of the media; and I've enjoyed that to the fullest. Stories have been written about our record crowds, our record salaries, our record executives. The Sounders? They're the mystery guests, treated as an after-thought by everyone except their fans and us.

I've got a personal score to settle here. The Sounders stomped us in Seattle 1–0 early in the season, and it could have been worse. Normally I wouldn't mind. But I *hate* being humbled on national TV.

As the Sounders begin their laps, I head toward

the gate. On the sidelines, a tall sandy-haired man with hairy armpits sticking out of a cut-off sweatshirt is fast-pitching a baseball to a friend. His back is to me, and I can hear the thwack as ball burns into the catcher's glove. Guy's not bad; maybe semi-pro. He turns around and sees me.

"Shit. Messing. Well, shit."

It's Jim Bouton, a former 20-game winner with the Yankees until his fast ball got fat. I had heard he was trying to get back into the game, stray-dogging it with some Triple-A clubs for bus tickets and cheeseburgers. Crazy bastard. But that's why I love him.

Soccerbowl Sunday. My roommate Smitty and I haul ourselves down to the coffee shop at 8:00 for one of Coach Eddie Firmani's sadistic little crack-of-dawn breakfasts—catchem-if-you-can eggs, guaranteed to coat the stomach better than a pint of Texas crude. Outside, fat, swollen rain clouds are roiling around and the waitress says it's a sure thing they'll let loose around noon. Fantastic.

Goalies, like parades, hate rain. You throw yourself at shots that come in as oversize spitters, dipping and skidding over the spongy Astroturf. Dive too soon and you'll end up flopping around the netting like a dying mackerel, with that white ball nestled snugly in the cords. Goddamn rain.

The coffee shop is dotted with players: Pele, Beckenbauer, Chinaglia, the best in the world swilling imitation orange juice at a sticky formica counter. I wonder what Pele can be thinking with just a 90 minute game standing between 22 years of glory and retirement.

The night before I had asked him what he felt when I stopped by his hotel room after the team dinner. He was sitting on the edge of the bed, wearing a lime green jacket and a sphinxlike smile.

Sometimes, Pele can look a thousand years old. He acted as though I'd asked him a difficult riddle, and he didn't answer right away. While I was waiting for him to speak, I noticed his hands, so black against the cream colored bedspread. For a man who makes his living with his feet, they are abnormally calloused, cool and hard when he grasps yours, as though the millions of handshakes have worn them smooth as stone.

"When I retired from Santos, it was different," he said. "I still played exhibitions, still busy with the football. Now it is really the finish. I will stop playing, and that part of me . . ." He paused, smiling again, "That part will die. But it's okay, because another life is born. In my mind, it will be hard. I think someday I will wake up and get my things and go to the stadium, because this is what I do all of my life. Now, I must remember to go to the office. I don't know how I will like this, to sign papers, to speak on the telephone, because 22 years of my life is soccer.

"Now, I will know my children better. So many times Rose tells me I must have more time for my family. So many times, Edinho wants to play, to have me go to his school, and I must always be leaving. Leaving for the airport. No more.

"I have been very lucky. If I could not have been a football player, maybe I would be a housepainter. Maybe work in the factory, in the shop. I would have the same life as everybody else in my town, and I would only have tried to do my best job, wherever I am. For me, it has been simple. I never wanted to be anything but the best I could."

This morning, I'm watching him closely. I think everyone is, secretly, looking for a clue, an omen in that inscrutable face. The way he's attacking his steak, he hardly looks like a condemned man eating his last pre-game meal. I wonder how I'll feel when it has to end.

Smitty interrupts my reverie by flinging a forkful of home fries at Tony Field's head, and we finish our meal laughing.

11:05 I am sick to my stomach. Not nervous sick, but travel sick. Embarrassing, that a hardnosed goalie can't go across town without Dramamine. As the team bus lurches toward the stadium, my stomach stays at the curb.

Portland, Seattle, Tampa, L.A., the seating arrangement on the bus is always the same. More than once it's reminded me of long, rowdy rides on a high school field trip—teachers up front, bad boys in the back.

Behind the driver is Coach Eddie Firmani, who took over the fractured team in mid-season when Gordon Bradley was forced out. Firmani got us back in shape, making hard, ruthless decisions that didn't win him many friends, but did help us start winning games. He had taken Franz from his virtuoso sweeper position and forced him to play midfield. He had moved Pele back to give Chinaglia more room to score. He was given to jerking players all around the field until the chemistry was right. Grudgingly, we respected his expertise, but Eddie isn't the kind of guy you have a beer with after the game.

Next in line is Werner Roth, a 29-year-old American, and team captain. He and I are the only Cosmos that date back further than the vintage LeJeune Brut already on ice in the bowels of Civic Stadium.

"Can you believe it?" he had asked me two nights before as we were standing in the hotel bar having a couple of beers. Our faces were flickering on the television over the bar. It was an interview we'd taped earlier for the evening news, and Werner

14

was coolly analyzing the Sounder defense, leaning into the mike as naturally as he'd been to kiss a woman's cheek.

"Four years ago, we couldn't even get on goddamn cable TV on a goddamn Long Island station."

"Back in the toilet bowl at Randall's Island."

"Back with the old guys."

"Here's to the old guys."

"I offer this toast to Siggy Stritzl."

"Jorge Siega."

"Randy Horton, that crazy fucker."

"Len Renery."

"Here's to the old Cosmos."

"Here's to the new Cosmos."

"Here's to the survivors." We clinked glasses, and emptied them.

Goalkeepers have few better friends than their center fullback, the last vital link between defense and goal, a prowling stopper and jammer who has to remain cool and decisive under attack. On as well as off the field, Werner is graceful and elegant, with a smooth confident step that suggests he grew up negotiating the slick deck of a yacht instead of the pitted streets of the German ghetto in Ridgewood, Queens. Born in Yugoslavia, then forced to move to a halfway camp in Hessen, Germany, he and his family whiteknuckled a harrowing 48-hour flight in 1956, fitting numbed fingertips into the Communist bulletholes that pocked their plane's belly once it had safely touched down in New York.

Werner grew up in the immigrant German-Hungarian leagues, has a degree in design and often talks of designing his own "dream house." Women love him, seem to find his feline magnetism overwhelmingly attractive. But if they tumble for his poster-perfect body and chestnut curls, I value his extraordinary calm, which keeps my confidence afloat when we're being blitzed. Strangely, his

15

aloofness gives me a sense of kinship. As center fullback and goalie, we're the loners on the team, the men whose mistakes are glaring and costly. Werner, the ice man. He can bite the stem off a maraschino cherry and tie it in a knot, all in his mouth.

The next four seats are occupied by the English, sitting like model schoolboys. On opposite sides of the aisle are the two wingers, Tony Field and Steve Hunt. It is the winger who is expected to run the ball along the sideline at lung-breaking speed, stop, and chip a soft balloon crossfield to his strikers lurking around the goalmouth. The wingers are the detonators and, in a sense, their job is the most diversified. First, they must create and seek action; second, they must seize the right moment for finishing it off—for taking up the striker's duty and driving the ball into the opponent's net.

Field plays his position with the finesse of a hyperkinetic jackhammer. At 31, he possesses an inexhaustible store of energy, and the Englishman's enthusiasm for warm lager. Although only 5-7, he can fall off a six-foot barstool in mid-joke without missing a line.

Across the way is Steve Hunt, Field's left wing counterpart, an electric player with the hairtrigger temper of a London street kid. Early in the season we were playing our archrival, the Tampa Bay Rowdies, on national television, and things were not going well, for us in general and for Hunt in particular. Unable to defuse his own competitive appetite, Hunt was speeding up and down the left flank refusing to give the ball up except on wild shots goalward. Pele tried to calm him, extending his arms downward and saying "Easy, Steve, easy. Pass the ball." Hunt whirled around and in full view of everyone, impudently plugged his ears.

"Fuck you," he screamed at Pele, and for a moment I felt like decking him. For me, abusing Pele is akin to spitting on the flag.

Hunt blew up once again and this time it nearly landed him on his ass. Mired in a slump, George botched one of Hunt's passes in practice. "Stupid," Steve yelled. And when George missed a second: "Idiot." George promptly staggered him with a right cross. But he forgave Steve just as quickly, as did Pele.

Once I got to know Steve better, it was easy to see why two older, experienced players would take his tantrums in stride. They must have understood the situation. At 21, he's confused and unsure of himself. He's never been away from his home in Birmingham, England, for so long, and for his 19-year-old wife Sue, the loneliness and isolation of being an athlete's wife is more than she can endure. The Cosmos have settled them in suburban New Jersey, quite far from the rest of us, and coming into New York City frightened them to death. Just before the playoffs, Sue returned to England, saying she couldn't wait until the end of the season. I know that with all the craziness this year, I'd have gone mad without Arden. No, I couldn't blame Steve Hunt for an occasional outburst. All that frustration had to escape somehow.

The other two jolly Englishmen are Mike Dillon and Terry Garbett. Terry is the epitome of relentless British intensity, a powerful midfielder who has worked himself to near prostration in the last few playoff games. Terry is one of the reasons we were able to pull it all together. He dismissed all the season's ugliness with characteristic nonchalance: "When you mix a cake, there's a helluva mess until it comes out right."

Just beyond their impassive faces is the boyish

17

grin of Franz Beckenbauer, the Kaiser of Bayern Munich who abdicated his European throne to play in the New World. When former Cosmos President Clive Toye signed him, West Germany took the news of Beckenbauer's defection in traditional style. The reaction was the same as when the *Bismarck* sank.

There is no doubt that Franz is the finest player alive. He is a sleek, courtly midfielder who slips serenely into the fray and strips the ball from an opponent with the finesse of a Continental jewel thief. German papers branded him a traitor and a mercenary at the time of his departure but he is a quiet, cordial man who speaks excellent English, without a trace of arrogance. At certain moments, he appears wide-eyed, almost naive, delighted to walk down Fifth Avenue without being mobbed, giggling when I talked him into scrapping his blow dryer and letting his curly hair dry by itself into a "natural." The only time I saw him stiffen was in the locker room after his first game when I began joking with reporters. He said he couldn't believe I could be so open with "those people," and the next night, after dinner at my parents' house, he explained his discomfort:

"The negotiations with the Cosmos had been going on for two years. But I never expressed any interest until January 1977. You know, I was 31 years old and the time of glory for my club, Bayern Munich, was over. After the tremendous success we had enjoyed, there was not much appeal to fight at the end of my career for a mediocre position in the league table. So I decided to visit New York and was very impressed with the Warners people. They were making jokes with millions. Steve Ross told me to call him Steve. Never in Europe have I heard of calling your boss by his first name. I was struck by the contrast between the relaxed atmosphere in New York and the narrow bourgeois habits I was finding in Germany.

"When I arrived home, I told Bayern president Wilhelm Neudecker about the Cosmos offer and he spoke to the national team coach Helmut Schoen. The next day I was asked to be Schoen's assistant coach. There is much pressure to take the job and stay in Germany.

"In my mind, I decide not to make a change of clubs until after the 1978 World Cup. But then on April 6, a story appears in the newspaper *Die Welt* with the headline, "The Kaiser's Private Life Is Tense." Using anonymous sources, the story accused me of adultery, tax evasion, bringing Bayern Munich to bankruptcy and betrayal of the national team before the World Cup.

"This is the start of the most unpleasant three weeks of my existence. I am a human being, with a good many defects, but because I am the Kaiser, the press thinks my private life is for the public.

"Those were days of pure horror for me and my family. I discovered the other side of glory. After the stories I realized I could no longer live in Munich. I told my manager Robert Schwan to call Clive Toye and tell him I am ready to consider the Cosmos offer. But if the press campaign had not taken place, I would not have left."

In the center of the bus is the Brazilian rhythm section, singing, chanting, clacking samba cadence on seat backs with Zippo lighters and ballpoint pens. At the center is Pele, laughing and singing like a kid. He is the village elder, the spokesman, the lifesaving buoyancy that keeps this small bit of Brazilian flotsam afloat as the five men navigate the bewildering rush of American sport. Pele will tell them when the bus leaves, interpret a plane

19

schedule, shepherd a homesick couple to the friendly Brazilian restaurant on West 46th Street that warms the soul with spicy, steaming black beans and fish stews.

Sitting beside Pele is Nelsi Morais, his former Santos teammate, a short, aggressive defender with a baby face and hundred-year-old eyes. Behind him is Ramon Mifflin, the quintessential soccer vagabond, a Peruvian native who has bounced across South America, playing first for his country Peru, then with Pele at Santos, now as a midfielder for the Cosmos. Ramon answers to the nickname "Cabeza," which means "head," the highest compliment for an intelligent midfielder charged with the difficult task of choreographing the attack.

Sitting slightly apart, feet barely tapping to the carnival din, is sweeper Carlos Alberto, the sturdiest thing between me and the opposing front line. Carlos is Señor Supercool, a man who always knows exactly where he's going and just how long it will take to arrive. Carlos established our team's traveling style by wearing his French-cut sport coat flung cape-like over his shoulder; just as it was Carlos whose watersmooth passes finally linked the concepts of poetry and defense. His are never the blind, desperate clears of trench warfare; miraculously, his balls float lazily out of danger, touching down at a point immediately adjacent to a teammate's right instep. Off season in Brazil, he paints sensitive portraits of clowns that have earned him one-man shows.

My wife Arden and I once visited Carlos in Brazil. He is a different man on his native soil, much more talkative as we drove through the streets of Rio. "Pele and I represent two different levels of the Brazilian poor," he said, smiling. "He was the poor boy from the country, from the beaches. Me, I come from the city where every street is filled with young boys, all playing football. For them, football can be the key to heaven."

We were passing along the fringes of the battered residential sections that lie between the gleaming modern city of the travel posters and the *favelas*—slums so horrible they make Harlem look middle class. Carlos' story sounded familiar, like those of inner city basketball players who make it to high rise apartments on the strength of their jump shots. Now Carlos has a duplex in Copacabana and a happy split-level life.

At the back of the bus, the Rough Riders are doing their usual thing: George Chinaglia, Bobby Smith, Erol Yasin and me, rumbling along like the class cut-ups.

George, our striker, is an uncontested superstar in Italy but misunderstood in this country. A large, good looking bear of a man, he spreads hundred dollar bills around like the Godfather dispenses favors. His friends knows a warm, generous, witty Chinaglia; his critics describe an arrogant, calculating man who plays soccer with the grace of a gangland enforcer. Actually, he's both a formidable enemy and a loyal friend—a hard-nosed businessman touched with the mischief of a ten-year-old. He'll spend the day poring over his investments and the night playing electronic baseball, feverishly computing box scores until he's sure he's won. George loves VIP dinners, fast cars, his lavish New Jersey home, Chivas Regal, and winning. He's an armful of contradictions, and I enjoy the hell out of him.

George's other friend on the team is Erol Yasin, the quiet, capable Turkish goalie who is the particular favorite of two Cosmos executives. These men are brothers. Turkish brothers. Ahmet and Neshui Ertegun's dabbling has caused some problems, but never between Erol and me.

Last we come to Smitty, my roommate, the bearded imp. Smitty is a congenital, congenial crazy. The story goes that when he was born, the doctor slapped him and Smitty coldcocked him. He's had a terrible temper ever since. This year it cost him a 16-game suspension when he demolished a blackboard and challenged Coach Gordon Bradley to a fight because he had been left out of the starting lineup. "I'd do the same thing again," Smitty says, repentent as always. "The bastard lied to me." For Smitty, the game is all that matters. He would rather get his kicks than his paycheck. "When I'm on a soccer field, I feel invincible," Smitty once told me in a Wild Turkey dither. "Walking down the street, I'm just another asshole."

Together in a hotel room, we regress a few years, playing Frisbee in the halls or skimming cold pancakes out the window. It's Smitty and I who get the bedchecks, Smitty and I who get the curfew warnings, the late-to-practice fines, the coach's nasty looks. In fact, the only real difference between us is that he's still running on heart and guts alone, while I've become wise to the feeding habits of the corporate giants.

At this point in professional sports, Smitty's an endangered species; and oddly it's George, the quintessential capitalist, who's taken on the task of teaching Smitty to survive: "Man, I don't need your goddamn $300,000 house in New fucking Jersey with the goddamn tennis court and the hot shit chandeliers." This is Smitty talking to George. They are into their running act on the evils of capitalism just two hours away from the championship game.

"Yeah, I know lots of communists in Rome," George is saying; "they live like rats for all your Marxist bullshit." Yasin is wearing his keys-to-the-harem grin, saying nothing. Up front the Brazilians are getting louder.

"Phew, it stinks, this singing," George is going mock-berserk, banging his head on the window. "Shut up, shut up, can't a guy relax a little before a big game?"

It's like a bad Fellini movie—George is cursing in Italian, falling back from time to time into his weird Welsh accented English. Steve Marshall is in the aisle trying to tango. I'm under the seat looking for my can of tobacco, hoping a small pinch of wintogreen will keep down the breakfast eggs.

Suddenly, in the middle of a large suspension bridge, the bus screeches to a stop. Somebody is shining lights in our eyes. It's an English film crew, clattering aboard for a little of that journalistic jive. My stomach doesn't want any part of it and George is furious. The two of us charge down the aisle, threatening to make them swim to the game. Peace returns.

11:35 The bus hisses to a stop beside the curb at Civic Stadium. George points over his shoulder to four black Lincolns that have just pulled up behind us.

They have arrived. The motorcade. The same glittering entourage that used to ease in under the bombed out hulk of Downing Stadium. And while the hoi polloi tossed down hot dogs and Schaefer, they would feast on lobster and steak done to a turn on hibachi grills by their chauffeurs. These are the same men who are now delivered to Giant Stadium by helicopter. This is the Warner's brass, making its customary entrance: Chairman of the Board Steve Ross, Office of the President Jay Emmet, vice president Rafael de la Sierra, record mogul Nesuhi Ertegun, and a string of cultured women.

"Should I know them?" one fan asks.

"Maybe it's the Governor," answers another.

Like a school of minnows spooked by a sudden change in current, the crowd flashes an about face and darts past the limousines to where the Sounders bus has just pulled in. They're mobbing the players, surrounding them, tugging at them, pressing hands: "All right, all right, show 'em, run 'em, do it, do it, do it."

As we head toward the locker room a girl clad in a skin-tight Cosmos T-shirt, made somewhat tighter by the rain, leans over the rail and asks for my autograph. "Got a piece of paper?" I ask. She shakes her head, smiling. "No, sorry," she says. "You can just sign here." And she sticks out her chest.

12:00 Most of the team is dressed, busied with the little pre-game rituals that lie somewhere between careful preparation and outright superstition. Players move through their own routines in the spacey posture of sleepwalkers, winding tape, pulling and adjusting ace bandages, flexing and extending their muscles under the flesh-toned elastic.

I like to get to the locker room early and relax, read the program, get taped up, stretch a bit, check my hair, stretch some more, until the muscles in my calves and thighs move easily over the bones and joints. George has a routine that lasts exactly forty-five minutes, no matter what. Silent as a monk, he walks into the training room and gets massaged in a rotation as unbending as the sign of the cross: First the right foot, then the right calf, then the left foot, left calf, thighs, stomach, shoulders, arms. No one dares speak to him, especially when he gets to his shoes, talismans possessed of such mystical power that George will spend five minutes measuring the laces and evening them out, and another five softening the tongues between thumb and forefinger.

While George is communing with his shoes, Pele is blissing out under a towel, looking for all the world like an Egyptian pharaoh about to be embalmed. Massaged, taped, dressed and warmed up, he is lying still as death on the tile floor, feet elevated on a bench, the stark white folds of the towel covering all but one cheekbone. He is gone for ten minutes, floating over some ghostly South American stadium or running along one of those crystalline Brazilian beaches he's always talking about.

"Is good," says the Professor, pointing to the compact dark form Pele's wandering spirit has left behind. "When he meditates, when he is so far away so long, is always a good sign." By now, everyone is watching him silently, stepping wide arcs around him, talking quietly as though the harshest tone, the merest nudge will rupture his trance and pierce the fragile aura that surrounds us all. A legend is retiring after today, and we've got more than a trace of sentiment. I'm not ashamed to say that I love the man. And we're going to win this one for him.

12:45 Eddie is going through the final litany. Slow them down, hold the ball, watch the wetness, careful of the field, take the smart shot, run like hell.

Now, as the captain, Werner is up and says, "Let's win this one for Pele." But everyone is still unusually quiet, waiting, as if for some final benediction.

He knows. Pele gets up and motions for us all to put our hands on the scarred practice ball Werner is holding. I can hear him breathing, and down his left temple a little rivulet of sweat is running toward his jaw.

"Please," he says, his voice is a little choked. "Please, one more game."

Now everybody is getting loud. Smitty is screaming let's beat the shit out of them, let's kick ass; I'm yelling, too. At the fringes, Beckenbauer looks astonished. I don't know what I'm saying, just the usual jockobabble that stokes the boilers in a competitive brain. Steve Ross and Jay Emmett appear with some corporate kids in tow, smiling nervously and shaking hands. Everybody is rolling now, shouting, stoking it for 30 seconds or so. Then Eddie throws open the door and we steam out onto the field.

Twelve thousand of the Seattle faithful have come down the coast to swallow raindrops yelling for their Sounders. The rest of the crowd is a mix, but all I can see are Sounder banners: "The Year Seattle Slew the Cosmos" and, for Franz, "Cosmos: You Vill Lose Und Like It."

After the warmup I walk across the field, stepping over the patched seams in the Astroturf, like a kid avoiding cracks in the sidewalk. But hey, what's this bullshit? I'm not nervous, sure as hell not superstitious. I stomp on a seam and look up to see George, who's standing stock still, grimacing like a crazy statue of Garibaldi. I know what he needs.

"Show 'em all, George," I scream at him. "Put the sucker right in the back of the net."

He doesn't smile.

The noise in Civic Stadium is incredible, rushing, surging—the kind of a noise a river makes when you turn a corner on its rapids. Two minutes to game time.

Behind the goal, some Seattle fans are arguing with a security cop over their bedsheet sign that says "Cosmos Suck" in chartreuse day-glo. Perhaps in the interest of TV decorum, some fellow sheathed in Hefty trash bags against the rain is working on a cleaner version. He holds up the result.

SHEP CHEWS.

I grin, in spite of myself, glad of another free commercial for the guys who pay me to savor a pinch of tobacco on national TV. The garbage bag man is jumping up and down and screaming at me now. I love it, whatever he's saying. God save us from indifferent fans.

I make a final check of the cords, tossing aside hot dog rolls, flashcubes, plastic cigar tips. Then I see it. It's lying on the ground right next to the left post, a horrible little rubber figure with a shock of that cotton candy hair they put on those fake shrunken heads. Tony Chursky's voodoo doll.

This Seattle goalie is too much. Terrific player but before a game he gets downright schizophrenic; brings six pairs of gloves onto the field and changes them every five minutes. During team introductions, he's a hyperactive golliwog, arms and legs flapping, head shaking. It annoys hell out of me. And now this. I pick up the doll and fling it into the crowd. Just then the whistle shrills.

Forget what the game looks like from where you sit. Suspend the notion of seeing a crisply lined field where you can neatly dissect the game into backward and forward, offense and defense, green shirts and white.

From down here the horizon is neck high and the perspective is tunnel-like. Alone in my rectangular cage, 24 feet long and eight feet high, I battle the mirages of depth perception, figure angles of attack, and worry about sight lines. The goal is often a godawful lonely place to be.

Then down they come: A small brigade of white Sounders shirts is bearing toward the goal, mad dogs and Englishmen with such names as Robertson, Jenkins, Scott, Ord, and Cave. All I know about them is that they are English and they will test me as all English teams do, with long, high balls into the middle, hoping for an error.

I would rather play against 11 Englishmen than one South American because at least with the English I know what to expect. It's all so predictable, so devoid of imagination. Their game is built on long balls and speed, on advancing through the air instead of on the ground, on hurtling attacks and paper cut passing. At its best, this is a volcanic, spectacular game. At its worst, it is a futile series of nonsensical rushes from one end of the field to the other, with scant reward for player or spectator. It's sloppy, boring and unworthy of the Queen.

But just now, boredom is not my problem. Out on the right flank, Bobby Smith is dueling Jocky Scott shoulder to shoulder, and they're carving each other's ribs with enthusiastic elbows. Scott has the better of it and he traps the ball with the inside of his foot. Wheeling on it, he heads for the corner flag with Smitty an agonizing, unforgivable split-second behind. Now the white jerseys are streaming into the penalty box in front of me, their forwards jamming the front of the goal to wait for the floating bomb, the dangerous crossing ball.

But not just yet. Smitty has anticipated Scott's turning the corner and he is correct. Just as Scott cuts in, Smitty slides feet first, making a clean tackle that leaves the undersides of his thighs burning; the two players sprawl on the ground.

"Get up, Smitty. Goddamn it, get up." The ball has rolled free and the Sounders have it. I crouch low expecting a shot but instead the ball is curled away from me toward the edge of the box. Two uniforms climb after it, fighting to get in the proper heading position. Mickey Cave deflects, the ball screams over my head—wide.

Three minutes have passed, but I don't yet feel in the game. I need a save to loosen up, to get the adrenalin rushing. Seattle is surprising me. Instead of running pell mell, they're whipping the ball around at midfield quite artfully, launching their sorties with quick, precise passes. Thwack. There's a hard volley from 25 yards out; I lean to my right, then realize the ball is curving to my left. I dive, get a finger under the ball and deflect it up, off the crossbar. It rebounds straight to Cave who nails a lunging header. The ball hits the back of the net as I hit the ground. I am just beginning to curse when I hear a whistle. Oh, what a lovely sound! Offsides.

Cave is snarling, but the official waves him away. Tough break for him, but for me, the shot was like an overdose of adrenalin. I'm awake, in the game. My mouth tastes like old nickels, but my body feels alive as I watch the bobbing jerseys diminish in the distance. Your turn, Chursky my boy.

I can see Franz probing from midfield, a seismologist searching for cracks in the Sounders defense. From where I stand it looks bad. Pele is stopping, accelerating, twisting to avoid vicious tackles and not succeeding. George can't shake Mike England, the Sounders formidable center back, who shadows him all over the field. Seattle is wired for an all-out game but we can't seem to plug into the same frequency.

The crowd is screaming now, and I follow the knot of players to the left, focusing on Steve Hunt. He's dueling with one fullback, now two, then he uncorks a blazing shot of about 25 yards, a clean comet to the upper left corner. Chursky gets it. Somehow, our forward line comes up with a brief salvo of shots, and Chursky is playing out of his mind, diving, leaping, punching balls back into startled faces. The crowd starts chanting, "Chursky, Chursky, Chursky." I feel a tinge of jealousy, wish the suckers would come and try some stuff on me, their best stuff, see what I've got. And then it happens.

Steve Hunt has bird dogged a pass from Chinaglia right to Chursky's feet, and Chursky gets it, flinging himself sideways. He's standing now, holding the ball to his chest, and he does an incredible thing. He drops the ball as though he's going to dribble it. Bad mistake. The second it touches the ground, Hunt is on it, nudging it loose from a startled Chursky. I can see the ball rolling lazily across the Seattle goal with Chursky and Hunt racing after it. Steve gets a foot on it, pushes it toward the goal, but something else is flying through the air; his left shoe, followed by Hunt, followed by Chursky, who's made a desperate goal-mouth tackle, tumbling them both into the net. Where is the ball? Hunt and Chursky are untangling themselves when I see it; that little red, white and blue ball, sitting neat as you please in the corner of the net.

Steve is up, running out to Pele who scoops him up like a baby and holds him there, hollering like a bastard. I don't even smile. I can't let myself, can't commit the sin, the unpardonable lapse that has left Chursky kneeling, head down in the goal. He fell victim to the worst thing that can happen to a goalie—he lost his concentration.

You make a save like he had, you look up, look around, because you never know where an attacker might be. Maybe a defender will yell, "Hold it, man behind you." Maybe some extra sense tells you he's there, hovering behind your left shoulder, just waiting for such a mistake. For a moment Hunt had blended in with the crowd over the end line and Chursky wasn't aware of the blind spot. Or perhaps he got caught in that deadly, hypnotic relief that can wash over a goalkeeper after a good save.

Whatever. The Cosmos are ahead 1–0 and in the personal duel that goalkeepers wage, I'm out in front.

It's what Chursky does just following the goal that gives me the edge. Twenty seconds after the score, he's still kneeling with his head in his hands, and this must have a deflating effect on his team. To see the goalie, the last line of defense, so weak, so vulnerable—it can be devastating. A goalkeeper has to exude confidence and control, no matter what. I've given up a goal right between my legs in front of 80,000 at the Munich Olympics, gotten right back up and said, "Let's get the bastards." And here's Chursky, openly admitting "the bastards got me," admitting it to everyone. And admitting it to me. After the game, I'll feel sorry for him. Right now my spirits are rising like helium; I'm ready to take a few feet in the face.

It sounds crazy, but when a keeper on the other team makes a good save, or when he blows it, I want them to come down and shoot on me. I want my licks, I want to rub it in his face. All ego, sure, but ego is what moves my kind of show. I eat it for breakfast. Suddenly, the churning, lunging bodies are coming my way; the chance is near.

As I tense, the strain in my muscles serves to increase my concentration, stretching it as tight as the ache in my jaw. I move from side to side in small, careful steps, a surveyor, calculating those angles that intersect the chaos of play. Suddenly, my careful geometry is blown apart, and they're unleashing shots from every direction. I catch a low ball and roll it to Carlos Alberto, my main man.

Carlos is a skillful defender, taking care of business with studied confidence. The man thinks nothing of halting a breakaway simply by thrusting his feet out and landing squarely on his ass, with the ball astonishingly glued to his soles, his opponent still running full speed until that awful second when he realizes he's been stripped of his purpose.

Now, with a graceful turn of the ankle, he flips the ball to Beckenbauer. It's a perfect pass but, incredibly, Franz has lost it at the edge of the box. The thief is Scott, who passes to Cave, who drops it at Ord's feet. Anticipating, I take two steps to the left, slipping on the slick surface just enough to foul my timing. The ball flashes by me like a meteor.

One fucking one.

Half time, and we're a little down. The performance of our Big Money men has been strictly penny ante stuff. Beckenbauer is guilty of sloppy passing; Chinaglia has been marked out of the game by England; and Pele looks strangely dislocated, as though just awoken from some terrible dream. The laxity of our play has offended Firmani, and he doesn't mince words telling us so.

He is strutting in front of the blackboard like one of those little wind-up toys, punching the air, the tips of his ears turning red, growling in his clipped South African accent, "If you can't work hard for forty-five minutes in the second half of a championship game . . ." It's not particularly innovative stuff, but neither do I think we need anyone telling us that we have to raise our level of play; the frustration masking Pele's face is enough.

Just as we're about to go back on the field, Firmani announces a lineup change for the second half: Vito Dimitrijevic for Terry Garbett. This stuns everyone, particularly Garbett who rips off his shirt and stalks into the shower. Can't say I blame him. Garbett had come back from an injury to play the most consistent ball on the team, and his first half performance had been rock solid. Vito, on the other hand, is something of a mystery. Few people have been in this country six months and learned less English. Too, he has an annoying habit of exaggerating small hurts to the point where a sprained ankle takes on the significance of two broken legs. There's nothing a team dislikes more than a malingerer, especially when he replaces an honest worker like Garbett. Yet Vito is more offensive minded, and Firmani hopes the enigmatic Yugoslav will stimulate our sluggish attack. One man's pride is negligible compared to the promising gleam of an engraved silver cup; no one knows that better than I.

The game resumes. I curse silently as I spot the ball coming in from the right flank. Should I stay put and let the defenders challenge the Sounders in the air, try to catch the ball in traffic and risk having it jostled out of my hands, or punch it clear for simple good riddance? I choose the last, and twisting high, thrust my fists out from my chest. They travel so close to the ear of a leaping Ord that he can feel the wind as his head meets nothing; my knuckles strike the ball with a thud and it lands softly in front of Nelsi, who flicks it to Carlos as the attack is repelled.

By now it's obvious the game will be a struggle of tempos. The Sounders had operated the first half at top speed, moving ahead with short crisp passes. For them, the nub was to keep it going; any slackening and we'd restore the hypnotic pace that was our preference. Once the leather-lunged Sounders begin to weary, the tide reverses. Twice Pele breaks clear, the first time dribbling a serpen-

tine path around Mike England, only to put the
ball yards over the bar. His game seems a paler
version of what it once was, slower, more fitful. But
the instincts are still strong as he sniffs for an opening, waits for a chance to do the one thing that no
one else on the field can. Finally, the moment arrives and Pele seizes it. The ball is played ahead of
him, into a small space occupied by two white
shirts. In a split second, Pele has left them kicking at nothing but air. There is one more defender
to beat, England, and Pele slows, as if out of respect for the imposing Seattle center back. This
gives England just time enough to strip the ball
away with a sliding tackle and the fairytale abates.
Momentarily.

12:04 remaining, and we're homesteading in the
Seattle penalty area. The throw in from deep in the
right corner goes to Hunt, standing 10 yards from
the flag. Mel Machin is on him, but Hunt curls the
ball around the Sounders fullback and sends it
floating in front of the goal.

There, at last, free of England, is Chinaglia,
leaping, heading, scoring. He's running past the
goal now, into his triumphant boogie, shaking those
lumberjack hips, fists clenched, a man vindicated,
sprung from the pressure cooker.

It's the final, perfect irony of this crazy season.
Chinaglia scores the winner on a pass from Steve
Hunt, the same Steve Hunt he punched out earlier
in the season. Chinaglia scores the winner with his
head, a part of his anatomy most sportswriters had
condemned. For many, it was an ending hard to
stomach, the sudden canonization of the heavy, the
player the press blamed for all the back stabbing
and divisiveness on the team. Yet with one powerful twist of his body, Chinaglia rose to the ball, the
pressure and the occasion to stick it down everyone's throat. I wanted to run out and hug him,

kiss him, tell him "You showed those bastards." But I don't move, barely smile. Because there are still 12 minutes left.

Seattle is swarming, and within the next two minutes I am forced to make three desperate saves.

On the first, I dive, to stop a low curving shot. I throw the ball to Vito at midfield but he loses control, and here come the Sounders again. The shot is high to my left and I pick the ball out of a quilt of jerseys, following its surprising upward path unflinchingly to punch it out. I allow myself a small grunt of satisfaction as I watch Steve Hunt settle the ball outside the box.

But suddenly Hunt is heading toward me. Toward me! My God, he's lost his mind. He's trying to take the ball through the entire Seattle team, moving by one, now two, now three Sounders and here he is, about five yards in front of me to my left.

"Kick it out, kick it out . . . oh, no." Hunt has lost the ball, Steve Buttle's got it and he hammers it to my left. I dive and get just enough finger on the ball to turn it around the post. Hunt gives me an apologetic wave as I clamber to my feet, and as I go to retrieve the ball, somebody dumps one of those giant containers of beer on my head. I towel off for the final blitzkreig, silently thanking the anonymous idiot for the short break.

Why does it always have to be this scary? All I can see are white jerseys as Scott shoots from twelve yards—wide, left. A minute later, England slams a ball by the right post and hangs his head in resignation. I look up at the clock; it reads 44:15. We may survive. Then George steals the ball at midfield, and I know the game is over. My body goes limp for the first time in two hours.

At the final whistle, Pele whirls, rips off his shirt and hands it to Seattle's Jim McCallister, the young American fullback voted Rookie of the Year. Within seconds, the sodden green surface is overrun with fans, players, all writhing, twisting, leaping into the air and through it all, somehow, I find Pele and hang onto him, half shielding him, half hugging him. "For you, for you," I tell him and he is crying, "Thank you, thank you."

Up on a table in the middle of the field, Commissioner Phil Woosnam is trying to make an announcement, a hopeless formality in the face of sheer bedlam. He's trying to present the trophy, and I'm tugging it down, grabbing it for Pele. For most of my professional career, Woosnam has treated me with all the deference he would an escaped convict. But now he is smiling at me.

After a few minutes of hugging, hollering and touching the trophy, the giant web of people begins moving us across the field. I crane my neck, looking for Arden in the stands, until the sweaty tide carries us into the tunnel.

On the way, I see a familiar face pinioned against a doorsill, and next to Arden's, it's the face I most want to see—that of Hubert Vogelsinger, the man singularly responsible for my being where I am. Hubert, the temperamental Austrian coach with the big Teutonic voice that bellowed at me in college, then again in the pros when I played for the Boston Minutemen. Goddamn Hubert, the only man who could teach me to play the goal in spite of myself. We do a victory pas de deux, and I drag him into the locker room, two hallucinating drunks interpreting the scenery.

I take a jersey and wipe the sweat out of my eyes. They sting a bit from the champagne that is now in the air and everywhere. I blink once, twice, and try to focus on this tangled mass of bodies, klieg lights and waving notebooks.

In one corner, George is knotting the sash of his

blue velvet robe, the only man drinking champagne
from a glass. With his free arm, he hugs Steve Ross.
Earlier in the season, their closeness had been the
source of divisive rumors: Chinaglia was running
the team, Chinaglia had talked Ross into firing
President Clive Toye and Coach Gordon Bradley.
"Wait," George had told him. "Wait and see." And
now we saw. "Yes," he is telling a knot of reporters. "Today I've won a lot of personal satisfaction
and a lot of individual battles." Steve Ross comes
over and George embraces him, laughing. Ross' hair
is dripping. After a trip to the showers, he had
changed his clothes. All that he could find were a
pair of green sweatpants with the number 9 on
them. George's pants.

"We forgot we were the Cosmos," I hear Werner
Roth saying a few feet away. "We stopped dancing
around the ball, and just went out there and kicked
ass." A reporter is pursuing him into the shower,
asking him how it feels to be the sole survivor of
the Cosmos 1972 Championship. Werner winks at
me, and points to Gordon Bradley. "No," he says.
"There's another survivor."

Bradley, whose face bears the look of a man not
invited to the banquet, finds Pele. Pele kisses him
and embraces him and they both begin to cry,
Gordon choking out that he is very pleased, Pele
sobbing, "Thank you, Gordon, thank you very
much."

Bill Schwing, a director with the television network that has covered us all year, waves a glass
of champagne over his head. "You guys were bigger
than all the bullshit," he yells.

Now the din is fusing into one voice, growing,
louder, more throaty.

"PELE, PELE, PELE." The players have taken
up the chant of the crowd and as Pele steps from
the shower, he shouts, "Get my wife." Out of the

steam and the throng, Rose appears, sobbing and the two of them embrace in one of the small air pockets the room affords.

On the blackboard where Firmani had sketched out his final strategy, someone has scrawled, "Cosmos: 1977 Champs." Now the lettering has begun to fade from the combined effects of champagne and steam. As if to restate the message, Steve Marshall, a man with the build of a giant Sequoia, gathers Pele in his arms and holds him aloft.

"See, Steve, you see?" Pele is laughing now. "I promise you this. Now do I keep my promise?"

All my daydreams are coming to pass, my mind is a blur, my body is on automatic pilot. I introduce Hubert to Pele, hold up the trophy with Beckenbauer, baptized Smitty with the Erteguns' vintage champagne. It's an hour of top-rated minutes, the kind you'd like to press gently between the pages of a book.

I've experienced other exciting moments in sport, personal triumphs. An undefeated junior high wrestling season. The chilly spring night I pole vaulted my lifetime best, with only the hiss of the cushion as applause.

But this is different, strange, It's the first time winning has been a team experience, the first time all season the Cosmos have approached the dictionary definition of a team. I'm crying like a child, grinning like a fool, lost for an unspecified period of time in the victory warp—a steamy twilight zone that marks the end for Pele, and the beginning for American soccer.

2

ROOTS

I'm told that 1958 was a pivotal year in soccer, that Pele—then 17—scored three goals in a World Cup match against France and the game was never the same. I'm told that Franz Beckenbauer, a Munich schoolboy, and Giorgio Chinaglia, a kid in Wales, saw this on television and their lives were changed. But what did I care. I didn't know anything about soccer in 1958—I was playing baseball.

I was born in the Bronx, so I suppose this conjures up visions of a youngster shagging flies in an outfield littered with empty bottles of muscatel. Tell a sportswriter that you were born in the Bronx and his eyes light up, real *Boys of Summer* stuff. By the sixth paragraph they have you collecting empty Yoohoo bottles and turning them in at the corner market for enough nickels to buy a bleacher seat. Pretty soon they have you talking like a Dead End Kid, and your parents looking like Dead End Adults. Well, it wasn't that way.

Though I was born in the Bronx, third child of Elias and Anne Messing, we left our apartment on Metropolitan Avenue when I was two. I spent my

Wonder Bread years in a comfortable tract house in Roslyn, Long Island.

One side of Roslyn is a white middle-class suburb. The land is neatly subdivided into half acre plots easily traversed by a standard garden hose. The houses are split level, ranches and modest Cape Cods. Children are expected to go to college, marry well, and do something useful.

The other side of Roslyn is a sheltered enclave of upper middle class and wealthy Jewish families. Here the land is parceled into larger chunks, attended by gardeners and separated by six foot hedges. The homes are Georgian, English Tudor and Spanish stucco; the children inherit corporations, law firms and medical practices. Our house, perched dead center, sheltered most of the town misfits.

There were eight of us: my parents, older sister Jeanne, then Marc, myself, brothers Albee and Roy and our black mutt Smokey. We were comfortable, but not wealthy, Jewish but not religious, middle class but not middle of the road. The radio did play Brahms but it also played baseball games, and while we were acquainted with Shakespeare, we knew the Mouseketeers on a more intimate basis.

We took family vacations, travelling across the country piled in our station wagon. I never saw the inside of a Holiday Inn, but I did see the Northern Lights, storm clouds over the Canadian Rockies, and wild geese, as I peeked out from under a pup tent.

My mother taught physical education at nearby Nassau Community College, plus an exercise class in our playroom. As the daughter of a furniture maker who emigrated from Russia and his Latvian wife, she had a stubborn pride in her working class roots. But of course, she wanted something better for us.

My father commuted daily, preparing for trials in a paneled office just a short walk from lower Broadway, where his own father had sold men's hats. Abe Messing emigrated to New York from Riga, Latvia, and was delighted when both his sons became lawyers. In America, the Messings had become a professional family, with doctors and lawyers on both sides. It is important to make a living with your head, my grandfather said. It is the mark of achievement to have a profession.

Naturally, that didn't include professional athletics. The whole family played sports, but they were always low on the list of priorities, behind homework, music lessons, and household chores. My father, in particular, didn't want me to grow up thinking that the greatest living writer was the author of the New York Giants playbook. I'm sure he took some measure of pride in having his four sons create Roslyn's first athletic dynasty. But always, he had a keener eye for our grades at school.

Whether the culprit is Freud or Grantland Rice, American male athletes are invariably linked to their fathers. But looking back over my experiences I'm sure that I was better off for the scant attention my own father paid to my athletic achievements.

I remember afternoons in the Munich Olympic Village in 1972, when I was playing on the U.S. soccer team, shooting pool with other American athletes and listening to stories about Mark Spitz and his father. Some were told in fun, and some out of jealousy, but Arnold Spitz did end his son's normal childhood prematurely. He enrolled Mark in a gruelling swimming program before he was nine, twice uprooted the entire family so the boy could have the best coaches in California, and constantly reminded him that he cared little for age group records. He wanted world records.

Mark was a nice enough guy, but on the few occasions I spent some time with him, he seemed awkward socially, literally a fish out of water. He didn't mingle much. I'd see him everyday, sitting on the balcony of his room in the Village, sunning himself and watching the rest of us laughing and playing Ping Pong below. I remember thinking he had paid a high price for his excellence, that being the best in the world could be lonely indeed. I am thankful for the quiet, low key way I acquired my values. Sports have a place in my life, but they aren't my life.

My father was a good athlete. He could play baseball, handball, basketball, and almost anything else we could talk him into. Our backyard was a perfect rectangle, with no annoying trees or flower-beds to cramp a sprint around the bases. It was always filled with kids, dogs, balls and neighbor-hood moms dragging their youngsters home to supper.

It wasn't until I came across an old cardboard box in the attic that I realized how much restraint my father had shown. He had been more than a good athlete. There were dusty bronze plaques, newspaper clippings, photographs from his years at City College. He had run track and played baseball well enough to get nibbles from the big leagues. Instead, he'd gone to law school. And become a professional.

"No big deal," he said when I asked him about the box in the attic. "When I walked in the door for the physical, I knew major league baseball wasn't for me. I had to see a manager, a trainer, a doctor, two scouts. I realized it was a business, panicked, and hit the street. For me, sports had been fun. So I decided to keep it that way. I wanted to enjoy them as just a part of my life."

Only a part of his life? At nine this was hard for me to understand. I was going through what mothers call "one of those stages." It was my Mickey Mantle stage. I *was* Mickey Mantle, lived, ate and slept Mickey Mantle. In those banner years, when the Yankees reached the World Series as surely as the leaves began to turn, my birthday present was tickets to the games. I can remember running alongside my father in the parking lot trying to keep up, then settling in along the third base line. I wore a first baseman's mitt to catch the foul balls that always landed a section or two away, and I'd drive my father nuts with my instant Mel Allen play-by-play. I'd drop my chin to my chest, take a deep breath and recap each inning:

"Two out . . . three and two . . . bases loaded . . . top of the ninth . . . Yankees trail 2–1 . . . Burdette looks in and gets the sign . . . around comes the right arm . . . here's the pitch . . . Richardson swings . . . line drive to right field . . . it's in for a basehit . . . McDougal scores . . . Slaughter scores . . . the Yankees lead 3–2 . . . How about that!"

Of course these stages came and went with the easy regularity of the seasons. When winter turned the baseball diamond to frozen mud, I became Jim Brown wearing a big number 32 on my jersey; spring found me leaping over makeshift high jump bars in the backyard; summers at the neighborhood pool turned me into an Olympic swimmer. It was all in my head. But I enjoyed these fantasies.

The only offbeat aspect of childhood involved my pets, and in that respect I've never grown up.

I still own a three foot South American iguana, two modest sized boas and a glider turtle, and it's a cinch that if I ever get a six figure contract, I'll buy a pet store. But at 10, I had a two figure allowance, 75 cents. So I had to start small, with hamsters, white mice, guinea pigs, rabbits, turtles. I had hamsters giving birth behind the refrigerator, mice escaping into the box springs. But snakes were my favorite.

It started when a friend of mine caught a small black snake in the woods and fed it his sister's goldfish. We watched that snake, circling the bowl, tongue flicking in and out, then slithering elegantly, almost disinterestedly around his prey when my friend finally beached the fish on his desk. It was the ultimate one-on-one. While I wasn't insensitive to the cruelties of the situation, I was fascinated by the snake and the way it moved, so graceful, and without wasted motion. A lot could be learned from snakes.

I now entered my most serious stage. I decided to become a herpetologist, a snake man. I poked under rocks on camping trips, saved up for a membership in the Bronx Zoological Society. I set about learning every species of snake on the east coast. I was a strange kid.

I remember my first boa constrictor as well as I remember my first girlfriend; both were slender, graceful and gentle unless provoked. "How much is that boa in the window?" I had asked the proprietor of a nearby pet store.

"$30 plus tax. Say, aren't you the kid who bought the matched salamanders last week?"

I tried to take out a revolving charge account at the pet store but was rejected. So I washed cars, mowed lawns, saved my allowance, and finally I had the $30. I ran to the store after school, plunked down the money and walked away with the boa and a pair of white mice for its next meal. I was excited, and a little apprehensive. In the same pet store, I had seen a 23 foot python crush three ribs of its handler with a single coil. The sickening crack and the pain on the man's face gave me a healthy respect for the animal's integrity. But my boa, only six feet long, was docile as a puppy when well fed. I made sure it was well wrapped, figuring Mom might draw the line at my having a pet that in a few years could swallow her whole.

"What now, Shep?" she asked as I sped by on the way to my room.

"Nothing, Mom."

Five minutes later, there was a tapping at the door.

"Shep? You in there? Come out this minute! And close the door behind you!"

I knew the jig was up. It seemed a neighbor had heard about Shep's monster snake from her son and called to ask if she could bring over her Cub Scout den. Mom and I went around for about half an hour. She said it was dangerous. I said she'd seen too many Johnny Weismuller movies. She said it was no kind of animal to have around the house. I said it would protect her from mice. She then parried with the ultimate argument: "Shep, I'm your *mother* and you'll listen to me." I riposted ingeniously, slashing home with a brilliant counter: "Mom, think how educational it will be." I had her there. My mother would rather be staked out on an anthill than deprive her son of knowledge.

"But I'm not," she said stiffly, "I absolutely *will not* vacuum your room anymore. And I don't care how much it likes water, keep it out of the bathtub, and away from your sister's room."

I got her drift. Though I tried to keep my menagerie confined to my room, there were occasional escapes, and naturally, my snakes found their way into Jeanne's room. But the only time I caught hell was the morning we discovered my grandmother curled up on the couch, having found her bed in the guest room occupied by Moses, my black snake. She took it well. In fact, she even supported my hobby.

Some years later, when she was in a nursing home, she suggested a little nature study to her friends. "Well now, I saw this nice little snake out by the garden," she told us, "and I knew Shep would like it, so I asked a few residents and one of the nurses to help me catch it. My, such a fuss. They told me an old lady shouldn't play with snakes, sooo," she looked at me apologetically, "I let him get clean away."

I guess if I had a role model, someone else to blame for my unconventional lifestyle, it would be my brother Marc. He is three years older and was the best athlete in Wheatley High School. A wrestler, track star, captain of the soccer team, he was the first guy who dared wear a T-shirt to school and the first to be suspended for it. He also grew a small goatee. When told it was forbidden by the wrestling coach, Marc covered it with masking tape. He was no troublemaker, just an independent guy who insisted things be explained to him. He wanted to know how a beard would influence his half nelson, whether what he wore would alter what he learned. Later on, in the midst of altercations with coaches who view every facial hair as a Communist encroachment, I'd find myself thinking of Marc. "Are sideburns going to affect the way I save a shot?" I'd ask. "Will they make me a poor goalkeeper?" After Marc, anybody just bearing the Messing name was enough to make teachers at Wheatley pull out their detention books. But I wasn't as politically committed as my brother so high school went smoothly for me.

I did well academically, assuring myself a place in some respectable university and a solid future. Having passed through that brief adolescent period when pants cuffs and voice are too high, I discovered girls. And the Wheatley H.S. marching band. And soccer. In that order. Identifying the common thread that ran through these diverse activities was simple: I love to perform. I would also do anything to impress a girl including, once, going to the opera. Playing trumpet, I enjoyed the solo spotlight as much as I loved the pyrotechnics of playing goal. Several times my showboat tendencies got me bounced off the school band. Because I was forever forgetting my music and adlibbing Shubert adaggios, our conductor Salvatore Signorelli would holler, "Messing, quit the fancy stuff! Learn to play with us!"

The sports I liked best were not team sports. I was a hot dog, loved attention and challenged myself by setting personal goals. Left unchecked, these tendencies might have caused serious ego trouble. That's if it hadn't been for Bill Stevenson, a physical education teacher and coach at Wheatley.

Our first meeting was hardly cordial. I was wrestling in eighth grade, 148 pounds of snot-nosed self-assurance. I had quick reflexes, a gyroscopic center of gravity, and a strange fixation for athletic tape. I loved tape. Loved the way it smelled, loved the way it looked. Thought it was definitely macho, especially when you rubbed it on the underside of the mat to get it a little dirty. I'd tape my wrists, my elbows, my knees, even my thumbs. The first day of practice, I was out there doing my mummy impersonation and Stevenson walked over. He looked me up and down, shaking his head.

"Messing," he said. "So help me. If you're ever

going to wrestle for me, if you ever want to do anything in this athletic department, take off that stupid tape."

I figured he was insensitive to the needs of an artist, but I tore off the tape and settled down. Stevenson coached me for the next five years in wrestling, soccer and track. He did even more for my attitude than for my skills. He taught me to handle myself—somewhat.

Almost every professional athlete I've talked to remembers his coach, the one man, early on, who is still The Coach long after trades and quirky management decisions have placed him under a dozen grizzled authoritarians. Stevenson was The Coach for me, and probably the reason I played soccer rather than football.

He was a character right out of Claire Bee, the perfect combination of disciplinarian and nice guy. His techniques were textbook, and his coaching ideals were the traditional litany:

Play your best, boys.

Play clean.

Don't talk to the referee.

Damn well don't argue with the referee.

Always pick up a fallen opponent on the field.

Never scratch your vital parts on the field.

Be stoic.

Be sportsmanlike.

And when the athletic director was not within hearing, he'd whisper these forbidden instructions: Have fun.

Naturally, I poured my energies into fun. Pole vaulting was fun, because it had great entertainment potential. By my junior year, I had established a modest reputation and exquisitely choreographed routine.

I had this girlfriend, Leslie. On the afternoon of a meet, we'd drive to the field in her '62 maroon

Chevy, find seats in the center of the bleachers, buy a couple of Cokes and settle down in the stands for the early events. I always wore my bathing suit. It afforded great freedom of movement and went a long way with Leslie. Also it was great for working on a tan. Like all my athletic outfits, from Little League to the Cosmos, it had to be perfect. In 1967, it was not just any bathing suit, but a genuine Speedo tanksuit, in the special pattern worn by the U.S. team in the 1964 Olympics.

I'd sit in the stands until the rest of the vaulters worked the bar up to a suitable height. Rules allowed you to pass on the lower jumps, provided you could make the later heights, and I'd pass half the meet away. It would drive the other vaulters crazy. Messing, that asshole, sitting up there in his tight suit while the groundhogs were clearing 8, 9, 10 feet. When it got interesting—around 12 feet—and most of the field was sending the bar whanging off the posts, I'd put down my Coke, pick up my pole, stroll on over to the runway and win the meet. At 16, it felt great. And in all honesty, winning was not the part I liked most. Looking good was just as important.

That was my act. But I found the purest enjoyment in those solitary hours of practice where the only competition was between the bar and me. I'd cut classes, or wait until late in the afternoon so I could practice alone. I could concentrate better, listening for the breeze in my ears that said I had cleared the bar, or the jarring clang that told me I had failed. I liked early evening best, when the cool spring nights kept my head clear and I could jump until the dull orange bar disappeared in the dusk. Some nights I pushed myself, setting the bar at an impossible height, hoping for a miracle, thudding time after time onto the cushion with a spreading purple raspberry where the bar hammered my calf.

Other nights I kept it low and comfortable, enjoying the lazy sensation of floating on my own jet stream.

On one such night it happened. I was feeling good, energetic but loose, and already I could see a thin sliver of moon over the left corner of the bar. I was jumping well, up to 13'2", approaching the indescribable isolation an athlete enters when near a personal goal. Logic and superstition began to overlap. You're conscious of the threshold, yet unwilling to shatter the ease with which you've arrived there.

Daring to spoil the moment, I moved the bar up to 13'6", higher than anyone had jumped in the county. I weighed the pole in my hands, looked hard at the bar for a minute or so and took off, twisting, hands up, watching the pole fall away, the trademark PORT-A-PIT growing larger as I fell toward the cushion. Silence.

I guess I lay there for about 5 minutes, flat on my back, looking at the bar bisecting the sky. And since that time, past the Olympics, past even the Cosmos championship, past everything except, perhaps, the first time I played with Pele, I've never enjoyed a more exhilarating moment. I made 13'6" once again in a meet for the county record, but it didn't compare.

In soccer, it took some time for me to find my spot in goal and experience the oddly sensual pleasure of being kicked in the face. Three factors brought me around. First was Marc's influence, since he was captain of Wheatley's soccer team. Second, Bill Stevenson was coaching. And third, we had a lousy football team that didn't score a single point my junior year. Soccer won out by default.

After one practice, I found I could play, and

play reasonably well. I could run and kick the ball, bounce it off my head and trap it dead with my chest. The sport was new and different, much faster than baseball or football, with fluid action for two 45-minute halves, and no annoying time-outs. If the ball goes out of bounds, you toss it right back in and run like hell after it. And though I wasn't crazy about team sports, I found soccer's requirements acceptable. The game demands intelligent rhythmic teamwork, but it's spontaneous and unprogrammed. You follow the capricious bounce of a small bladder of air, trying with your feet to impose your will on it. If you do so, the rewards are immediate—no waiting for some guy to bat you home. No measuring your progress with a 10 yard chain. I started out playing at center forward, and watching that ball arc and spin off my foot into the net was an instant thrill.

Physically, I loved the game's sensations. Thwack, the ball leaves my foot. Unngh, the goalie gasps as his body jars to earth. Swish, the sound of the cords. It is an act of pure aggression, but graceful as a swordfight.

The running is nonstop, 100 yards up the field on the attack, 100 yards back to wait a clear from the defense. It takes some guys a month of wind sprints to keep up the pace; the running can make you puke, and it can make you high.

Of course, though skill is paramount, at least in theory, there's contact for a guy who wants it; sliding tackles, goalmouth collisions, aerial arabesques. Some coaches from other schools stressed contact and offered generous praise for upending a dangerous opposing forward. There was this one coach with an awesome neck and a massive chest who used to run up and down the sidelines, screaming things like "Stick 'em, Davey," and "Good hit, Mike." I can only guess that he would rather have coached football. After all, soccer was still considered a sissy sport and poleaxing your opponent was generally frowned on.

Looking back, the soccer we played then was hardly soccer at all. It was more on the order of what writer Paul Gardner describes as "bootball," a clumsy, aimless game of running and kicking. Classic skills were as yet unknown, since few coaches were that familiar with the game. Ball handling consisted largely of booting a pass upfield and hoping it reached the right man. Most high school players came away from the game having had a lot of fun but knowing precious little about the sport. It's a problem I still see in my clinics each year, and always the kids' lament is the same: "I really want to learn, but there's nobody there to teach me."

To his credit, Bill Stevenson tried, drilling us in ball skills as best he could. But the lessons were quickly lost in competition when opposing teams rushed us with all the finesse of Genghis Khan's hordes. "Control," Stevenson would yell from the sidelines. "How about some ball control?"

I'd like to think I became a goalie by cosmic design, but really the reasons were mundane. Graduation had taken our best goalkeepers and a nagging thigh injury made running difficult for me. I discovered I was made for the position, a little crazy and a little hooked on body contact. I was in 10th grade, the only sophomore starter. I agreed to try goalkeeping, but in the beginning I was all set to hate it. Our first game was at Westbury High and I was frantic at the thought of being alone in that cage, with real opponents thundering down on me. I was used to scoring, not being scored on, and the responsibilities seemed immense. All of it was made worse by the fact that

I'd forgotten my "sticky stuff," the Toughskin spray many goalies put on their hands to goo them up.

As it turned out, my fears were unfounded. So powerful, so intimidating was the Wheatley team that in our first game, I never touched the ball. It didn't even roll over the midfield line.

"Take me out of there," I bellowed at Stevenson on the way home. "It's hell, I hate it."

"Wait till you get some action," he told me, but I was unconvinced. I hated the loneliness, the immobility that numbed my toes. I couldn't stand the hypnotic boredom of being a spectator.

Next game, I got some action. And after that day, I never left the cage again. Giving up a goal is what I imagine death must feel like, a blankness that descends the moment the ball crosses the chalk. It's still a tough thing to articulate, and for a sixteen-year-old, it was too confusing to talk about at all. I only knew that hurling my body against a ball or an opponent seemed the ultimate commitment. It felt right. And once I made that commitment, I got better and better. So did the team. By my senior year, we finished with the county championship. And I ended up with an injured thigh muscle, torn from the bone in that last championship game.

As graduation neared, sports made their bid for a place in my future. I had been offered athletic scholarships as a pole vaulter, and after coming off a .700 batting average in Babe Ruth baseball, I was approached by a scout for the Mets. He wanted me to come to Shea Stadium for a tryout. "Could change your life, kid," he told me. And maybe that's what I was afraid of when I told him no thanks. Like my father, I was turning down the other path. I was going to college, then to law school. I was going to become a professional.

My plans were reinforced by that torn muscle. Right after graduation, in June 1967, I had an operation on the thigh. The tear was so serious, so complete, so jagged that I couldn't walk for three months after I left the hospital. The surgeons told me I'd probably never play soccer again. I enrolled at the Bronx campus of New York University, intending to major in political science. Instead, I majored in partying.

Still, my two years at NYU were educational in certain respects: I discovered that you could not get a satisfactory education by studying beer labels, and I acquired the worldly skills of seven card stud and handicapping the trotters at Yonkers Raceway.

I also learned what it was like to play soccer in the "big time." Against the advice of my doctor and with the aid of some intricate taping rigged up by trainer Doc Farrell, I played soccer almost as soon as I shed my crutches. And quickly, I learned that big time American soccer meant being the only gringo on a roster of names I couldn't pronounce. I could yell "Hey, Papa" on the field and Papadakis, Pappadoupoulos and two or three others would turn around. They were either exchange students or local kids who grown up playing soccer in ethnic communities where baseball bats were things you kept behind the door to welcome burglars. These guys had ball skills that made American players look clumsy and absurd. To keep up, I had to play hard.

I was tough, fearless, reckless and bold my freshman year—but showed no special ability to protect the goal or organize a defense. And this caused me great concern when I met Varsity Coach George Vargas my sophomore year.

George Vargas was from Colombia, a dark, hawk-eyed man who could play the game as well as he coached it. In retrospect, he was one of the finest coaches I've ever played under; at the time we met, my only thought was to impress him enough to beat out the starting goalkeeper. Vargas took us to a place called Ohlers Mountain Lodge in Kingston, N.Y., for two weeks of preseason training. I couldn't do a thing right. One night, things were especially uncomfortable. The policeman who pulled me over for going 85 in a 55 mph zone also proved to be the town mayor and the judge. He held court in a gas station he ran, and fined me $150, payable on the spot. Though Vargas was not happy when he had to come down and bail out four of us at 2 A.M., he still played me the next day.

Our first exhibition game was to be split between starter Emilio Escalades and me. Emilio came from Cuba, and was a tremendous athlete. I liked him very much but hoped he'd break his leg on the day of the game.

We each played routinely, until at the very end of my stint a loose ball rolled out of a thicket of players, right to the foot of an opposing forward five yards in front of me. He slammed it full force toward the far corner. It was one of those saves a goalkeeper remembers well: I threw myself sideways, just getting my fingertips under the ball to deflect it—a mixture of reflex and pure, dumb luck. After the game, Vargas approached me and said, "You're my starting goalkeeper for the year."

I was stunned. Few coaches I know have the confidence to make a decision like that. Once I knew I had his trust I went all out for him. I played hard, and trained harder, listening intently when he gave me advice on how to play the goal. I wish I had listened as carefully when he commented on my attitude. "Shep," he said, "you have great potential but you're going to be your own worst enemy because of the way you act."

The NYU Violets had a fine season, making the NCAA regionals. I was named to the All-American soccer team and got my picture on the cover of the NCAA soccer handbook.

In the spring of my sophomore year, still clinging tenuously to academic integrity and a bit wan from winter debauches, I was selected to the New York State All-Star team. Only my beer drinking arm seemed in shape, so I started to work out at a gym in Queens. There I met Gordon Bradley, an English player laboring for a then struggling pro outfit called the New York Generals. This was the first time I came up against a rigid English disciplinarian, one of the group who would so dominate the NASL; and it was also the first time I met anyone foolhardy enough to play American soccer for a living.

When Bradley was named to coach the All-Stars, it was clear from the look on his face—as though he were smelling rancid English trifle—that he was less than impressed by us.

"Remember lads, you're here to do a job," he said in a clipped British accent. "Remember that your shoes are your livelihood, and they are to be taken care of. Polish them, respect them. And keep the laces neatly trimmed."

I had to stifle a laugh. Here we were practicing perfunctorily for some exhibition games, and this guy was lecturing us on our shoes. But the grin disappeared when Gordon started his workouts, and over the next four weeks, my amusement calcified into awe. This guy was serious about soccer. It was more than a game to him. In fact, he had all the grim determination of a northland coalminer, which he once had been.

Gordon had seen friends torn in half, decapitated by the cruel machinery of the pits. It was soccer, however, that got him out, when he bulldogged his way into the English third division. No, soccer was not a laughing matter to Gordon, though I didn't realize it then.

Soccer was still just a game to me, and from the outset Gordon and I had troubles. Our first meeting left me somewhat confused. I was being made aware of what it meant to be a professional soccer player, but at the same time I was just a kid from New York playing for kicks. My confusion deepened when Gordon refused to start me one day because I appeared wearing a black sweatshirt with a Jewish star painted in the center. Gordon shook his head and sent me to the bench.

The reason for the Star of David, I tried to explain, was just a spillover of my excitement at being chosen to represent the U.S. in the Maccabiah Games, the Jewish Olympics held every four years in Israel. I was thrilled because, besides traveling to Israel, it would be my first taste of international competition—yet another glimpse into "big time" soccer.

All spring and summer, the Maccabiah team practiced twice a week at Long Island University. There was another goalie on the squad, and we were competitors for the starting spot, but Mickey Cohen and I hit it off right away.

I had heard of him, read enough about him to convince me that his reputation as one of the best American goalkeepers in America was well earned. And when Mickey walked onto the field that first day, it was easy to see why crewcut American coaches and their regimented British counterparts refused to recruit him for any professional team. I stood there in my violet NYU sweatsuit, slack jawed at the sight of him. Mickey came bopping

on the field in a floppy hat, adorned with a ribbon
in the red, green and black stripes that had become
the Sixties symbol of Black Power. He was just
your average Jewish kid who believed in civil
rights, gay rights, women's rights, yippie rights
and athletic freedom.

"Ay, wuz happenin?" He gave me a ten part
soul shake and scrambled up into the bleachers,
where he began to rummage through a large battered leather bag. I soon realized he was getting
dressed, right there in the stands. He pulled off his
sweat pants, revealing a pair of baggy green ber-
mudas; tearing off the workshirt, he pulled on a
skintight beige bodysuit; rummaging some more,
he came up with one green and one brown sock.
The pièce de résistance was a pair of sneakers with
the Black Power fist drawn on each one in magic
marker.

He caught me staring.

"Hey, man, there's method to this madness.
Simple principle, dig? I have applied the techniques of guerilla warfare to playing goal. What
you gotta do, man, is blend in with your backdrop.
You see these jive guys, wearing red and yellow
and purple . . ."

I looked down at my royal blue pants and saw
nothing abnormal. "Shit, some opposing forward
comes roaring down on you, that dude is going to
see where you are from twenty yards. Nah, man.
You gotta *camouflage*."

To Cohen, this was an intricate process begun
a day or two before the game. He would recon-
noiter the field he was to play on and examine the
backdrop. Cement called for a grey sweatshirt; dirt
for a neutral color plastered with dried mud. Aided
by Salvation Army thrift stores, Cohen's playing
wardrobe could now blend into brick, terra cotta,

brown grass, green grass, chain link fences and multicolored scoreboards.

"You dig where I'm coming from, Messing?"

We've been close friends ever since.

In August, it was time to leave for Israel. The day before our departure, I was doing my afternoon diving show at the public pool in Roslyn Heights where I worked as a lifeguard. I always had an audience, even if it consisted of eight-year-olds. "Come on, Shep, a double jackknife." "Hey, Shep, a back flip." Afternoons tended to be long and boring, with the steady prattle of the radio, endless cheeseburgers, the same little wise acres dumping ants in my suntan lotion. Okay, I said, just one more for my farewell engagement.

Smiling the faintly aloof, supremely confident smile of an international athlete, I mounted the highboard to do a three-and-a-half somersault. Instead, I came down on the edge of the board, slammed into the water like a sack of pipes and spent the next half hour having my nose reset in the garage of a doctor friend. I got on the plane for Israel with two black eyes, a broken nose, and an ice hockey mask, the kind goalies wear for protection. Mark Spitz was on the flight. So was his sister. I focused more on her than I did on the Games, until I found out she was only 14.

Mickey Cohen had other pursuits in mind. He's a vegetarian and was then into Judaism. He took a sack of carrots and disappeared into the hills beyond Jerusalem for a few day. When he returned, he was dehydrated, as though he had tried to do 40 days in the desert without benefit of divine intervention.

He started in goal the first game, screaming something about psalms and Pharisees every time the ball flew into his net.

Thwack. One goal for Argentina. "On the wicked, He will rain coals of fire and brimstone," Mickey screamed.

Thwack. 2–0. "O Lord, how many are my foes? Many are rising against me . . ."

Thwack. 3–0. "And many are saying of me, there is no help for him in God."

Thwack. 4–0. "Deliver me, O my God."

And so it went. We lost 9–0.

I played the next game while liquids were pumped into Mickey. We lost 1–0. I didn't invoke the scriptures, but I did take the team bus ride to the Wailing Wall. The American team was eliminated in the first three days, and I spent the next two weeks tracing my roots in Jerusalem discos and hanging out with a blond Sabra whose family owned the only hamburger stand in Tel Aviv. Mark Spitz tagged along on one of our excursions but that one trip convinced us to leave him behind. His style was a little damp. He had this habit that made the women squeamish. Mark's knees can hyperextend or bend backwards, and he liked to do a contortionist act. Those knees may have given him six extra inches kick on his butterfly stroke, but the social rewards were scant.

I was late returning to NYU in August, and decided to skip practice the first couple of days to take care of some academic matters. By now, my jumbled priorities had earned me a regular spot on the probation list, and so I decided to transfer to the School of Education downtown and see if I couldn't soak up a bit of just that—education. I told this to Vargas, who suggested I discuss it with Ben Carnevale, Director of Athletics, late of the U.S. Navy and as charming as a medieval inquisitor.

I told Carnevale that I couldn't play soccer until my academic problems were cleared up.

"Son, I hope you realize the lifelong values of athletics at this university."

"I just want some education courses," I replied.

"If you're not a team player, you don't belong here."

"I can't play unless I pass."

"Sports and academics are, by nature, independent concepts. Now I take care of my boys. You just go out and play ball, and I'll see to it that everything is fixed up."

"Can you guarantee it?"

"Just play soccer."

"I have to know."

"Don't you want to play soccer?"

"I think I'm being reasonable."

"I think you're being ungrateful."

He was shuffling through papers now, putting on an end-to-the-interview act, dismissing me like an incorrigible child. In one awful moment, it was clear to me that the myths I'd heard about big time college athletics were alive and well behind that mahogany desk. I looked down at my gray T-shirt that said "Property of NYU Athletic Department" and knew that Carnevale took the words literally.

"Stick it," I yelled at him. "You don't give a damn about me as long as I play soccer. Well, screw you."

Storming out of his office I stomped around the block to an Italian joint where I ordered an anchovy pizza and a lemon ice. As I polished off the last slice, I realized what I had done.

"You idiot," I said. "You just dropped out of school. Now what are you going to do?" Yet the more I thought about it, the less I cared. The whole place had been wrong—wrong priorities, wrong curriculum. Wrong. I hung around campus for a few days, basking in the notoriety of such local headlines as "Golden Boy Leaves School" and "Messing and NYU—Not a Sweet Parting." At least they didn't say "Dumb Jock Flunks Out." Then I packed up my snakes, sold my books, and headed back to Roslyn.

I enrolled in Nassau Community College, where my mother taught. As a transfer student I was ineligible to play soccer so I settled for assisting my old high school coach, Bill Stevenson. It was a perfect leveller. I got straight A's, helped Bill coach in the afternoons and tended bar at night. When pressed I worked at Gigi's, a Long Island catering firm with a brisk trade in chopped liver cupids for weddings and bar mitzvahs. Soccer was a thing of the past—until a letter came.

3

SO THIS IS HARVARD

The return address in the upper left corner was embossed with five, multicolored, interlocking rings. I tore open the envelope and began to read.

Dear Mr. Messing:
I have the pleasure of inviting you to the preliminary trials for the soccer team which will represent the United States of America in the 1972 Olympic Games . . .

The rest of the typewritten letter was a blur. It was about midnight and I had just come home from work at the catering company. I sat alone in the kitchen, absentmindedly picking little bits of chopped liver and shrimp Newburg from under my fingernails. I read the letter again.

The U. S. Olympic Committee was inviting me to preliminary eastern trials in Baltimore in April, four months away. Survivors would advance to the regional tryouts in Philadelphia, and the country's best would then compete against each other in St. Louis in August. Twenty-two players would go to Munich in the summer of 1972. To the Olympics.

I grabbed a beer from the refrigerator and went

outside to sit on the patio. My breath rose in tiny clouds that drifted off into the darkness. The backyard looked different at night when I couldn't zero in on familiar landmarks: the worn patch over home plate where the grass never grew back and the stunted laurel bush that didn't have a chance with five kids hurtling over it. I closed my eyes, remembering.

On my tenth birthday, my family gave me an Olympic party, something I had lobbied for. We set up hurdles, improvised landing pits and invited everyone to compete. Somewhere, Mom has a photograph of me standing against the back door, beaming, with four or five medals clustered over the belt of my dungarees. I must have invited every klutz in the neighborhood who wasn't at day camp to win that many events. But, after all, it was *my* birthday party and as birthdays go, it had been one of the best.

The Olympics, however, were the ultimate fantasy; and at 21 I was still dreaming: I saw blue jerseys, a red on white U.S.A. on the back of each one; flags, banners, all the best athletes in the world. All the best athletes in the world . . .

Sharp as the piercing January cold, reality rushed in. Who was I kidding? I ran down the factors conspiring against me. One, I was competing with hundreds of the best players in America just for a spot on the team. Two, I wasn't even one of them since I had left school and stopped playing. I was out of shape, short on wind, and all my hands were good for was slicing pastrami. Three, American soccer teams have always been laughable, losing first round games to Third World countries.

Screw reality, I decided. Forget the improbabilities. I'm going to go for it. And I did.

For three months before the Baltimore tryouts, I worked every day with Eliot Klein, the assistant soccer coach at Nassau Community College. I ran, did sit-ups, stood in goal like a Moscow bear while Klein's players hammered shots at me. For endurance and reflexes I played basketball, and by the time it came to leave, I was fit and able.

As a final light workout, Eliot and I decided to play a little one-on-one. Two minutes into our game, I drove for a layup and came down on the side of my left ankle. By 10 o'clock that night, I was in pain—the combination of a hairline fracture and a bad sprain.

I spent the night buried in ice packs and despair. My mother hovered over me, remembering the broken nose of the Maccabiah Games. "Some mothers have sons with medals," she sighed. "My son has notches on his body like a gunfighter." By morning, I was unable to walk. Eliot had to talk me out of turning back three times before we hit the Long Island Expressway. "Explain to them," he said. "I'm sure they'll give you another chance. These are reasonable men entrusted with great responsibility." It sounded fine, but halfway through New Jersey I panicked. We stopped at every bar with a pool table between Trenton and the Baltimore Beltway. Pool is my therapy. Say what you will about one eight ball finding comfort in another, it calms me. This worked well, until we pulled up at the field in Baltimore.

"Really, sir, I'm an All-American from NYU. I'll do anything, I'll go anywhere in the country at my own expense. Please, give me another chance."

It was as close to begging as I've ever come, but the Eastern selection committee sat there stony and impassive. Shoulder to shoulder, jut-jawed, crewcut, their fists like Virginia hams, they resembled an American Legion disciplinary committee and stared at me as though I were Trotsky asking for working papers at the Pentagon.

"Play, or pack up and go home," I was told.

Eliot helped me limp onto the field. Not a great start. I stood there like a blind boxer, waiting for the first punch. When the ball came, I couldn't move, and it whistled by my ear into the net. No use. I limped off the field over to where Eliot sat in the bleachers. Anticipating the results, he had a supply of cold beers. We sat in the stands and started pounding them down, watching the rest of the scrimmage. Midway through, Eliot pointed out a strange looking fellow playing midfield.

"A cross between Harpo Marx and Stan Laurel," Eliot said. The guy was wiry with a thicket of red hair, black shorts and a polka dot shirt. Deftly, he was pickpocketing passes from opposing forwards all around him. He was everywhere, challenging, driving, orchestrating the attack. Len Renery was easily the best player on the field. We watched him the rest of the afternoon, dribbling the ball through legs, bumping perfect headers off the springy coils that flew like a fright wig when he snapped his head.

"Think he rode a box car from Haight Ashbury?" Eliot asked.

"No, he hitchhiked from the Maine woods," I said.

A new vision detonated with each pop top. Finally, tryouts were over, and we walked over to where Irv Schmidt and John McKeon, heads of the selection committee, were about to read a list of eastern finalists. I mustered up all my humility. I asked McKeon once again.

"Can I go to another regional tryout? Anywhere?"

"Sorry kid, forget it. Now excuse me."

Eliot and I were headed for the car when we saw McKeon talking to Renery. We couldn't hear, but Renery's face was turning scarlet, his fists clenching and unclenching at his sides.

"Screw you," he screamed, and hopped into a battered van parked in a nearby lot. Lurching into gear, the van peeled out across the playing field, scattering the committee, which fled for the bleachers. Renery made one last circle before he disappeared in a cloud of dust and track cinders.

Len Renery didn't make the team either.

If you want to debauch, there isn't a better place than Baltimore, home of Blaze Starr and The Block. Next to Hoboken, New Jersey, which holds the national record, Baltimore must have the most bars per square mile; and the worst of them are on Baltimore Avenue, The Block, which is where Eliot and I headed.

By 3 A.M., we had hit about 15 of the raunchiest, dirtiest topless joints, pool halls and 35 cents-a-shot saloons that generous city had to offer. As we stumbled into Mimi's Little Shangri-La, I nearly tripped over what looked like a matted wig.

I looked closer, recognized the shirt. Polka dots. It was Len Renery. Face down under a table, he came up swinging when I shook his shoulder. When I explained our common bond, he began hugging me. And the three of us then spent what was left of the night together, toasting our righteousness and cursing the system.

Back home, I tried to figure out how to beat the hodgepodge of the American Olympic selection "system" that seems to believe that in this Land of Opportunity no man should get a second chance. More than likely, my place on the NCAA All-

American squad had gotten me the first tryout, but I needed connections to get a second shot. Unfortunately, the American selection committees are bureaucratic hierarchies. Every year, good athletes go unrecognized because of the Byzantine protocol surrounding the whole selection process.

Immediately I began calling everyone I felt could help me: congressmen, officials, coaches, teachers. And at last I connected with Wayne Sunderland, the mayor of nearby Massapequa, who I knew enjoyed soccer.

"I saw you play at NYU," he told me. "I think you'd be an asset. Get in touch with Joe Bariskill in Philadelphia, tell him I told you to call, and you should get that tryout."

I had heard about Joe Bariskill. I had heard that he was a tough old guy of 90 or so with a hide as thick as his glasses. I dialed his number; it rang at least ten times before a hoarse, impatient voice answered.

"Yeah?"

I went into my spiel, and he stopped me mid-sentence.

"Hold it son," he said, the edge gone from his voice. "I've talked to Wayne about you. You really want to play Olympic soccer?"

"Yessir."

"You really committed?"

"No question."

"Okay. If you want a chance, you've got it. Go out and practice."

Down in Philly, the tryout went well. I played one game without a mistake and was halfway through the second game when Bariskill came walking onto the field. He was a small, frail man with a thatch of silver hair and a cane that belied his brisk, springy walk. I thought he was coming to yank me out.

"Messing," he barked, breaking into a wizened grin, "you're our boy. You made it to the finals 45 minutes ago."

I stood in front of the bathroom mirror and took inventory. Midsection could be tighter. The scarred right thigh, still an inch less in circumference than the left, would need strengthening. Arms could be toned. Calves were in need of limbering. I had three months until the national tryouts in St. Louis, three months to get my body and my soccer into the best possible shape. I started on a training regimen, alone, pushing myself.

Training is much more a test of will than of physical strength. The human body is capable of amazing improvement, but it's a bore for the mind. Determination must supersede pain and exhaustion. The brain must convince the muscles that it's all going to be worthwhile. This isn't easy.

I loathe training, detest its joyless repetition. There are small incremental satisfactions: ten seconds shaved off a mile, 25 more push-ups than the week before, but by and large the process is grim and lonely. The fierceness and dedication with which you train is directly related to the goal.

In my case there was the Olympic dream, rooted in childhood, now just an arm's length away. There was also vindication, the need to prove myself the best at the St. Louis trials. I had to show the world—or at least the Irv Schmidts and John McKeons of the Olympic world—that a top grade athlete could wear denim and long hair. I had a personal score to settle in pursuit of which no obstacle seemed too great.

And so, the routine continued. Each day, I would plot a different cross country course for the prescribed number of miles, counting on a change of scenery to ease the tedium. One day I'd run beside the Long Island Expressway; the next, along the Northern State Parkway; the following day I'd be on the undulating slopes of a nearby golf course. After running came exercises: push-ups, chin-ups, sit-ups. Half an hour with the barbells, building arms and shoulders. For the thigh, leg weights.

Last came the wall drills. Using a plywood backboard my father had put up against the garage wall, I'd bounce a soccer ball off it between sit-ups, first to the left, then to the right, then clapping hands before the catch. I'd end up by kicking the ball full force against the wall and trying to smother the rebound.

Finally came a test of nerve, the most important weapon a goalie has. I would toss my ball at the wall low and hard, and practice diving for it on the concrete driveway. I was pounding the hesitancy out of my body by conditioning it to smack against the hard, gravelly concrete. Hurl yourself down and natural instincts send arms and hands out to cushion the fall. A goalie can't do this. Arms and hands are for catching the ball; the body must fall where it will. By the end of the first week my hips were black and blue, my knees and elbows like chopped meat. But I kept at it.

Afterwards, there was always swelling. When you abuse your body in this manner, blood and fluids speed to the damaged areas; the swelling hinders mobility. Ice helps, however. And that summer, the family drank a lot of warm lemonade.

"The Obsession," as a friend called it, began to color my life even beyond the daily training routine. I watched television and read newspapers squeezing one of those $1.95 hand strengtheners that look like oversized pliers. Once, for a large Jewish wedding, I set 300 places—institutional-weight china cups, saucers, soup bowls, salad and dinner plates, flatware—all with my left arm, to build it up. My boss asked me why I wasn't using my right hand. I told him that side was for dairy, the left hand for meat.

I flew to St. Louis feeling invincible. When I boarded at La Guardia airport, I was just another guy from New York, nothing strange, nothing out of place. But when I stepped off the plane in St. Louis, I was a freak in long curly hair, moustache, the beginnings of a beard, sandals and jeans. My baggage included three pairs of shorts, a few shirts and five pairs of soccer shoes.

Bob Guelker of the Southern Illinois University at Edwardsville, and the 1972 Olympic coach, was at the arrival gate, shaking hands and directing us to the hotel. He looked at me but didn't offer his hand. Instead, he gave me directions to the hotel and a warning: "Dinner is at 7, but you will not be allowed to eat with the team unless you appear in coat and tie."

I wanted to show him my bruises and he wanted to see labels. It was the beginning of a long, trying relationship.

I had no jacket or tie and so I was exiled from team meals. Were it not for a sympathetic waitress who provided unauthorized room service, I might have starved to death.

Actually, the tryout only lasted two days. Short but dull. That first night Guelker gave a talk. Mostly about St. Louis, renowned for having produced more NCAA soccer champions (and smug coaches) than anywhere in the country. From the heavy local flavor of the team, it didn't take an eastern education to realize the kind of players Guelker was looking for. He wanted solid, muscular, run-all-day types. A squad of lemmings.

Guelker spent a full ten minutes telling us just

how an Olympic athlete was supposed to look, how only the finest gentlemen should represent our country. (Had I sparked this?) He stressed pride and dignity. And he would not tolerate sideburns, facial hair, long hair—in fact, almost any hair. Narc haircuts were the rage.

I was depressed as hell. It lasted until the first party where I met a player I had read about for two years, Mike Ivanow, an excellent goalkeeper for the University of San Francisco. He and Neil Stamm, a tough centerback from Centerreach, Long Island, became my friends; and I would room with Neil the rest of the way.

The Saturday trials went well. Ivanow and I celebrated by drinking until 4 A.M. On Sunday I played well again, better than in my toughest games at NYU. I walked off the field feeling confident.

On the sidelines, Guelker was congratulating the best players. He shook their hands, nodded, smiled, said things like "See you in a couple of weeks," and "Fine job." When he got to me, the smile disappeared. "Thanks for coming," was all he said.

I don't remember ever feeling as low. All the work, all the punishment, all the pain: there had been so much sacrifice, physical and mental. And so much foolhardy hope. I had paid my way out, played my guts out, and now nothing.

That night I partied with a vengeance. I didn't return to the hotel. I just couldn't stomach the jubilation of the guys who knew they had made the team. At 5 A.M. I found myself in the airport, unshaven and utterly wretched. I was draped over one of those little pay televisions watching a test pattern when a porter walked by with the morning paper. I bought one and fumbled until I found the sports page. My eyes focused on a small heading at the bottom: U.S. Olympic Soccer Team Selections. I skimmed down the list to goalkeepers:

Jack Bell, St. Louis
Shep Messing, New York

I slid off the chair onto the floor and cried.

I've always been a guy to push my luck. Deal me a pair of nines at blackjack and I'll take another hit, expecting a three. So once I had nailed down a place on the Olympic team, I aimed my sights higher still. With a dismal academic record from NYU and an "A" average from tiny Nassau Community College, I applied to Harvard. I wanted to finish college. So why not the best? Besides, I always wanted to go to a school with a polo team.

In June, Harvard accepted the first junior college transfer student in its long and distinguished history, the honorable Shep Messing, scholar. I would be allowed to enroll as a junior that fall. Life was falling into place. My parents were delighted. Their son, the Harvard man. After that, Harvard Law. And then the Supreme Court. Mom couldn't wait to visit Washington.

I left for Boston early in September, two weeks after the Harvard soccer team reported. Remembering my NYU experience, I decided to forego college soccer.

Harvard Yard was, sure enough, covered with ivy: the windows, the fences, the somber brick buildings. My little Long Island junior college looked like a shopping mall in comparison. A clutch of students walking by warned me not to "pahk my cah" so close to the walkway or I'd get a ticket. And I thought I had left the foreign accents at NYU.

I jogged up the stairs in Mather House, a men's dormitory, and down the hall to a door marked 4B, a suite of rooms with a common lounge. The door to one room was open, and on the floor I saw a pair of patent leather shoes with bows on them. Bows made of ribbon. On the bed was a black tuxedo, and a pile of starched stand-up collars. Peering into the next room, I saw a matched pair of African carvings, two Black Power posters and an antelope throw rug.

So this was Harvard. Fred Astaire on one side of me and a Zulu chieftain on the other. I started to unpack, but slowly. My wardrobe ran to extremes: lots of T-shirts and jeans, and a flashy white suit that looked great in a Broadway pool hall—but out of place in cashmere country. All the nonsense about clothes with Guelker had made me extremely sensitive about my image and more determined than ever not to change it. But neither did I want to alienate my roommates.

As it turned out, we got on quite well. Dick Spalding needed his tux for meetings of the Hasty Pudding Club; Charlie Thomas had brought the African carvings from his native Gambia, but his first love, after political science, was soccer. The three of us spent the first night discussing an 18th century nude that hung over a bar on Harvard Square, a funky campus shopping area with prices only a Harvard student can afford. By 2 A.M., I knew five variations of the Black Power salute and the entire recipe for hasty pudding. I also knew I'd like it there.

A week later, walking across the Yard from class, I ran into Phil Kydes, a soccer player I'd known when I was at NYU. Now he dragged me over to the soccer field despite my protests that I wasn't going to play. "Just take a look," Phil said, smiling like a real estate salesman. "Nobody will pressure you."

And nobody did. I stood on the sideline, listening to the thud and thwack of a dozen balls being volleyed at midfield. It was a clear, sunny day and over a small hill, the Charles River was dotted with the long, varnished pods of rowing shells. Cross country runners perspiring lightly loped around the perimeter of the field. Kydes had lured me into the center of a damned college idyll.

Oh God, I had to play.

By the next afternoon, I was sharing a dank, musty locker room with the oddest assortment of soccer junkies yet assembled. My roommate Charlie was one of two Gambians. We had one Nigerian, one Englishman, one Finn, a Greek and three guys from Choate. That's a prep school, not a country. Strangely enough, I was the most exotic nut of all—the token New York Jew.

The player I felt closest to was Chris Papagianis who arrived from St. Louis with a custom-made pool cue. Papa had scored an unbelievable 79 goals in his last two high school seasons. At Harvard he was the team's high scorer and my constant companion on forays to Boston's Combat Zone, a little downtown pocket officially designated for sleaziness by the city's governing fathers. A dozen bars promised topless college coeds. I'm sure they were: Barber College, class of '44.

Harvard had a superb team both years I played there. We were tough, fast and high scoring. Coach Bruce Munro was affable enough, but ineffectual. His complaint, oddly, was that he had "too much talent." He had to spend hours just deciding who to play. For the most part we coached ourselves, and while I didn't learn much about goalkeeping skills, I was well schooled in conviviality. I learned that I could enjoy being part of a team.

We loved to play soccer. We literally played. If you had an afternoon class, you were excused from practice; and some days only three guys showed up, especially during exam periods. But there were no reprimands, no benchings. It was like intramural soccer. I alternated games with the other goalie, instead of competing with him for the starting spot. Soccer at Harvard was fun, a Saturday afternoon fling. Just another healthy diversion for the well-rounded young gentleman.

In fact, legend has it that the venerable institution was at least partially responsible for keeping American soccer in the ethnic closet for so long. In December, 1873, a group of prestigious eastern universities proposed to form the Intercollegiate Football Association. Football meant soccer in those days. Representatives from Yale, Columbia, Princeton and Rutgers gathered at a New York restaurant to inaugurate their new league. Harvard, icily, declined the invitation to engage in this crude populist diversion.

Harvard stuck with its own "Boston Game," the precursor to college football. And because Harvard was playing it, the entire nation took notice. It wasn't long before college football became our great intercollegiate sport and soccer crawled back to the oblivion of back lots in Polish steel towns.

Since alumni didn't hold tailgate parties before games and threaten coaches with extinction, Ivy League soccer tended to be friendly, gentlemanly affairs. Except when Harvard played Yale. Then I reached into my laundry bag and transformed myself into Shep the Hippie, hellbent on freaking out the Yalies in their clean sweat socks. I'd wear a black shirt and black shorts, tuck my curls under a bandana, slip on my shades and be cool. Jack Kerouac, here I am.

The Yale players thought me weird. Hubert Vogelsinger, their coach, was convinced I was evil. Every game he conducted public exorcisms on the sidelines. The same scene was repeated every time we played:

Harvard is dominating, leading 3–0, keeping the ball in the Yale end. Finally, Yale manages to inch the ball over the midfield line toward my goal. I've been leaning against the post, chatting with Phil Kydes' girlfriend. Slowly, I straighten up and hand her my sunglasses. I make the save effortlessly and shove the ball back in their faces. As she hands me back my shades, Hubert is screaming from the sidelines: "You asshole, they ought to throw you out of the Ivy League. Hot dog! Bolshevik! Get that goalie the hell out!"

The animosity was so intense, Hubert and I once got into a shoving match before halftime. Players and the referee pulled us apart. He kept screaming all through the second half, so bent on rattling my concentration that he never noticed we had 12 men on the field for nearly 15 minutes. Hubert prides himself on being a master gamesman but this time he was cheated unwittingly by our coach. The combination of this lapse, a loss and my antics were just too much for him. When the final whistle blew, he headed straight for me. I dug in my cleats, ready to block the first punch. Instead, Hubert grinned. "Damn nice game," he said, and kept walking.

Arden came into my life about the same time as Harvard soccer, though for the first few months I managed to keep them apart. Yet she should have been suspicious when I showed up seven hours late for our first date. I'd been out after a game with Charlie Thomas and Papagianis, when at 3 A.M. they carried me up the stairs and dumped me in the shower at Mather House. Half an hour later, Arden found me there and rescued me. "What a woman," I mumbled before passing out.

77

It wasn't until November, when Arden saw my picture in the Harvard *Crimson*, that she realized I played something.

"That's nice," she told me. "But what is soccer anyhow?"

The first winter played itself out like a scenario from *Love Story*. Arden and I trudged through the snow in Harvard Yard, went to Crimson hockey games and actually studied. Arden went to nearby Emerson College but she spent so much time in Mather House that one day flowered curtains blossomed in my room. Fortunately, Arden got along well with my roommates, especially Mingo, the kinkajou who occupied the front closet.

Mingo, a little South American honey bear, was very sweet if he liked you. He came to live with me soon after I got to Harvard, a gift from my brother Roy. Mingo was about four feet tall. He liked bananas, climbing venetian blinds and relieving himself under my roommate's bed. Though I built a huge cage for him by tearing out a closet wall, he usually had the run of the suite. In warm weather we moved his cage outside so he could take a little sun.

Having pets was really against the rules, and when a custodian ratted on Mingo, I received an ominous note from the Mather House dean.

Dear Mr. Messing:

It has come to my attention that you have a bear in your dormitory room. Please be advised that the rules specifically prohibit the harboring of pets "possessed of feathers and/ or fur." I believe this applies to bears. Kindly remove yours, at once.

The dean's message was clear: no bears in the room. So the following day, I moved Mingo into the hall.

All during that first year at Harvard, I made weekend trips to St. Louis to train with the Olympic team. By spring, teamwork and friendships had begun to evolve. Ncil Stamm, the captain, was an experienced veteran of 29. Some of his German friends accused him of tilting at windmills, and took fiendish pleasure in calculating the odds against our ever reaching Munich.

"We'll show the suckers," Neil would say. "We'll send them all postcards from the Fatherland."

Between workouts, roomie Neil and I had a good time. In fact, we had many good times, and most of them centered around evading Guelker's maddening prep school rules. There were rules for dress. Rules for food. Rules for drink. And rules for sleep. Between us, we managed to break them all. Sometimes Guelker caught us, and when he did, we counted on the intercession of Julie Menendez, his assistant from San Jose.

Julie was everything Guelker was not, a warm, hilarious showman who smoothed things over with his improvisations and remarkable card tricks. Julie understood our conflicts with Guelker because he understood us. He was able to appreciate the uncertainties of the 22 men who were pouring so much energy, so much pain, and so much of their own expense money into what seemed a bottomless pit.

"It doesn't matter," Julie would tell me after each of my rows with Guelker. "Just do it on the field, Shep." I credit Julie for the fact that I *was* able to do it—Julie and the 21 other crazies who chose to spend so much time away from family, friends, school, all the facets of normality, just to run their guts out in St. Louis.

Did we run. We began each day with a four mile trip up and down a steep hill on the St. Louis University campus. Every time Mike Ivanow, who had replaced the original second goalie Jack Bell, reached the top, he'd throw up his beer from the night before. Then he'd follow the rest back down. After a week, we developed a scheme. We'd use Mike's pause to wait for the others to descend and lumber up again. Then we'd rejoin the pack. It saved two miles. Goalkeepers shouldn't be running that much, anyway.

Finally, we were to leave on a six week trip to play in the preliminary Olympic qualifying rounds. Our division included Barbados and El Salvador. We would play both teams once in the United States, and once on their home ground. Our opening game was against Barbados in Miami. The night before we left, I laid my new blue Team USA uniform out on the chair so I could see it from my bed. I felt like a little kid.

On the flight down, Guelker was nervous. Just how nervous became apparent when the jet landed in Miami. It was 8 P.M. Before the seat belt light went off, he stood in the aisle, barking orders.

"All right. Everyone drop your stuff in the rooms and be out on the track for a 12 minute, two mile run, at nine o'clock sharp." By 9:15 that night, there were four players with severe muscle pulls from plunging into the run without a warmup.

After such a night, it was natural to need a couple of beers. Body fluids must be replaced. Though it was forbidden, we snuck across the street to a bar. The foam was just tickling my upper lip when Guelker walked in. To avoid another sermon on the virtues of temperance and obedience, we next decided on a new tactic. Room service, of course. We ordered up a six pack, and left the empties outside Ivanow's door.

I found training in Miami even more exciting than the prospect of our first game. Guelker was assisted by a West German named Dettmar Cramer, one of the most respected soccer coaches in the world. He took me out and worked on my goalkeeping one on one, and he knew how to make me produce. He taunted me, yelled at me, threw his hands up in disgust until I got furious. I also got better. Once when I messed around a bit, Cramer stormed up and poked me in the chest with his index finger. "Vat? Vat is dis? Dis is not circus. You are not clown. Never do I want to see such showboating. Never again."

We tied in Miami 0–0, a well-played game. I made a number of key saves, but Guelker was still unhappy about my appearance. We went on to Barbados. Three hours before the game there, he came to my hotel room with an ultimatum: Trim your sideburns over the earlobe, or look hip on the bench. Calmly, I asked him to sit down. I reasoned: We are from different parts of this great country. America takes pride in its diversity. Yes? Yes. In New York, sideburns are perfectly acceptable. In fact, only foreign security guards at the United Nations don't wear them. It makes sense that on the American team, I represent my part of America, yes?

No. Guelker was unmoved. From between clenched teeth, I told him to get out of my room. I sat there for two and a half hours. Fifteen minutes before we had to leave, I cut the sideburns and instantly, I was sorry. I swore I'd never do anything like that again. I stomped onto the field and I wasn't concentrating. I let Barbados score an easy goal. I was furious at Guelker, and at myself for giving in. It was a miserable day, but it did confirm something once and for all—that you can't hope to get the best performance out of an athlete forcing him to be what he is not. That business about creating the Olympic ideal was bullshit. Guelker didn't want to coach a team, he wanted to command a platoon of the Master Race.

Life didn't improve after a little incident in San Salvador, capital of El Salvador. The poverty there was astounding, unlike anything I'd ever seen, but at game time thousands of people, rich and poor, jammed the stadium. This was a great event. The stands were bobbing with paper cone hats worn as shields against a baking sun. We played well, holding a skilled, gritty El Salvador team to a 1–1 tie. Our pictures were in the papers, and we were looking to unwind.

Though curfew was at 11 P.M., I was out on the back balcony with Ivanow and two other teammates at 11:15 going to a small place they recommended. We pulled up to an old warehouse with its windows painted over. Midway through the first frosty beer, I took a close look at the decor. There was none, just crates and cots and laughing women in lace and satin underwear and black fishnet stockings.

"Hey," I said to Ivanow. "This is no bar, this is a . . ." At which point the police crashed in through the front door and we dove out the rear. We hid in some bushes for a while and then hitchhiked back to the hotel.

We showed up at the airport grinning sheepishly the next morning. My smile disappeared when a long blue serge arm clamped down on my shoulder.

"Señor." It was the Chief of Police. The night before His Excellency, personally conducting the raid, had recognized me before we made our escape. The goddamn papers. He went into a harangue, half Spanish, half English about how we had dishonored America. Guelker nodded in agreement. It was the coach's finest hour until the police chief said he couldn't let us on the plane. After a long argument, however, he finally let us go. Guelker, of course, threatened to let me go permanently.

Next stop was Cali, Colombia, and the Pan American Games. Unofficially, the Pan American Games are a warmup for the Olympics, which are usually held the following year. For many athletes, it's a first try at international competition. Those that perform well will arrive at the Olympics with a reputation and a bit more confidence. Those that do poorly either disappear, or work that much harder in the ensuing 12 months. It's a crash summer course in competitiveness, international relations, intestinal fortitude—though we drank bottled water—and, as I quickly found out, political survival.

From the moment we arrived, there were ominous undertones. The days in Cali were bright and sunny, but once night fell, a palpable tension hung over our compound; government directives slipped under doors warned against going out after dusk. Each evening, as the lights flickered on, tree frogs set up an eerie murmuring that sounded like infiltrating armies. The place even looked scary. Moonlight shone on a cruel collar of barbed wire that ringed the enclosure, and bullnecked Colombian police patrolled its perimeter, creating more a sense of menace than security. I became the special concern of the captain of the guard, a huge, perpetually unshaven man in grease-stained fatigues.

"*Identificación, por favor,*" he growled nightly; he'd then inspect every comma and period on my papers, and turn my athletic bag inside out, runing his fat fingers along the insoles of my soccer shoes. Was he expecting to find something sewn in a jockstrap? There were already scores of young Americans in Colombian jails on drug charges. And in T-shirts, jeans, and long hair, I certainly looked the part. After the fifth or sixth search, I couldn't resist asking, though we had been warned not to antagonize these men. At all costs.

"You think I have grass?" I asked.

He spat, just missing me. "Nah. We look for the other things. For *terroristas*."

Terrorists. It had never occurred to me. What would terrorists want with a bunch of athletes? Back in the room, we all laughed it off. It was like being in a B movie about a banana republic.

"Next thing you know," I told my roommate, "we'll have corpses falling out of closets."

Turned out, I wasn't far off.

Two mornings later, I walked out of the building and into a dead man. One glance, and I knew it wasn't natural causes. He was lying face down on the lawn. Blood mingled with the morning dew. There were three small holes in his shirt, surrounded by spreading brownish stains.

"*Es un Cubana.*" A Cuban, the guard told me casually. He sounded like a tour guide pointing out a statue. As I stood gaping, two groundskeepers dragged the body across the lawn and tossed it into a waiting jeep. By 9 A.M., the grass had been hosed, and not another word was said.

The United States was playing Cuba and a troop of bayoneted security men arrived at the compound to escort us to the game. Fifty thousand people were crammed into the stadium, the first of those fabled South American arenas I'd seen with a moat around the playing field. Beyond the moat was a stretch of barbed wire—the nasty double-pronged kind outlawed in World War II. Outside the wire was still another deterrent, a three foot wide ring of poured concrete studded with shards of jagged glass. The glass was recycled Coke and whiskey bottles; the jagged edges shone like emeralds in the late afternoon sun. Up in the stands, people unwrapped bean filled cornflower cakes and long brown bottles of Colombian beer.

"Viva Los Estados Unidos" a small group of Colombians cheered as our hosts escorted us into the stadium. Our honor guard formed a double line around us, bayonets pointing at the crowd. But I was relaxed; these were friendly faces, come to cheer for the anti-Communist avengers—us. There was a flurry of small plastic American flags when we took the field, and only scattered applause and whistles for the Cubans. Trotting over to my goal, I began checking the net. Then I remembered the murdered Cuban and tensed. Was it significant that he was gunned down and left to die in front of our quarters? At which point 20 helmeted guards filed past me to take their places along the end line.

Standing alone in goal, surrounded by all that artillery, I felt uncharacteristically vulnerable. The moat, the barbed wire, the concrete and glass wall —why were they needed? Was there a sniper in the stands? Terrorists in the changing room?

One minute into the game, I realized that most of the terrorists were on the field. In Cuban uniforms. For it was the bloodiest, most vicious game I've ever played in. A Cuban striker made a tackle, spikes high, chopping down our left winger with deep, circular gouges just above the kneecap. The Cubans were going for the man; if a pass skittered within 10 feet of an American player, he was upended. Elbows were dug in rib cages and yellow caution cards fluttered in the air like helpless canaries until the referees realized the futility of their mission.

In goal, I threw myself at bullets, punched out high balls, wrapped my body around low ones and stayed down on the ground until the traffic had cleared. Once, twice I got kicked in the head after making a save. A third time, I wasn't so lucky as

I felt a searing pain in my right shoulder. For a second, the shoulder was pinioned to the ground by a Cuban player's shoe. He had spiked me just below the shoulder. When I got up, a liquid warmth spread over my ribs and ran down into my shorts. I was bleeding like a pig.

From that point on, I wasn't myself. Someone else was screaming at the Cuban strikers. Someone else was flinging his body out of the net and into other bodies. Shep Messing, hippie from New York, had become John Wayne, patriotic avenger.

The 80 minutes remaining was not soccer, it was war. The same athletes who had nodded amiably at each other in the dining hall now lunged at one another with murderous intent. By some insidious psychological process, we had been transformed from players into soldiers, staunch defenders not of a small white net, but of the American Way. It was frightening.

Had anyone told me beforehand that I'd end up shrieking "Viva Americana" like some jingo crazy, I'd never have believed it. But by the time the whistle blew at half time, I found myself clenching a raised fist and grinning at a guy on the sidelines who screamed, "Get their commie asses." That's what blood can do to a suave young liberal.

In the locker room, when our trainer cut my shirt off, there was blood all over; my clothes, my arms, my face. Julio Menendez, the assistant coach, took one look at me and whipped out a deck of playing cards. He spread them out on a bench and we watched, amazed, as he started to do card tricks.

Since Julio was originally from Cuba, I don't really know what feelings the game had aroused in him, but he knew a volatile situation when he saw one and launched into his bag of tricks to calm us down. "Listen, you guys," he said, riffling the deck along his forearm. "Remember this is only a game."

He paused, and drew an ace of spades out of his waistband. "It isn't goddamn World War Three."

With my shoulder stitched and a new jersey covering the damage, back onto the field we went. I was calmer but no less determined. The rest of the game was just as tough, but the referees maintained control. Though the crowd kept up a rhythmic clapping, chanting "USA, USA," when it was over, we had lost 1–0. Yet nobody lost his life.

There was a month break before the finals of the first round. Barbados had been eliminated, and all that stood between us and the second round were El Salvador and Mexico—not obstacles were scoffed at. Salvadorians are serious about their soccer, so serious that three years earlier a brutal war broke out after El Salvador eliminated Honduras in World Cup qualifying competition.

Actually, Honduras and El Salvador had historic bad blood centering on real or imagined mistreatment of Salvadorian immigrants living in Honduras. The game in question was played in neutral Mexico. But so great were the tensions that after El Salvador won, it sent 12,000 troops to invade Honduras. Somewhat simplistically, perhaps, El Salvador is remembered as the country that went to war over soccer. Yet we weren't about to take the characterization lightly.

The game was to be played in Jamaica, and it was to be "overtime plus sudden death—if need be." Not my favorite phrase. In soccer terms, this means that if the score is tied at the end of regulation play, and a predetermined number of overtime periods, each team takes five penalty kicks. Penalty kicks are nasty, primal situations. The goalie stands alone in the net and a player from the opposing team takes his best shot from a spot 12 yards out. As luck would have it, regulation time ended in a 0–0 tie. After two 15 minute overtimes, both teams had scored once.

Guelker left me in goal for the tiebreaker. I would have preferred a snakepit. Five times, our guys rammed the ball into their net. Four times their players put shots past me. It was us 5, them 4 with one El Salvador shot left. It was all up to me.

As their forward readied himself, I paced back and forth in my cage, muttering, cursing. Against Cuba, I had felt like a warrior. Now I felt like an animal. I was charged with enough adrenalin to fight a Brooklyn street gang. In that instant, something snapped.

I was charging out of the goal, ripping off my jersey, swinging it over my head. I ranted in pidgin Spanish and obscene English.

"Simon Bolivar is a *puta*."

"Your mother sleeps with burros."

I spat. I snarled. I ran at the El Salvador player and took a few licks at him with the jersey, screaming all the while. Then it was over. I was proud of myself. I had shown him I was crazy—and that any fool had better think twice about scoring on me.

I walked calmly back to the goal. "Ready," I said evenly, and crouched to await the shot. It sailed high over the bar. We would go to the final round. The El Salvador player would probably go to Honduras.

My senior year at Harvard was a wonderful one. The soccer team went all the way to the NCAA championships in Miami's Orange Bowl, where we lost to eventual champions Howard 1–0 in the semifinals and I was voted MVP of the tournament. I continued to practice with the Olympic team every few weeks, and to study as well, suffering my most serious academic trauma when Term Papers Unlimited went out of business. This was a fantastic operation in its heyday, where you could purchase a 25 pager on Existential Despair for $15—$2.50 extra for an annotated bibliography.

Arden and I were known as the Duke and the Duchess, that eccentric New York couple with the four foot bear. We were first on the dance floor, and last to go home. A few professional modeling jobs in Boston had left their mark on me, to say nothing of my wardrobe. I wore three piece suits, broad brimmed hats, carried a walking cane and trailed silk scarves. I often wonder what Guelker would have said if I'd dressed like that for a team meal.

During my last term, we had to play a final round of Olympic elimination games against Jamaica, Mexico, and Guatemala. It wasn't going to be easy; Mexico had finished fourth in the 1968 Olympics, and Guatemala had made it to the quarterfinals. We practiced in St. Louis, and in January we flew to Guadalajara to play Mexico. Unfortunately, a little piece of Harvard came with me. It was exam time, just a few weeks away from graduation. At Harvard, exams are taken seriously. So seriously, in fact, that they insisted I take my Humanities final on the very day, and at the very hour my classmates back in Cambridge were taking theirs. Only I would have to take mine in Guadalajara.

I had a choice of studying humanities in my hotel room or studying humanity on the beach. Bikinied humanity. "Go out and have a good time," the team manager told me. "I'm a sociology major, and I'll tutor you just before the test." Naturally, I obeyed so wise a man.

At the appointed hour, Harvard flew in a professor who was on sabbatical in Mexico City to monitor my exam. He sat me down at a table beside the pool at the Guadalajara Hilton, and after one glance at the questions I knew I was in trouble. I decided to wing it.

In a marvelous piece of expository writing I likened my exile poolside to Thoreau's experience at Walden Pond, somehow linking the perils of Mexican water—which included a concise entomology of Central American reptiles—to Henry David's civil disobedience. I thought it was pretty good. My professor thought it was bullshit. But I pulled out with a "D" for effort.

Effort was also the key word for our game in Mexico. I remember telling some writer that we can't play at 95% of capacity and beat any of these teams. We have to play 100%. And that's what we did, using an aggressive defense to disrupt the slow, graceful game of the Latins. We tied Mexico 1–1 and they were jeered out of their own stadium.

Next was Guatemala in April. Before the game even started we felt as though we'd been through a prolonged siege. This began gently, as the Guatemalans practiced a quaint local custom of raining orange peels on the visiting team's heads. At first, we enjoyed it; the humid afternoon acquired a refreshing tang of citrus as the peels showered like bright orange blossoms onto the green sod. Then players started slipping during the warmup. We tried clearing the field, running back and forth as if we were in some absurd game show relay, scooping up the peels and dumping them on the sidelines.

Just as we finished, the explosions began. The Guatemalans call thm firecrackers. They were six inches long and an inch thick. Tied together and detonated on the edges of the field, they looked and sounded like dynamite. Players stumbled through dense clouds of smoke, holding fingers in their ears against the deafening thunder.

Our ears were still ringing as the home team trotted out, calm, fresh and ready to kick ass. We held them as best we could, but it wasn't good enough. We lost 3–2. We were still in the running for a spot in Munich—barely. The next game was against Guatemala in Miami, a city with plenty of oranges, but very few soccer fans. Mike Seerey, whose father Pat once hit four home runs in a game for the Chicago White Sox, scored two goals for us and we won 2–1. Next obstacle: Mexico.

We played them in San Francisco, but not before they tried some sleight of hand with the team's passports. According to international soccer rules, all players must present their passports to the officials before each game. Oddly, the Mexicans arrived at Kezar Stadium without their passports. Twenty-two men had "forgotten" them at the hotel, although they insisted a courier could produce the passports by halftime.

"Sure," Guelker said, "and for the first half, they can flood the field with professional ringers."

Under protest, Guelker let the game begin, and when it was over, we had tied them 2–2. In the round robin standings, we were now dead even with Mexico. The deciding game would be against Jamaica.

We played Jamaica in St. Louis, and the game was not without its little ironies: fittingly, the final Olympic qualifying game was being played in the city that spawned nearly half our team. Second, as we deplaned on his home turf, Guelker informed me that I wouldn't be playing. I sat out the game in a bitter funk. I remembered the endless hassles of tryout camp. I remembered the penalty kick against El Salvador. I remembered the Alamo. It was only when the final whistle blew and the score read U.S. 2, Jamaica 1, that I remembered Munich. I laughed, I cried. I went out with Stamm and Ivanow and celebrated. Two weeks later I graduated Harvard with a place on the Dean's list and a ticket to Munich.

4

"YOU ARE JEWISH?
COME WITH ME"

Two days before the soccer team left for Munich, Vice President Spiro Agnew threw a party at the White House. President Nixon was absent, but the First Lady was on hand to greet each member of the U.S. Olympic Team. Looking back, it seems only fitting that a man later drummed out of office should provide the sendoff for the most perverse Olympiad since Hitler's 1936 propaganda circus in Berlin. But at the time, the pomp of White House hospitality and the glamor of meeting Mrs. Nixon and the vice president in a receiving line had to be the ultimate pep rally.

"So you're the crazy goalie I've heard so much about," Agnew said.

"And you're the lousy golfer I've heard so much about," I replied. He smiled. Politicians always smile.

The ballroom was brimming with beaming young athletes in red and blue Olympic blazers. Exploding flashbulbs haloed such familiar stars as swimmer Mark Spitz and pole vaulter Bob Seagren. Behind a stand of red geraniums, the Marine Band transformed Glen Miller into a march. At the dais, Agnew stood in glory beneath the blue and gold presidential seal. He spoke briefly of courage and patriotism and, to my surprise, was no better than your average athletic banquet keynoter. We listened politely to his lectern-slapping finale about honor at all costs. On the way out, White House guards stopped a wrestler with a Presidential salad fork hidden in his sleeve.

As our bus rolled up to the gate of Olympic Village, German schoolgirls flung chrysanthemums at the windows. Oompah bands played beneath clusters of bright, helium-filled balloons, and tiny blond children in lederhosen carried baskets of rose petals. Beyond the chain link fence, the gleaming steel needle of Olympic Stadium caught the late morning sun. The buildings were of dazzling white concrete, shot through with reflective mica chips. The West German government was calling this Olympics the Jungenfestspiel, the festival of the young, and they couldn't have been more gracious.

I felt as though I were at the gates of Emerald City. The late Avery Brundage, patriarch and chairman of the International Olympic Committee, thought he was Oz. He swept past in a Mercedes limousine just as we entered the gate, waving and smiling like a benevolent emperor on a tour of his kingdom. Certainly, the 20th Olympiad was his creation—a shimmering multimillion dollar extravaganza that he intended to rule with an iron hand. Ultimately, his politics would expose him as a callous, narrow-minded autocrat. But as the festivities began, his smile was benign.

We settled into our quarters, an ultra-modern stack of apartments with more comforts than home. The athletes' compound had discotheques, recreation halls, bars, a mammoth pool and a Ping Pong table every 25 yards. It was a sinfully expensive summer camp for the elite. For the few days prior to the opening ceremonies, I had a wonderful time.

One of my favorite pastimes was watching weight lifters eat. Discreetly, I would follow them through the line in the dining hall and stare unabashedly at their trays. For breakfast they ate trembling yellow mountains of scrambled eggs, dozens of strips of bacon, twelve or more glasses of milk. Lunch and dinner were astounding: five or six steaks or two roast chickens, mounds of mashed potatoes awash in butter and gravy, whole apple pies, half-gallons of ice cream. I watched one Russian heavyweight put down 17 hamburgers, dousing them in 2½ bottles of ketchup.

"Russians are suckers for ketchup," said a voice behind me. "I think they'd defect for it." Turning, I recognized David Berger, a 28-year-old weight lifter I had met at the Maccabiah Games. Born and raised in Shaker Heights, Ohio, he was now living in Israel, his adopted country. When I met him in 1969 he was a quiet, dedicated guy in love with his sport and completely enraptured by Israel. He said that he planned to settle there, and two years later he did, though the move cost him his marriage.

That August afternoon as we moved through the lunch line, he talked about his plans to begin law practice after the Games. He had a law degree from Columbia University, but had postponed his career to train. For the past two years, four days a week, two hours a session, he strained under the heaviest weights his body could endure. Israel paid him a stipend and a living allowance, since Berger was one of Israel's brightest hopes for an Olympic medal.

Most Israelis had given their youth, sometimes their lives, to national defense. In return for Israel's faith in him, David had agreed to postpone his career. He trained like a fanatic and, for five more hours a day, studied Hebrew.

On parting, we wished each other luck. "Shalom," David said—a word that means many things, usually peace. This time it meant good-bye.

Guelker was strung like piano wire from the day we arrived. Sensing this, Dettmar Cramer offered to scout the other teams for him. Instead of appreciating the gesture, Guelker exploded, screaming that he wanted no help from anyone. He spent the remaining days devising torturous workouts. The day before the Opening Ceremonies, he called a team meeting.

"I've come to a decision," he announced. "Due to the fact that we have a game on the third day of competition, we will not march in the Opening Ceremonies."

I couldn't believe my ears. We had knocked ourselves senseless for two years. We were the first goddamn American soccer team ever to qualify for the Olympic Games. We were proud as hell to be marching behind our flag, and suddenly Guelker was forbidding it.

We argued. Guelker ranted. I raved. It went on all day. I insisted that I would march regardless of his decision, even if I had to march alone. Eventually, Guelker capitulated, and a handful of us hurried to the stadium just as the ceremonies were about to begin.

Outside the stadium, the athletes were being organized for the parade. We would walk five abreast. Positions on the outside were most coveted, since they were closest to the crowd and the cameras. This was my best chance at a smile and a wave to the folks back home.

In my group of five, I got the best spot. Ecstasy.

American soccer was scheduled for 30 seconds of television coverage, but only if it fit after Pierre Salinger finished his live report from a Munich disco. So the parade meant a lot to me.

Just as I took my place, Bob Seagren came running up looking for a better place in line. With his controversial fiberglass Catapole, Seagren had vaulted higher than anyone in the world. Ultimately, the pole would be confiscated in a preposterous official raid on his quarters, and he would leave the Games in disgust, but at that moment, he was part of the Olympic hype. Seagren wanted to be on television. So did I. A fin to the guy next to me assured both of us a prime spot.

Amazing. Already it had started. Willy Brandt's "joyous games" were tainted with petty squabbles and show biz dazzle before they began. International bickering over apartheid had already resulted in the expulsion of Rhodesia. And right on the heels of warring nationalism came rampant commercialism.

We had all heard stories about athletes being paid by various manufacturers to wear their products in the Games, though I never saw any outright evidence of this. But there's a different kind of payola that's absolutely legal which results when a company pays a fee to become the "official" outfitter of a national team, or supplies the official Olympic coffee, milk, razor blade, toothpaste.

That year, the official outfitter for the U.S. soccer team was Adidas. Guelker didn't appreciate my preference for Puma. The people who doled out equipment at the two sport shops in the Village were most generous. Though to some they were more generous than to others. Everyone got an Adidas or Puma T-shirt, the cheapest form of advertising, and even we—the unglamorous American soccer players—managed to wheedle a pair of running shoes. But the stars were showered with products. Marathon champion Frank Shorter needed a small cart for his haul: warmup suits, shorts, dozens of shoes, bags, visors. The others were left to walk around in ill-fitting castoffs looking like orphans. Duane Bobick, the heavyweight boxer, was one of them.

Bobick is a big guy, a heavily muscled cornfed boy from Bowlus, Minnesota, with a torso like a century oak and a face like a choirboy. I met him at the Pan American Games. He's an affable, sensitive guy from a family of 11 children who doesn't seem the type to make a living knocking lesser men senseless. Before the Olympics Muhammad Ali had dubbed Duane "The Great White Hope," but when I ran into him in Olympic Village, he looked like the Great White Clearance Sale.

His sweat pants were tight as leotards, reaching just below his knee caps. His jacket was so tight it drew his shoulders back like wings.

"Piss on 'em," he snarled. "The hell with them all." He pointed to a group of U.S. officials eating yogurt on a nearby bench. "Those guys kill me. They go in and demand three sets of matching warmups, and because they're officials they get them. They're all so fat they take all the big sizes. I can't even get a goddamn pair of pants to train in." Finally he laughed in disgust and walked off to practice. The view from the rear was something else.

Two days after the Opening Ceremonies, we were to play our first game. Naturally, Guelker blamed me for the whole parade controversy. Any chance I had of starting the first game was gone because of that. Was it worth it? Hell, I guess so, if for no other reason than to prove to Guelker that we were more than puppets.

I wanted to play against Morocco because I wanted to be part of the first American soccer team ever to kick a ball in Olympic competition. I had played in 12 of our 14 qualifying matches and thought I deserved a place in the lineup. Guelker thought differently. He started Ivanow.

I went into a classic sulk and looked for a reporter. Who should I find but Red Smith of the *New York Times*. Finding Red Smith at a soccer game is like finding Jascha Heifetz at the Macy's Thanksgiving Parade. I had been reading Red Smith since I was seven and he was an idol. He could be so irreverent and yet so graceful, a combination I'm still working on. For the first time in my life, I was nervous talking to a sportswriter. But Red calmed me immediately with an easy question.

"Did you bring your snakes?" he asked.

"No," I replied. "I brought Guelker instead."

I went on to explain that the reason I was benched had nothing to do with soccer but stemmed from the Bill of Rights. Red Smith liked the angle and played it up in his column. I'm sure my team spirit must have delighted Guelker. Here we have the United States playing its first Olympic Game and, I might add, playing damn well, holding a more experienced, skillful Moroccan team to a 0–0 tie—thanks to some sensational goalkeeping by Ivanow—and the next day Red Smith's column in the *Times* focuses on "an uninhibited young man from Roslyn Heights, L.I. with a reputation for playing with boa constrictors."

Needless to say, I was benched for game two against Malaysia. This time Ivanow was shaky, letting in two easy goals, and we lost 3–0. Guelker was left with no choice but to play me. He knew the West German team would leave Ivanow flopping like a beached carp. Ever since I learned the draw matched us against West Germany, the team that would ultimately win the gold medal, this was the game I most wanted to play. Being part of the first game would have been a nice piece of historical trivia. Being part of a game against West Germany would be an athletic accomplishment.

The Morocco and Malaysia contests had been played in the hinterlands, in auxiliary stadiums, before crowds of 15,000 or 20,000. Against Germany, we would be in Olympic Stadium before 80,000 people screaming for the Fatherland. Make that 79,997. There would be at least three U.S. fans in the crowd—my mother, my father and my brother Roy.

I had the standard pre-game fight with Guelker. This time it was over my uniform. For some strange reason, he wanted me to wear number 19, which is usually assigned to a reserve forward. I argued that traditionally—I knew he could relate to that word—goalkeepers wear number 1 and that's what I intended to wear.

"You can wear it on the bench," he said.

"Okay, you win, I'll wear 19." So I did, all through the warmups. Just as the whistle blew, I ripped off the 9 and threw it behind the goal.

Guelker would have yanked me right then except he probably knew it would be worse punishment to keep me on the field. In the first two minutes the Germans took five shots. The first four I saved with dives, the fifth flashed by me, straight and unstoppable. 1–0. Time elapsed 1:50. A terrible thought occurred to me. At this rate, the final score would be 54–0.

Deep down, I knew we had no chance for victory unless the whole German team got loaded on schnapps during a half time celebration. After all, this was a team that included five players from Bayern Munich, the top club in West Germany.

Why would a bunch of pros be allowed into the Olympics? I wondered until Dettmar Cramer explained that these guys were technically amateurs since they hadn't signed pro contracts. They were paid not for playing soccer, but for shining shoes and picking up towels. I suppose they were no less amateurs than blue chip college athletes at American football factories, the ones who drive cars loaned to them by thoughtful alums.

Philosophy aside, these fine amateur athletes were using me for target practice. I wondered if the guys wearing red, white and blue were my defenders or some cruel mirage. With each assault, they wavered and disappeared. The only time we got the ball to midfield was for the kickoff after Germany scored a goal. I saved shots with my hands, my chest, my arms, my feet. I saved bullets from up close, volleys from far away and ricochets from everywhere. I was in what athletes refer to as the "zone," that special, almost mystical area you reach that allows you to transcend your normal level. Colors fused. I couldn't tell friend from foe. I was the sacrificial lamb.

Uli Hoeness, West Germany's World Cup star, unloaded a cannon right at me from about 10 yards and I couldn't get my hands up fast enough. The shot exploded in my face and bone-jerking pain ripped through my nose. I tried to get up and the ball hit me square in the back. I made the save with my back. I wouldn't have believed it except I saw a picture in the paper the next morning. It was right under the headline that said West Germany set an Olympic record with seven goals. And under the picture it said that this long-haired American kid set another Olympic record with 63 saves.

Sixty-three fuckin' saves. Five dozen and three. That comes to one every 90 seconds. It didn't mat-

101

ter that my hands were raw, my body bruised, my nose broken. I had set an Olympic record with 63 saves in front of 80,000 people who understood soccer. Amidst the rubble of defeat, I found my own high at the Munich Olympics.

Despite pain, I enjoyed myself the next few days. I partied all night, slept in every morning without sadistic practices to disturb my rest. On such a morning, September 5, a hand gripped my shoulder, rousing me from sleep.

"You are Jewish?" a thick, German-accented voice asked. I looked up into the face of a uniformed guard and for an instant, my blood froze. I was terrified.

He must have seen the alarm in my face, because he released his grip. "Is all right," he said. "There is a problem at Building 31. You must come with me."

As I rummaged for clothes, he explained. Before dawn, a group of Arab terrorists had climbed over the chain link fence into Olympic Village and taken members of the Israeli team hostage, shooting two dead. As one of twelve Jewish athletes on the American team, I was to have special protection. My mind raced. We had been warned, advised of the possibility that the Fedayeen might choose Munich as an arena to gain worldwide attention. But to come right into the Village, just a few hundred yards away . . .

The window was open and it was remarkably quiet outside. No gunfire, no sirens. I could hear only the faint sounds of the recorded Muzak unceasingly piped through the Village to maintain the festive atmosphere. Funny what the mind remembers. That awful morning, the loudspeaker was playing "Que Sera, Sera."

I looked down into the plaza. Fifty yards away, clusters of athletes played chess and sunned themselves by the pool. I heard the steady plickety-plock of a Ping Pong game in progress. Then I saw a terrorist.

He was standing on a balcony of Building 31, not more than 100 yards away. He stood with his feet apart, staring directly at me. His face was covered by a grey knit ski mask and he held a submachine gun. Below him on Connollystrasse, the street named for Harold and Olga Connolly, white ropes ringed the entrance to the building. Behind the ropes stood reporters and ambulance attendants, waiting, while overhead, the steady rotors of an arriving helicopter beat the humid air. It was a bright, overcast day, about 85 degrees. My chest tightened; I felt I couldn't breathe.

On the roof above the terrorist, police snipers dressed in brightly colored warmup suits crouched in readiness. I could see the thin blue muzzle of a rifle just five feet away from my nose on the next balcony.

"How many?" I asked, and the guard shrugged.

"Ten, maybe twenty hostages. No one is certain."

The phone shrilled. It was Neil Stamm, calling from another building.

"You heard?" he asked me. I told him I had. "Can you see that guy out there?" He was referring to the terrorist on the balcony. "I'd love to see the police blow him away. I guess they can't. He's probably got a half dozen buddies inside."

And those buddies had their guns trained on a clutch of helpless athletes. It must be horrible, sitting there under a fanatic's muzzle, wondering whether or not these were your last moments on Earth.

"I heard they're going to shoot one an hour," Stamm said. There was a knock on the door, and I hung up as the guard asked in German who was there. It was three American reporters. They knew I was Jewish and asked if I would come to press headquarters for an interview. "I've got nothing to say," I told them, but agreed to go anyway.

On the way over, I spotted Howard Cosell, scurrying across the plaza in tennis shoes.

"Howard!" I caught his sleeve. "I'm American, I'm Jewish—can you tell me what's happening?"

"Don't have time to talk," he yelled over his shoulder as he dropped to his knees and began crawling toward a forbidden observation post behind police lines.

In the solid concrete fortress that held press facilities, news bulletins ticked across television screens in seven languages. "Preliminary reports indicate two dead, nine held hostage." As I reached for a Munich newspaper, a German correspondent leaned over. "Don't bother," he said. "You will find nothing there. In this country, such a security breach is not easily admitted."

His words were an understatement. Not until the final grim body count was revealed did the West German authorities release an honest, straightforward news bulletin. Even in the press building, rumors were rampant. Twenty-six held hostage . . . three more killings . . . an imminent surrender. Nobody had any idea what was going on.

"Are you scared?" a reporter asked. By now, ten Jewish athletes from the American team had been brought to the building. We stood in a small knot, answering questions in dazed monotones. Yes, we were all scared, but few of us for ourselves. Clearly, the Arabs had what they wanted—international notoriety.

"What do you feel?" another reporter asked me. For a moment, I couldn't answer. Words seemed inadequate, completely absurd. The pieces of the unfolding tragedy had not yet come together; everything was still fragmentary. There was outrage, that these people would dare do what they'd done. There was grief for the dead. There was fear for the hostages. There was disillusionment. We had been fools to believe in an Olympic ideal, to swallow the nonsense about international camaraderie. Our happy little Village was no sparkling oasis, it was just as polluted as the world outside. Commercialism and petty vanities had found their way past the large blue and white banner proclaiming *Wilkommen die Athletiker.* Now death had arrived.

"How do you feel?" he asked again, pressing a microphone under my chin.

"Sick," I said.

Having wrung all they could from us on that, the reporters turned to more routine matters. What did we think about the upcoming marathon? Did Bobick have a chance against the Cuban heavyweight?

"How can you care?" I practically screamed and walked out, slipping past my guard. I wanted to get away from them all, to get out of that place. It was unclean.

Walking back to my room, I ran into Duane Bobick who grabbed my arm when he saw me.

"They're making me fight," he said. "Goddamn them, they say I *have* to fight."

He was scheduled to meet Cuban heavyweight Teofilo Stevenson at two that afternoon in what had been billed as *the* match of the Olympics. Bobick still bore a nasty bruise on his left cheek from his bone-crunching bout with Juri Nesterov, a Soviet fighter, two days earlier. It was strange that the Cuban match should be scheduled so soon after such a punishing fight, but Bobick had been ready. "It's the biggest fight of my life," he'd told me the day before. Now, in the face of murder, it meant nothing at all.

"Man, what am I going to do?" he asked. "I've trained years for this, but I just don't feel like fighting. It's sick, really sick."

"Haven't they stopped the Games?" I asked. I couldn't believe it.

"No," he said, shaking his head. "They say I have to fight or forfeit. It makes me sick."

Still shaking his head, Bobick trudged off to the Boxhalle, where Stevenson destroyed him. Just 200 yards from where the Israeli team members lay bound and gagged, a crowd of 2000 watched a volleyball game. At 3:30, nearly 12 hours after the first murders, Avery Brundage suspended the games—temporarily.

I spent the rest of the afternoon and early evening passing through cycles of anger and bereavement, like a small child experiencing death for the first time. It was big and ugly and hard to understand.

"Don't you have any goddamn human decency?" I snarled at a guy wearing a red Polska jacket. He was walking down a footpath, laughing and tossing a frisbee in the air. A maniacal scream came from inside me as I hurled the Polish athlete to the ground.

I don't know why I did it. I'm Jewish, yes, but religion has never meant anything to me. I guess I just didn't understand how anyone could play at such a time. But my anger fled as suddenly as it came. The next moment I was overcome by sadness and apologized to the Polish athlete. It wasn't him I hated, but the whole Olympic farce.

I had come here prepared to love everybody, to suspend ugly political realities and to act civilized. I had lost the struggle. We all had lost. I walked to my room planning to get away from the Olympics as soon as I could. Just inside the building, assistant coach Julie Menendez came rushing off the elevator.

"Did you hear?" he said. "They're free. The Arabs have let them go."

I pressed for details, but there were few. Julie had seen two helicopters leave the Village, supposedly carrying the Arabs and their hostages, followed by a third with police negotiators. And the late news reported that the terrorists had surrendered at the airport. I went upstairs to bed feeling relieved and emotionally spent.

Next morning, the Village awoke to the horrible truth. They were all dead: 11 Israelis, 4 Arabs, a German policeman. In the newspaper, I read through the names of the dead: Moshe Weinberg, Mark Slavin, David Berger.

No, it couldn't be. It had to be a mistake. Not David. The rest were faceless names, but David was a friend, and friends aren't supposed to die. I went to the building where the Israeli team was sequestered but a guard stopped me at the gate.

"No one is allowed in."

"I don't want to go in. I just want information."

"Sorry, I'm under orders to admit no one."

"Please, just tell me if David Berger was one of the dead."

The guard took a small slip of paper from his jacket and ran his eyes down it. He nodded sadly.

There was nothing left to say or do, nothing beyond a memorial service in the stadium that afternoon. On the way, I passed the Russian soccer team, practicing, and confronted the goalkeeper whom I had met at the opening ceremonies.

"Don't you feel lousy about this?" I asked him. "Don't you feel you should go to the service?"

He looked straight at me, then at the ground as if to hide the remorse on his face, not from me but from his coach. "Orders," he said. "We have orders."

He turned and ran off to take his place in the goal.

Outside the stadium, people were arguing with the ticket-takers. You could not get into the memorial service unless you had a ticket to one of the afternoon events. It was being handled like a double feature, for God's sake.

"This is sick," an American woman said over and over, pleading with a guard to let her in. She was crying. On her sleeve was a black armband with a small Star of David.

"Nein," the guard told her, shaking his head. He pushed her aside and resumed punching tickets. The air smelled of bratwurst and sauerkraut as people carried food from the concessions into the stadium. I was nauseated.

Shortly after the ceremony began, Avery Brundage took the podium to mourn his Games. His party had been ruined. When he announced that the Games would go on, the stadium exploded into wild cheers.

I left. I could still hear the cheers as I ran down the stairs and across the plaza trying to put as much distance as possible between myself and such monstrous insensitivity. That was it for me. I was going home.

Each year now, I attend a benefit dinner in memory of those eleven Israelis. And one December night in 1977, I heard Bruce Jenner, the 1976 Decathlon champion, give his impressions of those horrible days in Munich. He stood at the podium, a picture of youth and promise with his good looks, smartly tailored suit, wide blue eyes that met and beguiled the audience.

He and I are survivors, I thought, in more than just the obvious ways.

As I watched Jenner, my mind wandered to the other athletes I had encountered that summer of '72. It was like turning the pages of a high school yearbook—all those young men and women with talent, hope, the world in front of them. They really did have promise not so many years ago.

David Berger is buried in a neat, shaded cemetery in Shaker Heights, Ohio.

Duane Bobick is still training, I guess, but this time for a comeback. Ken Norton knocked him out 58 seconds into the first round of the pivotal fight of his career. At 25, Bobick became a has-been.

Steve Prefontaine, the American distance runner who laughed his way through the Munich beer halls, died the summer before the Montreal Olympics. He was 24. Pre's sportscar jumped a curb on a road in Eugene, Oregon, hit an embankment and flipped, crushing him beneath. Pre had held every American distance record over 2000 meters and in Munich he confidently predicted he'd bring home a gold in the 5000. But he didn't. He didn't even win a medal, losing the third place bronze in the last ten yards when his vaunted kick failed him. That night in Munich's famous Hofbrauhaus, we talked a lot about what was wrong with the American Olympic system.

"Listen," he told me: "I'll train my ass off for Montreal. I'll go home and take one, maybe two jobs to support myself while I run. I'll knock myself out every goddamn day. But if Brundage and all those pompous asses think I'm doing it for America and the flag and all that bullshit, they better have their heads examined. I'm the one who's giving up my time and income. And if I win that gold in Montreal, brother, I win it for myself."

"Amen," I said. And that was the last time I ever saw him.

Mark Spitz, the Golden Boy, lives in California with his wife, seven gold medals, a roomful of trophies and a handful of endorsement contracts that will not be renewed. He never got to dental school, either.

Mike Ivanow, my rival in goal and partner in crime against Guelker's beloved rules, is facing three years in a California penitentiary.

In a way, his story is the saddest, the American Dream gone askew.

Mike was born in Shanghai of Russian parents who emigrated to Australia, then settled in San Francisco. Like me, he was a soccer fanatic with a second job to supplement his salary as reserve goalkeeper for the Seattle Sounders of the NASL.

Mike was an administrator in a Russian-American credit union in San Francisco. He worked hard during the week and played soccer with the same maniacal intensity.

"Why can't you be more like Ivanow?" Guelker would ask after one of our disagreements. Mike was his model of dedication and hard work. To him, Ivanow was the perfect success story.

I never resented the comparison. Ivanow was my friend and we had great fun trying to outcrazy one another during those two years we prepared for the Olympics. Then he was arrested for embezzling $70,000 from his employer. True to form, he confessed voluntarily. He just walked into a board of directors meeting and blurted out the whole thing before they even knew the money was missing. He had been shuffling accounts for six months. The F.B.I. was called in to confirm the crime and Ivanow was sentenced to the federal penitentiary.

When the Cosmos played the Sounders for the championship in August 1977, Mike was still on Seattle's roster, awaiting the start of his sentence.

5

VIVA SHEP

In the fall of 1972, I had but one small problem:
what to do with the rest of my life?

Though soccer was not a serious consideration, I
could have played professionally outside the States.
After my 63 saves in our Munich finale, I got an
offer to stay and play for a West German club.
And based on my performance in the qualifying
rounds, I received a firm offer to play in Mexico
plus a feeler from Morocco that was withdrawn
when the Moroccans discovered I was Jewish. But
my roots were in New York, and so was Arden.
We were married in December of 1972.

To make ends meet, I worked part time for
KLM Airlines and, occasionally, at nearby Westbury High.

KLM, like many European firms in New York,
fielded a weekend soccer team, paying as much as
$50 a game. It was a good team with players like
Gordon Bradley, the Englishman who had benched
me years ago over the Star of David incident. At
the same time, I signed on to play with Blue Star,
an all-Jewish team in the local German-American

League. For a big game, Blue Star might up the ante to $75.

Some weekends, I'd play three games, alternating for Blue Star and KLM, an interesting counterplay of grit and glamour. OK, maybe $50 a game doesn't sound glamorous but every now and then, KLM flew us to Europe to play other KLM teams in cities like Amsterdam or Rome. We would play preliminary matches in front of 60,000 fans before such major teams as Ajax of Holland took the field. Most KLM players were professional or, like myself, semi-professional. The league operation was strictly amateur.

You just threw your stuff in a bag, changed in your car, and ran onto the field in time for the whistle. Every game, one hard drinking Englishman named John McCover would stumble onto the field, throw up his Saturday night beer during the national anthem, wipe his moustache, and play. The guys kept an eye on McCover. Run over his slick spot and you could break a leg.

The German-American League was not so civilized. Soccer fanatics engaged in small wars of transplanted nationalism on the mucky, glass-strewn fields of Metropolitan Oval or Schutzenpark. Serbs, Croatians, Haitians, Greeks, Yugoslavs—every loyal son of a Baltic principality obliterated in the last century showed up on Sunday to honor his homeland on the playing fields of sport. It was ethnic soccer, bad joke soccer.

Disgruntled Serbs skewered loud Italians on the sharpened handles of the tiny national flags they waved on the sidelines. Referees required bodyguards. Bodyguards required referees. A writer named Paul Gardner once lobbied for the formation of a German-Hungarian-Argentinian-Sicilian-Transylvanian-Luxemburger-Yakuts league. He wanted to call it the GHASTLY League.

I usually asked Arden to stay away from these games as I didn't think she would enjoy participating in the halftime activities, which were riots. But one day when Blue Star was scheduled to play Dalmitinac, a predominantly Yugoslavian and Greek team, she and my younger brother Roy came anyway.

We were playing at Schutzenpark, just beyond the Lincoln Tunnel in New Jersey. From the main road, Schutzenpark looks like a miniature battlefield, completely isolated and set in a small ravine with a pitted, grassless oval serving as the playing surface. Somebody once carved on the goalposts, "Custer Was Here."

As we pulled on our shoes, one of my teammates said, "You know, of course, that these guys are supposed to be anti-Semitic."

"Come off it," I said. "Somebody's always starting these rumors. Let's just play the game."

Play we did, for about a minute and a half.

"Lousy Jew bastard." A Dalmitinac player slid into me on a save.

Roby Young, one of our forwards, stole the ball from a Dalmitinac defender inside the penalty area. "Kike," he gasped.

Play became vicious. Spectators joined the screaming. I started getting worried. During a lull, I was glancing in the stands for Arden and Roy when I felt a sharp pain in my left leg. I looked down and saw blood spurt all over my socks. A tiny six- or seven-year-old boy deftly removed a penknife from my calf and stood poised to stick me again. His father, who had given him the knife, stood 30 feet away shouting encouragement.

Figuring juries go harder on child killing than manslaughter, I went after the father. A full scale brawl erupted. I ran off the field long enough to hustle Arden and Roy into the car. Then I picked up a tree branch and ran back into the fray, swinging it over my head like William of Orange or Eric the Red. I was berserk, fighting for my life. Spectators, crazed on Retsina, pulled out billy clubs and brass knuckles from their ice coolers. It wasn't a soccer game, it was an ambush. Somehow, bloody and bruised, we got out alive, driving away in a shower of rocks and beer cans. From then on, Arden decided she'd find other things to do on Saturdays.

Most players for the KLM team had more sense than to risk their lives in the German-American League. Some were moonlighting for a club out at Hofstra University Stadium on Long Island where the crowds were small *and* sane. The team was called the New York Cosmos, one of eight franchises in the unlikely North American Soccer League.

I knew a bit about the NASL since I had been included in the spring player draft before I left for the Olympics. That draft was a joke. I had been up for grabs with such luminaries as Abbadia El Mostofia and Flash Oliviera. To my surprise, however, Montreal took me—giving them the rights to sign me for 1973. Still I never gave the NASL a thought until Bradley, one of the KLM players on the Cosmos, began talking seriously about my joining the team. He was then player-coach, though it was only a part-time job.

The Cosmos. The name intrigued me. It stood for the endless possibilities of professional soccer in this country. But at the time, there appeared only two: slim and none. The Cosmos had won the league championship in 1972, a feat the American public put on a par with the wrist-wrestling championships at Petaluma. Their offices were a tiny suite near Grand Central Station; the General Manager a quixotic English newspaperman named

Clive Toye. For reasons I still don't understand, Toye left a successful career as chief soccer writer for the *London Daily Express* to fly west and bring the game to the colonies. Toye and Bradley did their negotiating on a lobby payphone with a fistful of dimes, wooing players over tea and datenut sandwiches at a nearby Chock Full O'Nuts.

The Cosmos were a tortilla flat operation owned by a company from Hollywood and Vine. Warner Communications paid $25,000 for the franchise because record executive Nesuhi Ertegun, a lifelong soccer aficionado, convinced the board of directors that soccer was entertainment's next growth industry. And if he was wrong, it would make one hell of a tax write-off.

Warners has a way of guessing right on some things. They signed a nasal singer from Hibbings, Minnesota, named Bob Dylan; they bought movie rights to a small musical gathering in New York State that became known as Woodstock; they turned a gleam under Gloria Steinem's mascara into *Ms.* magazine. Add the voices of the Rolling Stones, Frank Sinatra, Fleetwood Mac and Linda Ronstadt, the faces of Robert Redford, Dustin Hoffman, and Clint Eastwood, as well as a string of such hit movies as *The Exorcist* and *All the President's Men* and it's easy to see why investors have trusted Warners hunches. It's just fortunate that no stockholders were on hand when chairman of the board Steve Ross attended his first Cosmos game in St. Louis in 1971.

"It was pretty depressing," Ross told me later. "There I was surrounded by 30,000 empty seats. But I didn't let it get me down. Instead, I thought about the possibilities. The growth potential from ground zero was tremendous."

Cleverly, Warners surmised that a Serbo-Croatian team would never be a hot ticket. The last

Serb to get ink in this country murdered some Archduke and started World War I. So to add box office appeal in the Long Island suburbs, Warners started looking for All-American lads. Yes, I was one of them.

Bradley suggested I express my disinterest to the Montreal Olympiques so they would get rid of me. I called Montreal, told them I was about to sign a baseball contract with the Mets and they traded me to the Cosmos for rights to Flash Oliviera and future considerations.

The Cosmos already had Werner Roth, a naturalized American citizen, and they added Stanley Startzell in 1972, an All-American golden boy from the University of Pennsylvania. It didn't take Stan long to realize that he had been drafted for his good looks, talk show talents, and local birth certificate. He spent more time at chicken dinners than at training meals. We were token Americans, a minority in our own land.

Before I signed with the Cosmos I agreed to show my stuff, although Bradley had certainly seen enough of it with KLM and Blue Star. I arrived at Hofstra Stadium one Saturday morning for my tryout and was sitting in the bleachers tying my shoes when I saw a guy with long red hair come bounding out of the fieldhouse.

Lenny. The last time I had seen Len Renery was on that barroom floor in Baltimore. He hadn't changed a bit, except his hair was longer, his eyes redder, and his outfits wilder. We embraced like brothers. He'd also been approached to try out for the team, so for the next week we hung together along with another young local, Joey Fink, a scrappy forward from Queens.

"Think I'll hold out for $10,000," Lenny said. Joey insisted he wouldn't lace his shoes for less

116

than $12,000. We all knew what we'd really get—about as much as the parking lot attendants. I got my offer in the locker that was Gordon's office just behind the showers of the Hofstra fieldhouse. In his thick Northland accent, Gordon started talking dollars and cents. I panicked. Shouldn't I have a lawyer here? Wasn't this supposed to happen in some panelled conference room?

"$2300 for five months," Gordon said. "I sign players according to ability. I put yours on a par with Lenny—that will bring you $2300."

I stood there contemplating and trying to keep my bath towel from slipping to my ankles. Not realizing the strain I was under struggling to coordinate both tasks, Gordon decided I was stalling.

"I'll tell you where you stand, Shep. I put Stanley Startzell and Joey Fink at $1800 for the season."

At $2300, I was going to be one of the big money players. I thought about it for a minute or so. A Harvard man making $76 a week. But I still had a teaching job in the fall; and with Lenny around, I knew we'd be in for some good times.

"How would you feel if I didn't sign?" I asked Gordon.

"Wouldn't bother me at all," he said.

"Okay, I'll sign."

So, nearly as naked as the day I was born, I toddled into the world of professional soccer.

"Can't you talk him into law school instead?" my mother asked Arden. "Some sensible profession that won't make him a has-been by the time he's 30."

Arden told me to go ahead and play. She was still in college, studying speech therapy at Hofstra. We lived in a studio apartment that was so small I had to store my soccer equipment—shoes, bags, balls—in my parents' garage. The way we were going, $76 a week would raise our standard of living.

We practiced twice a week that first season, but only when Randy Horton, our center forward, could get time off from his job at Warner Brothers Jungle Habitat, a wild-life park in central New Jersey. We were never sure whether Randy jumped out from behind bushes or took tickets. I was always hoping some catastrophe, like Randy being eaten, would cancel practice so I could take the time for a nap.

That spring, Arden's father died and we moved in with her mother in Stamford, Connecticut, to help her over the first rough months. This meant I left Stamford at 5:30 A.M. to get to my teaching job on Long Island, 100 miles away, by 8. After school, I practiced with the Cosmos and, for a time, was night bartender at Gigi's, my old catering house.

I usually got back home at 2:00 A.M., just in time to catch a quick three and a half hours sleep before the routine started again. Once I explained the situation, Gordon was most cooperative. He let me run two miles instead of four.

Every player had a second job those days, and some, like me, even a third. Jorge Siega sliced salami in his Queens delicatessen. Werner Roth designed prefabricated housing. Stan Startzell, Barry Mahy, and Joey Fink worked in the executive lounge for KLM. Charlie McCully was a bricklayer. Lenny delivered ice before he found his calling driving a beer truck. And Jerry Sularz delivered unspecified cargo in and around Passaic, N.J.

Jerry's wife had come out of Poland with him.

She was a sweet, quiet girl who spoke better English than he did, and said over and over how thankful she was Jerry had a trade, so he could make money. But she wasn't nearly as bouyant when she learned just how little America actually thought of her husband's vocational skills. "I must find a job," she told Arden mournfully. "Before it gets cold."

There were as many nationalities as occupations. Everald Cummings was from Trinidad, Sularz and Dieter Zajdel from Poland; we had Bermudians, Czechs, Yugoslavs, Britons, Scots. On the team bus, we looked and sounded like a rolling refugee camp. The foreign players who tried blending into the Long Island landscape dressed in mock turtlenecks, screaming plaid polyester jackets, two-tone platform shoes, flowered Qiana shirts, and gold chains. They drove Mustangs with chartreuse racing stripes; wore enough Old Spice to gag a bull. And wherever we went, they asked loudly for Coca-Cola and Budweiser to wash down a "chizburg" and fries.

Despite our differences, there was more camaraderie on the team back then. Soccer hadn't become a business yet, and there was no front office interference to engender fear and loathing among us. Not that there weren't problems. The Americans were forever fighting to get off the bench. Werner Roth played a bit, since he'd been on the team the previous year, and at 23 he was a grizzled veteran of countless German-American league battles. Joey Fink got the shabbiest treatment. He scored a hat trick in one game and was back on the bench the next. Why? Bradley had to "go with experience." Experience was spelled European. Experience was the same excuse Bradley pulled on me when he made Jerry Sularz the starting goalie.

For the entire season, I played about two full games. My brand new white shoes never even got scuffed.

Cruel as it sounds, I'd sit on the sidelines and hope Jerry would play miserably. I had second stringer mentality, wanting the team to win 7–6. Still, there is a bond between goalies, and when Jerry did have a bad game, only I could understand the full magnitude of his disappointment. For that reason, we got along well. I would commiserate with him at Bill's Meadowbrook Inn, the watering hole near Hofstra where we had our post-game parties.

Since the New York Jets also held their training camp at Hofstra, and drank at Bill's as well, this was one barroom where we picked fights carefully.

It was here that Mike Battle of the Jets once challenged me to a glass-eating contest in which, contrary to many reports, I never made it past the warmup. However, Battle really did eat glass— carefully—and ultimately had to spend $3000 on restorative dental work. But in 1973, his incisors were at their prime.

On the afternoon in question, Bill's air conditioning had broken. We'd all been through a particularly gruelling practice and were now hunkered down over the bar trying gamely to lower our body temperatures with icy fluids. I was drinking next to Battle. Finally, I got cooled out. So cool that I got into one of those really adult conversations.

"You think you're tough?" I asked him. "Just because you outweigh me by about 50 pounds?"

"Yeah."

"Oh yeah?"

"Yeah."

"Prove it."

120

He threw down the rest of his beer, and started on the glass. I was still cool.

"Big deal," I said.

"Shit," pipes up my loyal friend Lenny. "Shep can do that. Can't you Shep?"

"Sure." I'm getting nervous, grinding Lenny's toe into the linoleum with my heel. But it's too late.

"Awright wise ass," Battle says. "Meet me here in a week, and we'll see who's the better man."

Sweet Jesus. The entire front room has heard the challenge. Lenny, what have you done? And I've only got a week to prepare!

Quickly, I assembled a panel of advisors: Lenny, Randy Horton, and Everald Cummings. "Just take all the drugs you can and eat the sucker," Lenny suggested. Randy advised a hot meal. "Light one up. You know, heat the glass first, to smooth out the rough edges, douse it in alcohol for sanitary purposes and go to it." Everald just giggled.

Scouting reports were hardly encouraging during the week. Battle, I heard, was warming up on light bulbs. Had a 60-watt sandwich for lunch. Meanwhile, I was still working at swallowing the stuff once it was chewed.

Well, it was all for naught. At high noon on the specified day I sauntered into Bill's with fire in my eyes and the number of the Hempstead ambulance service written on my palm. But Battle never showed; I was a hero by default.

Playing at Hofstra was like what I'd imagined Mexican League baseball to be. The locker room was dingy, smelly and dank, coated in murky grey paint that had blistered and peeled from the heat and humidity. You'd leave the place looking like the guy in the dandruff commercial who used the wrong brand.

Visiting teams dressed on the third floor of the

fieldhouse, while the Cosmos were treated to the more permanent fixtures. There was a portable whirlpool, available when the custodian remembered to leave the keys to his supply closet. There was sufficient toilet paper, but all in one stack and of the folded type that you find in bus stations. Each player was rationed one thin, fraying towel a day. The trainer's supplies—tape, gauze, styptic —were stored in one of those carryout cardboard cartons from Burger King. To say the conditions were humbling is an understatement. Nor did it help when, on the first day of practice, a Hofstra student walked over to me in the locker room and asked, "You here for the intramural touch football game?"

Conditions on the practice field were only slightly better. The Astroturf field bowed in the center, perhaps from weariness. Passes hit slightly to the left or right of center would gain momentum on the hard green slope and curve at bizarre angles, while the intended receiver scrambled vainly in pursuit. On dry days, it was as soothing as sandpaper; our trainer's biggest function was smearing salve on nasty "astroburns" that seared thighs and buttocks. When it rained, anything moving, man or ball, experienced a hydroplane effect on the nonabsorbent plastic. Sliding tackles were obscured by great geysers. In goal, Jerry thrashed around like a drowning man.

The stadium—two sets of wooden plank bleachers facing the Long Island Railroad tracks—was built to hold 13,600. If we got 3000, it was cause for celebration. Not that Warners and the Cosmos didn't make every effort to pack them in. At one point, any kid dressed in so much as a piece of a Boy Scout uniform could talk his way in for 50¢. There were always gate promotions. On alternate Sundays, 2000 plastic soccer balls, Cosmos T-shirts,

Cosmos bumper stickers, and Warner/Atlantic record albums were given away. Suburban couples looked somewhat puzzled as zealous ticket-takers handed them copies of *Cream, Vol. II, Live at the Fillmore West*. Against St. Louis, paying customers were treated to Burger King Night, a discount on your Whopper.

Halftime might have inspired the Gong Show. Desperate for local support, Warners dreamed up a host of bizarre attractions. Men dressed in fuzzy pink and brown fur cylinders cavorted about as Burger King milk shakes. In exchange for tickets, small-fry soccer leagues supplied teams of eight and nine year olds to play halftime exhibitions. They were beautiful to watch, skinny, knock-kneed little kids in baggy shorts, wiggling through defenders with dirt stained rear ends. When they had run themselves senseless, a high school band took over, blaring their special versions of "Baubles, Bangles and Beads" and that eternal favorite, "Theme from a Summer Place."

Then came Harold, a five-year-old chimp, with a passion for eating hamburger rolls and peeing on his handler. Fittingly, he was the Cosmos mascot. Knuckles scraping the ground, he would scamper to the center of the field, and either boot the ball or chew on it. Once Harold had entertained, and the fans could stand no more fun, we'd take the field.

"Why all the promos and freebies?" I heard a reporter ask Clive Toye as we sat at Bill's Meadowbrook one night. Clive looked the guy in the eye and said: "Because in this bloody country, Americans think that any guy who runs around in shorts kicking a ball instead of catching it has to be a Commie or fairy."

This did seem to be the prevailing attitude of the New York press. Our publicity director John

O'Reilly spent his days making the rounds of sports editors, trying to fan their interest with thick packets of tickets. They either used them as book marks or foisted them off on the Spanish printers. Typical game coverage consisted of three paragraphs back on the page with the tire ads. Clive heard that baseball commissioner Bowie Kuhn was visiting all the sports editors in town to make certain they weren't allotting too many column inches to that foreign sport.

"You gotta understand what we are," Randy Horton told a sportswriter at Bill's one night. "We're not revolutionaries. We're not trying to undermine the Little League. We're just a bunch of crazy fuckers who love to play soccer."

A poet couldn't have put it better. We were crazy, and Randy was one of my favorite madmen. A tall, fierce-looking black man who played on the national team of his native Bermuda, Randy was studying for a post-graduate degree in economics at Rutgers. A bushy Afro added at least 4 inches to his imposing 6'2" frame. Huge eyebrows and piercing dark eyes made him one of the scariest dudes in professional sports. He liked to call himself "the meanest nigger in Newark." Randy also sported a full beard. He totaled more facial hair than the rest of the team combined. It stood to reason: American kids who warmed the bench were expected to see their barbers as regularly as they mowed their lawns. But Randy was a permissible exception, because Randy scored goals. Lots of them; enough to earn him the MVP award in the 1972 season. Enough to let him wear a beard, shades, rainbow dashikis and anything else he wanted, as long as that springy Afro kept heading high crosses into the net.

Randy was also a bright, sensitive doctoral candidate, though I had never seen that side until I

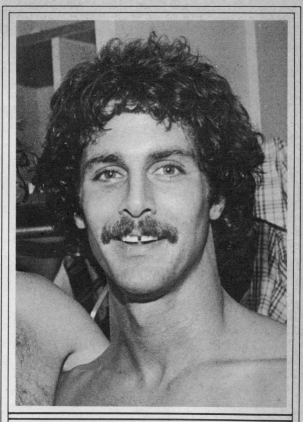

SHEP'S STORY

Above: Even at 3, I had my eye on the corners. Left to right: Marc, Albee, me, Jeanne.

Right: At Willets Road Elementary School, there was no getting by me.

Opposite, top: Mark Spitz (far right) and me with girl at the Maccabiah Games in 1969.

Opposite, bottom: The NCAA cover boy.

Above: At Harvard, my
problem was those half-
time pep talks in Latin.
COURTESY OF HARVARD

Top, right: When my iguana
Sam speaks, I listen for
a change. N.Y. DAILY NEWS

Right: Eusebio was the best
player in the world next
to Pele until fouls like
this ravaged his knees.
WIDE WORLD

Top: George Chinaglia. Whatever they say about his style, the Godfather scores goals. N.Y. DAILY NEWS

Above: Chinaglia saves his Chivas until after his shower. JERRY LIEBMAN

Right: Without my roommate Smitty, they'd have no one to blame but me. JERRY LIEBMAN

Top: Some of my happiest
moments are still spent
playing in the backyard
with my family.

Left: There's no defense
against my wife Arden.
N.Y. DAILY NEWS

Right: The author
is on the right.
DON POLLARD

Above, left: Werner Roth
heads one against
the Aztecs. N.Y. DAILY NEWS

Above, right: Playing against
Chinaglia and Pele in Boston:
the painful aftermath of a
goalmouth collision. JERRY LIEBMAN

Right: July 12, 1973.
Lenny Renery and I at Hofstra
Stadium a half hour before
game time. BARBARA PFEFFER

Top: August 14, 1977. A crowd of 77,691 filled Giant Stadium for the game against Ft. Lauderdale. Though Lenny and I arrived early, our seats were taken. JERRY LIEBMAN

Middle, top: Clive Toye and I always got on well, especially after I sued him — and won. JERRY LIEBMAN

Middle, bottom: My best friend in the game, Wolf-gang Suhnholz (left), and our partner in crime, Chris Agoliati. JERRY LIEBMAN

Bottom: Bending over backwards against Tampa. BOB KRIST

Opposite, top: Diving in the rain against Lazio of Italy. HARRISON FUNK

Opposite, bottom: Flying in the championship game against Seattle. UPI

Left: Changing of the guard: Out went integrity (Gordon Bradley, right) and in came deceit (Eddie Firmani). N.Y. DAILY NEWS

Bottom: Mick Jagger was asked how it felt to meet Shep Messing and Steve Hunt. WIDE WORLD

Opposite, top: Franz Beckenbauer hits a savage volley against Seattle. JERRY LIEBMAN

Opposite, middle: I brought Henry in to keep peace between Cosmos President Ahmet Ertegun and me. KEN KOROTKIN

Opposite, bottom: Who else? BILL SERNE

Above, left: One of these men has been declared a national resource. JERRY LIEBMAN

Above, right: Pele's Farewell. JERRY LIEBMAN

Right: Holding the Championship Cup with Franz. At left is Pele's bodyguard, Pedro Garay. JERRY LIEBMAN

Above: The 1977 NASL Champs:
(from left) Erol Yasin, Paul Hunter, Jomo Sono,
Gary Etherington, Vito Dimitrijevic, Pele,
George Chinaglia, Steve Hunt, Tony Field, Franz
Beckenbauer, Terry Garbett, Nelsi Morais (obscured),
Carlos Alberto, Werner Roth, me. JERRY LIEBMAN

JERRY LIEBMAN

dragged him to speak at a Westbury High sports banquet. It was the usual stuff: a bunch of itchy high school athletes forced to sit through over-cooked roast beef and six boring speeches before they could tote off their spray-painted trophies. Through dinner, Randy charmed the administrators with his erudition. But when he got up to address the kids, the principal nearly spit up his apple betty.

"Lissen you guys," Horton began, "I know you hate these jive banquets. You don't want no bull-shit, just the silverware. Am I right?"

Stunned silence.

"Yeah. Well dig a short message here. Sports take dedication. I said ded-ee-cay-shun. No reefer. No booze. No fuckin' around."

The place went wild; the dietician went pale.

"So come on up. Get your silverware. And be cool."

In 30 seconds, Randy had done more for sports morale than the Notre Dame fight song.

As the NASL's high scorer, Randy was the favorite target of every hatchetman in the league. They'd start chipping away at him early in a game, tripping him, elbowing him, even rolling under his legs to try and topple him. Randy hardly ever played a game without getting into a fight. Every third game, he'd be ejected for brawling.

His main eventer with Peter Silverester of Baltimore was a classic. One minute into the game, Silverester came up on Randy's left and kicked him hard in the shin. Ten seconds later, Randy charged up the field, knocking Silverester down. He got up, took Randy by the beard and butted him, water buffalo style, splitting Randy's forehead. Randy fought for control; his fists opening and closing. He grabbed Silverester and dragged him in front of the referee. Randy looked the ref in the eye, blood dripping down his face from the cut.

"Okay. What are you gonna do?" he asked the ref.

"Play on," the ref said, stepping back a bit.

"Okay," Randy said, and started pounding Silverester. A minute and a half into the game, Randy was ejected.

In 1973, we played 19 games and won 7. Our style was, in a word, primitive: Lots of hard running, long aimless passes, and precious few skills. We communicated like Neanderthals, grunting and gesticulating when the language barrier proved insurmountable. Everald Cummings yelled for passes in his calypso patois; from the goal, Jerry Sularz screamed instructions in Polish. Czech Josef Jelinek refused to pass the ball to German Siggy Stritzl.

"Peeg," he spat at Siggy during one game. "You take my money in poker, I never give you ball." I stood on the sidelines and cheered. It was the first sensible bit of English I'd heard Josef speak. For six months he had gotten by on Hello, I want ketchup, Goodbye.

As a former player for Dukla Prague, a powerful European team, Josef was one of the highest paid players. We could only guess at the sum, maybe a magnificent $4000 a year. But the true magnitude of the gap between what the Cosmos paid the foreign players and what they paid the Americans wasn't clear until midway through that first season, when Lenny, Joey, and I went to visit Malcolm Dawes and Ralph Wright, two third division English players the Cosmos had imported for defense.

We drove to the address in Hempstead, and found a handsome apartment building, far nicer than any of us could afford. When no one answered the bell, we walked around to the courtyard. Malcolm and Ralph were lying by a shimmering pool, holding beer cans slippery with suntan oil. So this was how Dawes and Wright spent their days, while the rest of us stiffs were toiling away at the salami works. The Cosmos paid the rent on this suburban shangri-la, and threw in a couple of new cars as well. Thus were sown the seeds of bitterness. We realized we were being used.

During those early days of the NASL, the English overlords were nearly as successful at rankling the few Americans in the league as their ancestors had been with the uppity colonists. Their prejudice was blatant, and their rule autocratic. And it hasn't changed much. Bobby Smith once told me that he overheard a reporter ask Ken Furphy, who has bounced from the Cosmos to Ft. Lauderdale to Detroit, what he'd do to raise the standard of play. Replied Furphy: "If I had my way, I wouldn't let a fucking Yank on the field."

In England, as in all of Europe, signing a pro contract is the equivalent of selling your soul. "In England," Barry Mahy said, "being a football player is like being a factory worker or a lorry driver. It's a job, and a bloody tough one. You never disagree with your employer, or you're out in the streets."

I'd argue with the foreign players that in America we do things differently. You don't just do, you ask questions. And ask I did. I asked Gordon why he let a man's citizenship papers determine his salary? . . . why bench American kids as soon as they begin to score? . . . why fine me for taking my shoes off on an airplane? Simple questions. I never got any answers.

Needless to say, in such an atmosphere, Lenny and I were considered a bad influence. We might persuade other players to think for themselves, talk freely to reporters, and loosen their ties at team dinners. To isolate this perfidious disease, Lenny and I were made roommates. The Cosmos, I'm sure, hoped it would kill us.

At times that wish nearly came true. There were sunburn and screwdrivers in Miami, motorcycles and Mai Tais in San Jose. In Dallas, we nearly drowned—thanks to Randy Horton and Everald Cummings.

Next to Lenny and me, roommates Randy and Everald were the two ugliest Americans on the team; and they weren't even American. The four of us constituted a loose brotherhood of rogues, always rooming side by side on the road. That night in Dallas, we were at a small motel just outside town. Lenny and I had spent the night drinking. At about 4 A.M., we found ourselves out by the pool, weaving among the chaise lounges. To sober up, Lenny suggested a dip. So we struggled out of our clothes and dove in, splashing around like palsied water spaniels. Only my summers as a lifeguard kept me from sinking. Then, behind some bushes, we heard giggling. We couldn't see anything and went on splashing. Soon it started again.

"Awright, who's there?" Lenny gurgled.

And then, a wondrous sight. Three of the most beautiful black women, completely naked, came walking toward the pool.

"Omigod," Lenny shrieked. "I've drowned and gone to heaven."

"Watch yo ass, honky," a man's voice growled, as Randy suddenly leapt from behind a bush, followed by Everald. They seemed to have lost their clothes, too, and were laughing like madmen. All five dove in, and soon we had a fair game of water polo going with an empty beer can. Could be we were making a little noise, because someone threw open a window on the balcony above the pool. We looked up, and there, framed in the light, was Gordon. He stared for about thirty seconds, shook his head, and closed the window.

Gordon never said a word, though as he brushed by me in the coffee shop the next morning he muttered, "You boys are crazy. Bloody, outright crazy." Later that afternoon, he fined us each $25 for being late to the bus.

That first year, Lenny and I were fined more than we made. Dress code violations, curfew violations, late to practice. Since we rarely played, we worked hardest at having a good time. It didn't hurt as much to nurse a hangover on the bench.

Our troubles with Gordon started on the first road trip, when Lenny discovered there was a dress code. Show up in jacket, tie, and shoes or you don't get on the plane. Lenny's solution was revolting. He went to the Salvation Army thrift shop and came home with some ratty dress duds a wino wouldn't wear: black shirt, green plaid jacket, a red, white, and blue polka dot tie. As Gordon became more strident, Lenny's outfits got uglier. Gordon countered by keeping Lenny on the bench, until one day an injury to Dieter Zajdel decreed Lenny must play.

The night before the game had been typical. After curfew, Lenny and I snuck down the hotel fire escape to some jazz workshop Lenny loved. Like the old saying, when in Bohemia, do as the Bohemians. Lenny smoked marijuana until he was paralyzed. We got back at 6 A.M., and needed 45 arduous minutes to climb back into the room. We fell into bed and passed out. At 8 A.M., there came a knock on the door. Lenny opened two bloodshot eyes and shrank back in horror at the apparition in the doorway.

"Gordon?"

"You're playing this afternoon," Gordon said.

"Matter of fact, you're starting." He stalked off down the corridor.

Lenny pulled the covers over his head, moaning like a plague victim. "Aieeeeee. What do I do? Oh shit, what now?"

I dragged him out of bed, dumped him in the shower and ran down to the lobby for some emergency aid. First, a bottle of Visine to pry open his eyelids. Next, a Bloody Mary. Then, another Bloody Mary. In the locker room, I slapped his face until his cheeks glowed and he looked alive. Lenny played that game in a purple haze, but he was fantastic. He was everywhere, sliding, tackling, stripping the ball from stunned opponents. He hit a 25 yard rocket off a direct kick that the goalie never even saw. Lenny's first goal as a pro.

"Man, you must have been smoking some good stuff last night," said Horton.

True to form, next game Lenny was back on the bench.

Since they didn't use us much in games, the Cosmos sought their $2300 worth by farming us out for promotions, speeches, award dinners and youth clinics.

One such assignment took us to Poughkeepsie in a raging snowstorm. Lenny and I piled into his rickety van with Cosmos traveling secretary Steve Marshall and Lenny's dog Toots. We're five miles outside Manhattan and Steve screams, "Stop this thing!" Lenny screeches to a halt. "Can't go anywhere without a beer," Marshall says, and tells Lenny to find a store. He doesn't want *a* beer, he wants a case of beer. Finally he's calmed down, pulling noisily on one beer after another, with Toots licking the empties.

Suddenly, Lenny hauls to a stop again. "Gotta have some grass," he says. Sorry, no grass distributors on the New York Thruway. Lenny pulls into a service area where a guy is tap dancing while he pumps gas into a pickup truck. Half of it is going into the tank; the other half onto the ground. His eyeballs look large enough to dribble upcourt.

"There's our man," Lenny says. He pulls the car in.

"I'll take $4 worth of gas."

Ten minutes later, we have the gas.

"How 'bout some oil? Gimme a quart of oil."

We get the oil.

"Got any of those things for the windshield wiper? Gimme two new wiper things."

We get the wipers.

"Got any grass?"

The guy straightens up. "You fuckin' crazy or somethin', man? The fuckin' New York Thruway? You nuts?"

"Come on. Come on. You ain't the Marlboro man. How about it?"

They go around for ten minutes, and the guy gives in.

"Okay, but if you're the Man, I'm busted."

Lenny buys some grass and we float on up to Poughkeepsie. It's midnight, and we realize that after buying grass, beer, gas and wipers we have $8 left and no place to stay. Eventually we found a spot like the YMCA, only not so posh.

Perhaps this is an appropriate time for a few words about drugs. With professional athletes getting busted for cocaine and Olympians accused of everything from hormone popping to blood doping, it's generally assumed that athletics are a hotbed of drug abuse. I'd guess the percentage of athletes heavily involved is about the same as for the rest of the population, no more or less depraved than housewives hooked on "mother's little helpers" and the truckers who swallow bennies like jellybeans.

131

Personally, I stay away from all that. Honest, I'm clean. A goalmouth collision is all the speed I need. I don't trust things that make me feel like my body belongs to someone else. In fact, I have a relatively low tolerance for any odd substance. Three beers and I start challenging football players to feats of lunacy.

In sports, the focus of most illicit activity is the bathroom. Players go there to sneak a butt, gulp a beer, down some Darvon. I knew one player who took his pills by the fistful—ups before the game, downs afterward. "They allow me to see things in perspective," he said.

A couple of players on the Cosmos that year would do a line or two of cocaine. One guy felt he needed it. He did a little before the game and slid into the bathroom during Gordon's halftime pep talk to do a touch more. He claimed it helped him run faster and longer. Run he did, like a super-charged top, spinning all over the field. He felt his running helped compensate for any lack of skills. Watching him, I could see it robbed him of some of his poise and ball control. It was hard to tell where the confidence ended and the coke took over, and, as he confessed to me later, there is a fine line between drug enhancement and crazed wanderlust. "Ten grains too much," he said, "and the ball starts looking like the Goodyear blimp."

Naturally, the most intensive use of drugs is in coping with pain. Imagine somebody whacking your knee with a hammer, or what it's like to go tumbling down a flight of stairs. Professional athletes deal with such sensations as a matter of course. They may have a higher pain threshold; but since the pain is frequently constant, it can turn them into mad dogs. They'll do anything short of chewing off a throbbing leg with their own teeth.

This feeling leads to many dumb and downright dangerous home remedies. If a trainer gives a guy two Darvons after a game and warns him not to drink, he's sure to wash them down with a beer. Atheletes will take any pill they can get—some a veterinarian wouldn't prescribe.

"My hair hurts," Lenny screamed after a particularly rough game. The chorus joins in.

"My teeth are throbbing."

"Somebody amputate my shins."

"Aauugh."

The best treatment for aches and pains is ice packs and rest. Believing this cure to be far worse than the ailment, I embrace a more active form of therapy. Dance, drink and ignore. Crush two aspirins in a jigger of Amaretto, rub it on the affected area and don't think about your pain until the next morning.

Sleep can be excruciating. As soon as we had saved the money, Arden and I bought a king size bed. In anything smaller, her big toe would inevitably ram a sensitive area, making me howl like a wounded moose. That first year, our neighbors must have thought us unusually ardent newlyweds.

That 1973 season I played well enough in my few appearances to be selected for the national team. I was all set to go on the European tour, until one of those fall weekend games for Blue Star landed me in the hospital.

I had made a save on a low ball, and was turning to toss it back into play, when this opposing forward came steaming in late, feet high, and sunk his spikes into my leg. Howling with pain, I jumped up and started to pound him. When someone finally separated us, my knee locked, jammed with a piece of torn cartilage. Fingers slipping in blood, I unlocked it and hobbled off the field. When my adrenalin level dropped enough for me to feel the full impact of the injury, I checked into Beekman-Downtown Hospital.

After the operation on my knee, I awakened in a semi-private room with an armed guard. Looking over at the next bed, I saw a huge, heavily muscled black man. Another orthopedic case, I figured. Probably a professional football player. Must be big time if he has a bodyguard.

"What are you doing here?" I asked; he scowled.

"Shit. I just knifed some muthafucka in the lobby," he said. "Damn guy cut me fo' he died."

Still groggy from the anesthesia, I persuaded an ambulatory patient in the hall to help me down to the lobby. Arden found me there the next morning, fast asleep.

For three months, I worked to get the knee back in shape, lifting weights, running, lifting more weights. It was coming along nicely when I started getting strange phone calls from Gordon Bradley in mid-February. It was 20 degrees with six inches of snow on the ground, but Gordon wanted to get together for a little practice. Just him and me. I was puzzled, but agreed.

On the way to meet him it dawned on me. Gordon wanted to see if I was in working order. Soccer was becoming a business and I was a property, a piece of meat. And coaches are very fussy shoppers.

Fortunately, Gordon was pleased with what he saw, and I signed on for another year at the amazing salary of $10,000—$7000 for playing and $3000 for promotional appearances in the off-season.

Not long after I signed that second contract, I got a phone call from Jim Bouton.

"Listen, how would you like to pose in the nude for a woman's magazine?" he asked.

"Get your head in one piece and call me back," I said.

"No, I swear it's on the level. They asked me to do it but . . ." He was laughing. "My pitching arm's too big and ugly."

He explained that *Viva* magazine wanted to do a nude photoessay with male athletes from the New York area. Randy Newman the fighter had done it; Jim Brown had agreed to pose at a later date. Bouton gave me the number of Barbara Pfeffer, a Manhattan photographer.

"Call her," he said. "You won't regret it."

I didn't want to get Arden upset before knowing the whole story, so I told her it was just a modeling assignment, like the ones I had done in Boston while we were still in school.

At 11 A.M. on the appointed day, I rang the bell to an apartment on Central Park West. I was relaxed—it was only an interview—and more than a little curious about a woman who photographed naked men. Maybe she was a porn queen in disguise, or one of those engaging nymphomaniacs I'd heard so much about.

The handsome blonde woman who opened the door was neither. As I passed into her apartment I noticed that her hair was lightly scented with developing solution and the walls were covered with excellent photographs of musicians, prime ministers, landscapes. She was a respected professional and when she spoke, she looked at my face, not at where I was afraid she'd look.

"You should know this whole thing is driving me crazy," she said. "I've interviewed over 50 men and none of them have been right."

She explained that the N.Y. Jets and Giants were too big and musclebound. Being offseason, the baseball players were flabby and out of shape. For three months she had been looking for the perfect body, and was ready to give up.

"It's gotten so that I stop men on the street,"

she said as she made some tea. We talked for a few minutes about soccer and which athletes should have the best bodies. Handing me a mug, she pointed to the vinyl couch. "Let's start the interview."

Dutifully, I sat down and talked until she held up her hand.

"Okay, take your clothes off."

My tea slopped. I hadn't really thought about this moment. I figured she just wanted to talk. But of course, she had to see me. As I hemmed and hawed a bit, Barbara sensed my nervousness.

"I have to do something in the other room," she said. "Undress while I'm gone." She left.

I fumbled with my zipper, feeling about ten years old, a kid undressing for the school nurse. I took off all my clothes, except my briefs. Barbara returned and frowned.

"I meant everything," she said. I tugged my underwear down and stepped out of it, about as self-conscious as I've ever been in my life. I sat down on the vinyl couch and shot up as though stabbed. Vinyl on a bare ass in February is a rude shock.

"Walk," Barbara commanded. I walked. "Hold it," she said, and began circling me, checking for scars and lumps.

"Terrific," she said after what seemed an eternity. "You're perfect. Well built but not muscle bound, slim but not skinny. You're my man." I grinned, happy that all my efforts in soccer had finally paid their first dividend.

Back home, Arden and I weighed the consequences. I was intrigued with the idea. There's a little narcissism in all athletes, I guess. Besides, it would be a good story for our grandchildren. Arden wasn't thrilled, but she wasn't opposed either. So when *Viva* called and offered a fee of $1000, we both agreed it would be a happy experience for the bank account.

Shooting took about four months. Once it began, my reservations grew. I had envisioned some moody, black-lighted semi-nude shots. Boxer Randy Newman's spread had been a good one. He wore almost as much as he did in the ring. I figured I'd have to take my shirt off, maybe cavort around with a towel. Not so. I was to play Greek statue.

The first session consisted of Barbara, six lighting assistants and me in a drafty downtown loft. Half a day was spent setting up the backdrop while I sat shivering in a terrycloth robe. Then someone hollered, "Hey you!" and I was suddenly being moved around like a bowl of fruit. Poetry in motion on the soccer field had become just another still life.

Next, Barbara announced she wanted some action shots. I must say I was relieved to learn these would be taken in the locker room; to which, for some strange reason, Gordon and Clive Toye agreed. It was early spring, and we were well into practice for the 1974 season. The Cosmos would be playing that year at Downing Stadium on Randall's Island but we worked out before the season at Hofstra.

Barbara came out one afternoon and was busy setting up lights when word spread that there was a photographer in the lower locker room. A female photographer. Siggy Stritzl came running. He walked in front of Barbara's lens, turned around and dropped his shorts.

"Hey, lady, check this out," he whooped. Barbara looked bored.

"I'm sorry," she said. "This is a camera, not a microscope."

I was teaching at Westbury High the day *Viva* came out. I couldn't understand why the halls were so empty, until one student told me that there were about 50 girls in each bathroom, with as many copies of the magazine. The Westbury newsstands were bought out in an hour. I walked around the halls with my sweater pulled down to my thighs the rest of the afternoon. All those little wide eyes . . .

The next morning, I began receiving invitations. The superintendant wished to see me. The principal. A homeroom teacher. The PTA. Petitions were drafted, letters of protest sent. There was a lot of smoke but, ultimately, no firing. The kids supported me. They thought freedom of expression was great, just like the folks who wrote the Bill of Rights. As far as the school board was concerned, the matter died quietly.

At home, though, things were just beginning. The phone calls were amazing. They came from everywhere in the country, at all hours and in all varieties. Some just breathed. Others made sucking noises. The language was off a bathroom wall. I was big on the slumber party circuit. One little 12-year-old voice would say hello and ten others would giggle until I hung up.

The mail was unbelievable, a pornographer's dream and Arden's nightmare.

Arden started calling travel agents, seeking a temperate spot 1000 miles away. I can't say I blamed her. She would visit friends in their dorms at Hofstra and find me winking from over their beds. Strange women walked up to her and said things like, "Gee, your husband is well hung."

"I feel like I'm the one on display," she told me.

In retrospect, I'd never do it again, not for any amount of money. Not that I'm ashamed, but a wife doesn't need such things.

The guys on the team thought the spread was terrific. "I'd do it for free," Lenny said, rolling his eyes à la Groucho as he calculated the fringe benefits. "Messing, it's the best thing you've ever done."

"Messing," cautioned a league official, "it's one of the most deplorable things you've ever done." Seems the league considered the spread bad for its image. But it certainly didn't hurt the gate. I got the sport more exposure by dropping my pants than the league did in a year of passing out its press releases.

After a rousing start like that, my second season with the Cosmos could only get better. Gordon let me play some exhibition games and then made it pretty clear I'd be starting regularly. The day before our first regular season game, he changed his mind.

"Shep, this is the hardest decision I've ever had to make . . ." he said after practice.

Hoooooboy. Here it comes.

"I think you're great, but I've got to go with Jerry tomorrow. You'll come around, but I have to stick with experience."

There it was. Experience was sticking it to me again. Or rather Gordon was, and blaming it on my lack of experience. At that time I knew I was the better goalie. I settled back on the bench and into another funk.

Sitting there I became aware of my public for the first time. Some guy in the stands about 10 rows back bellows through a megaphone: "Hey Bradley. This isn't Liverpool. This is New York. Play some goddamn Americans. Play MESSING, fer chrissakes."

My brother-in-law, Bobby.

A band of little kids from Massapequa, Long Island, is there with bedsheet signs that say "Don't Mess Up—Play Messing," and "Get Hep, Play Shep."

That first game was at Randall's Island against the Baltimore Comets. I wanted nothing more than for Jerry to look terrible. With six seconds left in the game, I got my wish. Jerry fielded a Comets shot and rolled the ball to fullback Frank Donleavy who tapped it back to him, the usual move unless there's an opposing forward in the way, which there was. Baltimore's Peter Silverester intercepted the pass and slammed it past Jerry to give the Comets a 3–2 victory. After the game, the problem became clear to everyone. Jerry hadn't warned Donleavy because he couldn't. He didn't know enough English to scream, "Watch out!"

I started the next game and stayed in goal for the rest of the season.

Before our last home game, Gordon called me over to the sideline. "Shep, I don't know how to say this . . ." Gordon was wearing that look of his once again refusing to meet my gaze. "It's not easy," he continued. "But you're not in our plans for next year."

Not in our plans. Another of those coaching euphemisms for take a walk, sucker.

"What do you mean?" I asked him. "I have a contract for the rest of the year. Is it my play? What the hell is going on?"

He had no answer, but it was obvious. The Cosmos had their eye on another one of those "experienced" players. The odds were, his experience was gathered on some coal town team in a basement English league. It stood to reason, jettison the centerfold.

In the locker room, the guys began avoiding me as though I had a terminal disease. I couldn't blame them. I remember how hard it had been earlier in the season when teammate Tibby Vigh flew down from his home in Montreal, started to dress and was told by Bradley not to bother.

"Sorry lad," he had told Tibby. "I thought

someone had called you. We put you on waivers two days ago."

What do you say to a guy at a time like that? How can anyone make it easier when his whole family is out there waiting for him to run onto the field? Now I knew. There is nothing anybody can say. As he passed, Werner squeezed my arm. Lenny kicked his locker. The rest were handshakes. Good luck. Don't let them get to you, man. Stay cool.

I walked through the game and the next three days in a stupor. Dumped. This possibility had never really occurred to me. Dropped by the same Gordon Bradley who had told reporters, "Shep will be my goalie for the next ten years." Then, without warning, I'm a non-person.

By the time the letter came formally announcing my release, I was bitter and furious. My father, who has always handled my legal affairs, confirmed the fact that I still had a contract. Under its terms, the Cosmos owed me $3000. Clive Toye thought otherwise, and so we filed suit in New York Civil Court.

Meanwhile, I wrote to every coach in the NASL. I knew they were looking for Americans and I was a genuine native son with two years experience in the league. I had gate appeal even if I wasn't yet known for my goalkeeping. As more and more coaches ignored my letters and phone calls, it soon became apparent that I was a victim of what Lenny called *Viva* backlash.

"Get that fucking flake away from me," one coach said to his assistant after I'd had an interview with him. By the second week I was beginning to feel blackballed. No coach wanted a blithe spirit who tossed off opinions and clothes so easily.

Ah, America. Home of the free. After two months of scrambling around, only two teams expressed interest. Tampa was one. Gordon had been decent enough to speak to them and they were sufficiently interested to get me into a law school and help us find a place to live. But when Arden and I went down for a look, we decided our roots were up north.

The other possibility was the Boston Minutemen coached by the esteemed Hubert Vogelsinger—the same Hubert Vogelsinger who had cursed me so creatively when I was at Harvard.

"I've seen you play," he told me. "And frankly, I don't care what my players do off the field, so long as they do their job during the game."

I couldn't believe my ears. Was there really a coach who would judge me on my ability alone?

"Ah, the hell with all that model athlete bullshit," Hubert said. "I like a player with spirit."

Enough said. Within a week, I had a contract to play for Boston. Arden and I made plans to move and my case against the Cosmos was settled out of court. I think Clive respected me for standing up to the Warner empire. It was the most amicable lawsuit in history, as he and my dad got on quite well.

Shortly thereafter, I received the following letter on Cosmos stationery:

Dear Shep:

In 17 years as a journalist and 8 years as a general manager, you were the first person to sue me.

How, then, could I possibly harbor hard feelings? Without you, another experience of life would have eluded me. Or, at least, eluded me until the more costly future.

Now, we shall not sign Pele unless he swears his father is not an attorney (joke).

Regards, or as they say in Mexico, Viva Shep.

Sincerely,
Clive Toye

6

"YOU GUYS
ARE SICK"

"Harvard Star Leads Soccer Revolution."
Who me? I sat on a clothes carton reading the
paper in the apartment Arden and I had rented in
Brookline, a suburb of Boston. The article said
American kids were the hope of the NASL's future.
Far be it from me to thwart history. I slid into a
pair of jeans, rummaged through the boxes for my
Borsalino hat, and went off to the wars, humming.

"I can't start you." Hubert met me at the locker
room door on my first day of practice. "I know you
expected to play, but I have to go with Michniewski. It's only common sense."

This was no way to treat the hot young revolu-
tionary, Che Messing. Not start? It certainly didn't
make common sense to me. No sense at all. I challenged Hubert. He got angry.

"What do you think I am? A hypocrite?" He was
yelling, backing me up against a locker. "It just
so happens I have another goalie who won a lot of
games for us. It just so happens he got us to a division championship last season. I play him first. I
owe the guy."

I couldn't argue. Jan Michniewski had earned
his spot. That gave me the problem of winning it

away from him. Some players will do extra wind sprints, showcase themselves in scrimmages. I won't. I'm not lazy, just egotistical. If a coach doesn't have confidence in me, I'd rather not play for him. I settled into lackadaisical practices, waited.

I didn't have long to wait. Michniewski played four games, gave up 10 goals. Something wasn't working for him—reflexes, timing, it's hard to say. But after that fourth loss, Hubert came to me, while Michniewski sat dejectedly on the shower floor.

"You are my starting goalie," he said. Now that the Minutemen were my teammates, my defenders, I began paying attention to them. We opened that 1975 season with 8 nationalities: an Austrian coach, the English, three Portuguese, a Pole, a German, some Yugoslavs, Dutch and Greeks, as well as four Americans. Stan Startzell (also late of the Cosmos), Chris Agoliati, Ben Brewster and I were the restless natives. Except for me, the Americans didn't see much action but they were playing behind more than English journeymen. Boston had signed international stars and just watching proved an education.

At the hub was the Portuguese Connection, three world-class players who enjoyed the adulation of Boston's considerable Portuguese population. They had a rotating entourage of beautiful, young women. Jokingly, we called this threesome the How Much Gang. Because anytime Hubert asked them to do something, a Portuguese lawyer in sunglasses would show up and ask "How much?"

Jorge Colado was the tough guy of the trio, a big black sweeper-back with a huge Afro and permanently bloodshot eyes who walked around team meetings with a coffee cup. I always figured he was trying to straighten out from the night before until I sniffed his coffee pot one day. It was Jack Daniels, 100 Proof. "For the blood," he said.

Colado thought America a funny place. "Where else?" his lawyer translated, "can you drive up and get sandwiches in your car? Cash from little machine?" And big pain, as he soon found out, from playing soccer on Astroturf. Colado had his ankles taped heavily for our first away game. By the second half, his ankles were swollen over his shoes because of the hard artificial surface, and he was whimpering in Portuguese. The final whistle blew, a tie; there would be overtime. I saw Colado hobbling off the field.

"Jorge," I screamed. "Is overtime. *Uno mas.* One more period. *Veni, veni.*"

"No, no, no," he shot over his shoulder. "I speak to my lawyer."

In contrast, Antonio Simoes was the team intellectual. Trim, elegant and soft spoken—a former member of the Portuguese Parliament who now served as scoutmaster for his countrymen—he was known for his silver cigarette holder and peerless right foot. Simoes had been a World Cup star and Benefica teammate of the Black Panther, Eusebio.

Any locker room that houses Eusebio should be declared a shrine. The day the powerfully muscled black man walked into ours, he was unrecognized. We figured he was just another guy looking for a tryout. Tryout, my ass. Eusebio was, at that time, the biggest soccer star to ever play for an American team. "It's like waking up and discovering that Babe Ruth has joined you," said Chris Agoliati.

Hubert completed Eusebio's curriculum vitae: 6–0, 175, one bad leg, the hardest shot in the game. He had a gleaming string of triumphs: a storybook game in the 1966 World Cup when he scored four of Portugal's five goals in a remarkable comeback against North Korea. For three years, he was

Europe's top scorer. In 1966, he was voted the best player in the world. Yes, even better than Pele.

Hubert was ecstatic. We were in awe. Playing with Eusebio gave me my first close look at a genuine world class superstar, even though he was 33 years old and in need of an overhaul. The magnum force shot, timed at 100 mph and reputed to be the most powerful in the world, was still intact, but countless injuries and seven operations had mutilated his legs.

Never was there a more graphic illustration of the ravages of professional sport than these two limbs. They were legendary. Guys would stare at them across the locker room, unwilling to believe that a simple, nonviolent game could do that to a man. They made Arden nauseous. Torn tendons, surgically removed and discarded like spent rubber bands, left deep gullies on the undersides of his thighs. Long, curving scars, raised half an inch high, criss-crossed his legs. His knees were puckered and dipped like a moonscape where the flesh stretched over bone fragments and calcium deposits. On one leg you could see the outline of the bone where a chunk of muscle had been removed. His shins were a ladder of greyish-white scars, his feet scaled, calloused and gnarled. No wonder that Eusebio hated practice.

But if his legs were a study in sacrifice, his face was lit with enjoyment. Eusebio loved life, America, women, poker and high times, sometimes all at once. Wherever he went, to play in special exhibitions or to do a promotion, his wife was two countries behind. She'd arrive in Boston, he'd be on his way to Toronto. She'd try to catch up with him, he'd be on a plane for Brazil.

The team had just as hard a time charting his movements. One day Eusebio would be at practice, and the next day we'd hear that he was in Rio for some charity game. He'd play on the weekend and turn up the following day in Cannes. For someone with such a hurting set of wheels, he sure got around.

Eusebio had special friends wherever he went. Seeing them swarm over him gave me my first look at the wild, wonderful world of soccer groupies: doe-eyed Americans in short skirts, lanky African beauties, devastating ash-blond Swedes. They were always waiting for him, bribing chambermaids to sneak into his room, sending him sizzling notes tucked inside his Spanish omelets, nuzzling against him in hotel bars.

When Eusebio wasn't playing around, he was playing cards. I think the first words of English he learned were "I raise you." The guy lived to play poker. He played on buses, planes, in locker rooms, hotel rooms, coffee shops, bars. Eusebio was always slipping away from his women to round up a game.

"Jes a frenly game, boys," he would whisper long after curfew, riffling a deck at the keyhole.

Eusebio had willing victims in myself, Chris Agoliati and West German Wolfgang Suhnholz. He also had a huge bankroll. Knowing we couldn't handle his stakes, he'd pass out bills like monopoly money. He was just a big kid who wanted to play. Chris would borrow two, three hundred at a time. The rest of us tried to talk him into playing for peanuts.

"Yeah, yeah, okay, okay. We play for the little nuts—I beat you anyhow."

Games would last all night, towels wadded under our hotel doors to keep the light from Hubert on his nocturnal strolls. Since there were usually six or seven women clamoring to get into Eusebio's room, we held the game in the one I shared with Wolfgang. Occasionally, Hubert would throw open

147

the door two hours before gametime, coughing as a cloud of Wolfgang's cigarette smoke billowed into the hall. "Enough with this bullshit. Get on the bus," he'd say. Eusebio would scoop his winnings into a gym bag and we'd continue the game in the locker room bathroom.

Fines ate up all my winnings. Late to practice, late to suit up. I led the team in fines. Wolfgang and I were Hubert's Bad Boys: Our training regimen was rigorous, but simple: the night before a game, we'd load up on carbohydrates, the kind found in barley malt, walk briskly between bars and never, ever put lights out before 4:30. Our travel kits contained Visine, Alka Seltzer, matching ice bags, bottle openers, smelling salts, tape, aspirin and several decks of cards. Wolfgang became my best friend in soccer. It was no accident that we decided to room together.

This guy drank life by the case. Also beer. He had come from the prestigious Bayern Munich club and was renowned for his lean good looks, elegant midfield play and fierce loyalty. Let an opponent upend me in goal, and ten seconds later the guy would be lying on the ground wondering what hit him. Ten yards away, a smiling Wolfgang would be dribbling the ball upfield.

He was as hard on himself as he was on dirty players. Wolfgang believed in sweating off his sins every night. Wherever we were, San Jose, Tampa, Dallas, he would turn the heat to 85, bundle himself in a sweat suit, and seal every window and door sill with balled-up towels. I'd suffocate until he fell asleep. Then I'd take the cigarette out of his mouth and turn on the air conditioning. If he complained about a stiff back the next morning, I'd set it right with a brief stroll up and down his spine.

Wolfgang and I told everyone we were writing the Bon Vivant's Guide to Boston. His wife was in

Berlin, still trying to keep track of him. She'd call up at 3 A.M. in the morning. "Ist Wolfgang der?" she'd ask. "He's out jogging," I'd say. Arden just gave up. She threw us out of the apartment every night at around 11 so she could sleep. Wolfgang and I would then cruise the neon watering holes of Boston, places like Zelda's and Daisy Buchanan's until dawn. Dressed in white linen suits, we sat beneath Tiffany lampshades in dark mahogany booths, drinking rum and coke and playing backgammon. Spotting a lissome stewardess at the bar, Wolfgang might disappear for hours, but I stayed cool, staring distractedly into the singles scene like the guy in those ads for 12-year-old Scotch. I might fall down the locker room stairs next day, but I never missed a game or practice. Not once.

Hubert never said a word. He couldn't. That season, I led the league in goalkeeping and Wolfgang scored seven game winning goals. "You guys are sick," he told us. "I hope you never get well."

Thanks to Hubert, I was becoming more than a human sacrifice in front of the net. For the first time since I had worked with Dettmar Cramer on the Olympic team, I got decent coaching on goalkeeping. "A goalkeeper is like a piano player," Hubert told me. "He has to train his hands to react automatically. Hands cannot spend time thinking." We worked on ball handling drills—catching crosses, high balls, diving backwards into the goal and holding onto a shot. I learned how to gather in ground balls, squatting so that my knees would back up my hands if they fumbled the ball. I worked on anticipation, positioning my body, adding education to reflex.

"You're less flamboyant," a fan told me after one game. I could detect a note of disappointment in his voice. Sure, I used to be long on flash, but that was only because I was short on skills. Hubert's logic was simple, and it worked: First, handle everything cleanly, so no one can ever say you gave up a "bad goal." Next, work at handling routine plays. You'll be stopping more weak dribblers to the far post than you will acrobatic bicycle shots. It made sense to work hardest on basic saves. Finally, I learned never to think about playing for the great save. Charging out to parry a ball you know your fullback can get is an unnecessary risk. This can leave you sprawled in the penalty area with the ball in your net.

The more I played, the better I became. Because in goalkeeping, experience is the cornerstone of performance. That's why so many of the great goalies like Russia's Lev Yashin and England's Gordon Banks reached their peak in their mid-30's. All that time is spent developing a sixth sense, one that can read a striker's mind from 40 yards.

Of course, I learned all this in spite of myself. If Hubert had just lectured me, I'd have tuned him out entirely. But he came on the field and wasn't above using a little Viennese psychology.

"Ptui." Hubert screams after a practice save. "You play like my grandmother. You look like shit." Thwack, he blasts another. I get it by the fingertips.

"You got hands like Mickey Mice." Another shot. "What now? You forget how to jump?"

Inside ten minutes I am so furious that not even an innocent gnat can get past the white line. "You must understand Shep," Hubert explains to Arden. "The man is an exhibitionist. He likes to look good. And if he thinks he looks bad, he will work."

He had me there. Most of my career in soccer has been spent trying to prove my worth to other people. To Guelker, to Bradley, to Hubert, to the fans, and often to the press. I'm compulsive about reading a game story the following day, furious when the only mention of my play is something like "slipped by Messing's legs for a score," or "beat Messing on a high cross." It's the goalie's unfortunate lot to be remembered for his mistakes. That's the way it is, but it can still make you crazy. Knowing how I reacted to these journalistic injustices, Hubert made sure he saw the newspapers before I did. He would check the newsstands on his early morning jogs wherever we were. After one bad game, be bought out the entire supply in our hotel.

My relationship with Hubert is hard to explain. It was the 100 Years War of soccer. We started off hating each other during our early Yale-Harvard rivalry. Now he's one of my closest friends. Between, there were gentlemanly disagreements, screaming arguments, threats, curses, fines and suspensions. It took me a while to understand a guy who makes his bed in a hotel room, takes cold showers at 5 A.M. and jogs at 6 A.M. We often passed in hotel lobbies at that hour. He on his way out, Wolfgang and I on our way in.

"You fellas," he'd yell over his shoulder. "You chust better do it on the field." Sometimes, Hubert would try to get through to me with a flurry of concerned phone calls to Arden. "Dear," he'd caution, "you'd better speak to your husband. He's digging the hole he'll never get out of. The kid's on Cloud 7." Cloud 7. It was one of our favorite "Hubert-isms" along with "double up in single file" and "pair up in threes."

On the field, Hubert was an embattled general. We could be killing a team, and to him its Waterloo: brooding, muttering, squeezing a plastic bottle until it bursts and water runs down his pants. But Hubert was cool. Let a Boston player get hot on the field, in danger of getting thrown out and Hubert rushes onto the field, screaming at the official in a torrent of English splattered German.

He was invariably getting yellow cards, warnings of imminent ejection. "Yeah, sure I gotta yellow card," Hubert would say. "But I still got a fucking player on the field."

Hubert is pig-headed. So am I. Our explosions were loud and frequent. We argued over curfews, technique, practice workouts.

"You are a schoolgirl. You play that high ball like this is kindergarten."

"You don't know a high ball from a draft beer."

"You better practice one half hour more."

Unfortunately, Hubert always had the last word. It was "waivers." Hubert loved to put me on waivers. It started as an idle threat, but by July it was almost a bi-weekly occurrence. Arden got regular calls from Linda, the Minutemen's secretary. "Arden, Shep's on waivers again," she'd report. "I'll let you know how it works out." Then she'd read Arden the letter she had just typed. They all read the same.

Shep:

    As of today, March 22, 1976, you have been suspended from the Boston Minutemen because of your unsatisfactory behavior. You have also been taken off the Boston Minutemen payroll. Furthermore, you have been placed on waivers effective today.

But I was still a Minuteman on June 10, 1975, the day soccer in America changed forever. I drove into Boston to pick up the New York papers. There had been rumors, rumblings of something big. It was to happen with the Cosmos. I had caught the end of something the night before on TV. It was just a name, two syllables that caught my ear. I flipped open the New York *Daily News* before I got back to the car.

"Pele signs 3 year 4.7M Cosmos Contract."

Sweet Jesus. It was true. They were going to take the greatest player the game had ever seen and plunk him down in the middle of that sewer on Randall's Island. Jorge Siega, Werner Roth, Mark Liveric—they were all going to be teammates of Pele. I drove home with mixed feelings. Boston was great. But to play with Pele . . . in New York . . .

For the next few weeks, I traveled into town to get the New York papers. It was a media orgy. Soccer had finally nudged its way into the national headlines, and onto the front page of the New York *Times*. Pele's first game with the Cosmos drew 21,278 spectators to Randall's Island and was televised to 22 nations from Australia to Zaire. It was covered by 300 domestic and foreign journalists. And we were next.

Boston owner John Sterge was enthralled. Dollar signs danced in his head as he made arrangements for the largest attendance in Minuteman history. His considerable entrepreneurial interests were stimulated to the point of prostration by the coming event. The rest of us were in similar shape. The Boston papers were hyping the Pele-Eusebio matchup. Stuff like "Can the Black Panther Savage the King?" In ten prior meetings, Eusebio's team had won only once.

"I want Minutemen beat Pele," Eusebio told reporters. Not until half an hour later did this sink in. We weren't playing the Cosmos, we were playing Pele. Suddenly, Eusebio was spending less time in the sauna during practice. Day by day, his shots got harder and faster. He'd practice direct kicks against me for forty-five minutes. The day before the game, he blasted one to my solar plexus that knocked me to the ground, semi-conscious. He also swore off poker. Eusebio was ready.

Just before the Pele game, as we had come to call it, Hubert called a team meeting. He spoke as though the other side had some terrible, secret weapon, destructive capabilities unknown. Can you go one on one with a legend? Reluctantly, Hubert had decided it was the only way.

"Look here," he said grimly. "You all know what I could do. I could put five men on him, like a pack of wolves, running him down. This kind of thing is no good for soccer."

Oh shit, I thought. The hell with soccer. I was going to be in goal. I didn't care if they planted land mines. I wanted him out of range.

"No," Hubert continued. "We play him like anybody else. The people are coming out to see him play, and we will let him. But we will *not*," he focused his gaze on me. "We will *not* let him score." That night, a Boston reporter called to read me part of an interview with Pele. "I think the first big American star in soccer will be a goalkeeper," Pele had said. For the first time before a big game, I didn't sleep well.

Sterge had rented Richardson Stadium at Boston University for the big event. It was built to hold 12,000, but estimates of the crowd that day ran upwards of 18,000. Later, an audit would show that the stadium was shamelessly oversold. On the day of the game, that fact was clear a mile away. Traffic was incredible. Futilely, Wolfgang kept hopping out of the car and pleading with people to let us through. "Me soccer player," he screamed at a large Italian family occupying an overflowing Buick. The man behind the wheel shook his head. Wolfgang started kicking the air, screaming in German, English. In a final burst of inspiration, he rushed back to our car, tore open his athletic bag, took out his jersey, which he waved in the face

154

of a startled cop in a cruiser. We sped to the game along the shoulder of the road, the whirling red light running interference.

When we arrived at the locker room, Hubert was already pacing. "I don't like this, I don't like this." He had gone out in the tunnel and had a look at the crowd. Normally, he'd be overjoyed at seeing people instead of empty seats. But there was something ominious about the atmosphere. Already, the guards had ejected a dozen tenacious celebrity hounds from the dressing area.

Inside the tunnel, the din of the crowd rose and fell against the concrete walls, punctuated by the blast of an airhorn or occasional firecracker. I tried to place the sensation. "El Salvador," I yelled at Wolfgang over the noise. "It sounds like a soccer crowd in fucking El Salvador." Hubert gave the signal and we ran out onto the field.

The stands were thick with people, clogging the aisles, wedged into stairwells, ringing the field twenty and thirty deep. Those standing were openly hostile at paying as much as $10 for a square foot of mud. A walkie-talkie squawked in the pocket of a guard on the sideline. "This is gonna be hell," a voice rasped through the static. "They're still coming in."

Finally, the moment. We stood lined up in the center of the field, facing the small opening in the crowd that led to the visitor's locker room. The team announcements started. Nusum . . . Roth . . . Lamas . . . Liveric . . .

"And now, wearing number 10 for the Cosmos . . ."

The announcer didn't have to finish. Detonated by the sight of a small black man emerging from the tunnel, the crowd roared, leaping to its feet. Flashbulbs shot tiny comets through the air as

Pele trotted to the center of the field, arms raised, fingers spread in twin "V" salutes. And then, the cheer.

"PELE, PELE, PELE." It came crashing down, echoing, hanging in the air like an invisible vapor as Pele ran a wide circle, sidestepping to face the crowd.

I felt chills. It must be incredible to be assaulted with so much love. How could a normal human being handle it? I had seen emotional ovations before, thousands standing and cheering for Mantle, Mays, Namath, Ali, but never anything like this. It was as if 20,000 people were hugging Pele with their voices. I looked over at Eusebio, who was radiant. Suddenly, he was back in the world of big-time soccer, back on the field with the only man in whose presence he ever felt humble. A tear hung at the corner of Eusebio's right eye.

How do you defend against the greatest player in the world? Fall to your knees and salaam? I fell on my knees all right, but it was to stop two point-blank shots. My knees were shaking even before they came. I was nervous as hell. Nobody had ever done this to me before. I watched Pele pick up a pass 60 yards away. He started toward me, legs churning, arms out for balance, dipping and bobbing through a parting sea of defenders. Pele was dribbling the way you would in your mind but could never do with your body. Desperately, Colado fouled a Cosmos player outside the penalty area. They lined up for a direct kick. Oh my God. Pele was going to take it.

Usually, a goalkeeper places his wall of defenders where he anticipates the guy will shoot. There are ways to tell: How the player eyes your cage, for instance, or knowing the kind of shot—bullet, curving, spinning, floating—he's best at or watching his forwards for some little sign. But with Pele, there was nothing. He could hit any shot brilliantly; and his face, a blank mask of total concentration, was terrifying.

He hit a rocket. It screamed over the defenders' heads and then dipped, heading for the right corner with uncanny accuracy. I knew I couldn't catch it. Instinctively I dove, felt the sharp sting. For a second, I didn't know whether I'd gotten there in time, until I saw the ball sailing out toward midfield. The velocity of Pele's shot had sent the rebound 30 yards.

I felt like walking off the field. Game's over, folks. Messing, Bronx-born Shep Messing has stopped Pele. Press conference at 4. Cocktails at 5. Testimonial dinner at 6. But hold the applause. Pele was still playing out there, still a threat. I settled into the game, finally concentrating.

A few minutes later, we sparred again. Pele was scrambling to reach a short corner kick our defender had misplayed. I was after it, too, running flat out to get there first. We were running side-by-side when something took hold of me—and I took hold of Pele. By his pants. Just a little tug, so quick the referee didn't see, and I made the save.

It went on like that. I came up with the ball in the goalmouth, knee up, and gave him a good shot. On the next save, as I wrapped myself around the ball he cruised by with a little two-fisted punch. Nothing menacing, just a message. I think we understood each other. The next time I fell to the ground he could have danced a samba on my head. Instead, he gave me a playful pat, smiled and trotted off. You had to love the guy, even if he stood to blow your net into a pile of fluff.

Throughout the game, the overflow crowd had been barely contained. When Eusebio scored a goal, they tried to overrun the field. Somehow, the handful of police managed to keep them at bay. I spent half the time flinging garbage out of my net. When I went into the goal to do my housekeeping, fat fingers poked and jabbed at me through the netting. It was getting scary.

As Pele ran up and down the field, the crowd rippled and bulged at points closest to him, a great wave of howling humanity. Weary security cops tried to keep pace with the occasional locos who broke from the pack and made a run for Pele. So when the real trouble came, the guards were too exhausted to be of much help.

This happened late in the second half. Mark Liveric hammered a shot that I just got a hand on, deflecting it around the left post. The ball flew into the crowd, and someone must have bounced it back in, right to Pele, standing in front of the goal. Since this happened so fast, I doubt the referee saw the ball go out of bounds; he was 20 feet behind Pele and the roiling crowd back of the goal was effective camouflage. Seizing the opportunity, Pele takes the deflection and slams the ball into the net. Knowing it had first gone into the crowd, I made no move to stop the shot. I bent to pick up the ball and when I looked up, Pele was leaping in the air, well into his goal salute. My God. Pele was pulling a Messing! I believe in gamesmanship, but this is too much. I run, screaming at the referee to disallow the goal. But it is too late. Within seconds of Pele's triumphant gesture, there are at least a thousand bodies on the field, just trying to touch Pele, crazy with love. It was a horrifying thing to see.

In the midst of all this, the referee waved his arms disallowing the goal. He had seen the ball go over the touchline after all. Now the crowd gets ugly. Enraged by the referee's decision, they swarm out to Pele.

"Pele, get down," a voice screams. "It's me,

Pedro." Pele's bodyguard was yelling from somewhere in the mob. Five yards in front of me, Pele obediently drops to the ground, holding his leg where someone had stepped on him. I'll never forget the look on his face: a look of sheer terror, eyes, rolling left and right, mouth twisted in a strangled yell. As I watched, someone yanked his shoe off for a souvenir, twisting his leg grotesquely.

I had started toward him when I saw people flying through the air, hitting the turf like limp rag dolls. Pedro was on his way, plowing through the crowd to throw his body over Pele. With my back to Pedro and Pele, I tried to block some onrushing bodies. A small cordon of police finally arrived with a stretcher, and wheeled Pele off.

Clive Toye ordered the rest of the Cosmos off the field, and both teams stayed in their locker rooms until things quieted down. There was a flurry of messages and negotiations and the game finally resumed. But Toye announced that the Cosmos were playing "under protest."

"Protest, my ass," Hubert said when he heard the news. "Who are they trying to kid?" The Cosmos were playing poorly, and now they would be without Pele for the remainder of the game. Knowing a suspension of play could touch off a full-scale riot, the Cosmos figured to save lives by finishing the game; they could save face, in case they lost, by lodging an official protest. And that's exactly what they did. We won 2–1 in overtime, but the Cosmos won their protest and NASL commissioner Phil Woosnam ordered the game replayed. "Woosnam has no guts," Hubert said to me. "He'll do anything not to alienate the Cosmos. He knows which side his butter is breaded on."

After the game, I tried to get into the Cosmos locker room to see if Pele was all right. Three beefy security men barred the way. "Orders," one barked.

"This locker room is sealed for security reasons." Half an hour later, on our way to the parking lot, Arden and I passed the Cosmos bus. Looking to either side, Pele sprinted to the bus like a rabbit. He saw me and grinned. Later that night, the Cosmos issued a medical bulletin. Pele would be incapacitated for a few days due to ankle and thigh injuries.

All that season my *Viva* notoriety pursued me. The phone would ring in our hotel room and when Wolfgang answered, he would hear only heavy breathing. "Shep, it's for you," he'd say.

Strange gifts appeared for me: flowers, candy, lewd little poems and phone numbers. Once, in Vancouver, I got a gift-wrapped girl.

The Vancouver Whitecaps were a fairly new team, and the press was pretty stirred up. When we arrived at the Vancouver airport, Hubert opened a paper to the sports section and winced.

"Male Centerfold Nudist in Goal Against Caps."

Hubert was cursing in German. Wolfgang, the only guy who could understand him, was falling out of his seat. I was amused until trouble came to my hotel room.

She was about 5'7", a frizzy blond, scantily clad in ribbons and some kind of filmy wrapper. She was incredibly tenacious and also a little crazy. Clutching a copy of *Viva*, she pounded on the door, shrieking that she must have me. I yelled back that I was married, wasn't interested, had nasty communicable diseases. Nothing worked until Hubert came to the rescue.

"No ugly scenes, please." He arrived through the door of an adjoining room and together with a chambermaid restrained my potential seducer until I had escaped down the hall and caught the team bus to the game.

Somehow I survived the season with both my virtue and my statistics intact. I led the league in goalkeeping with a .93 goals against average. I was 26, American, and proud as hell. The Minutemen clinched the Northern Division championship and we played Miami at home to begin the first round of the NASL playoffs.

It was one of those games when nothing went right. Miami's first goal ricocheted off Simoes' head into the net. Cursing the Gods of Deflection, I told Antonio to forget about it. There can be no emptier feeling for a soccer player than to score an own goal, especially in a critical game. I once read about a guy in Italy who scored an own goal, went home and hung himself. Against Miami, we needed all our players.

Late in the second half, Miami's Warren Archibald and Steve David burst clear at midfield, facing me with the prospect of stopping a breakaway by the two fastest players in the league. In a situation like that you can do one of two things; lie down and play dead or gamble and lunge at one player, hoping to force an errant pass. Coming way out of goal, I dove at Archibald's foot—where, I believe, part of my nose still remains. Somehow, Warren got the ball away and Miami scored and we lost 2–1. End of season.

After a farewell tour of the Back Bay bars, I drove Wolfgang to the airport. We had about 45 minutes before his flight. "Chizburg. Got to have a chizburg." I shook my head. Wolfgang was about to go into one of his cheeseburger frenzies. Ever since I introduced him to those greasy, onion-laden little things, he averaged three a day. Suddenly, realizing he would be without them for six months in Berlin, he bolted for the coffee shop and ordered a plateful. Naturally, he couldn't down two pounds of ground gristle without a beer. Or six. Just as he was nearing the end, he let out a shriek, pointing to the window.

His plane. The fat Lufthansa jet was lumbering away from the gate. We ran down the corridor, pounding on the door, trailing luggage, soccer shoes, bits of bun. Wolfgang started yelling at the gate attendant in German. The attendant yelled back, also in German. Wolfgang mentioned the magic word.

"Bayern Munich."

Instantly, the clerk was on the phone. To my amazement, the jet returned to the gate.

"Was terrific," Wolfgang told me some time later. "All these people look around in their seats to see who's big shot they bring the plane back for. Here I come, this bum in overalls, eating a chizburg. Just me, Suhnholz. With much ketchup on my face."

From the beginning of the 1976 season, Hubert was unusually irritable. Once he irrationally placed eleven players on waivers, took us all back the next night, suspended us again on the third.

"Something smelled bad in front office," Eusebio speculated. And that something bad was Sterge.

We noticed the little things like changing fields four times in nearly as many weeks. We shuttled like gypsies between Foxboro, Cambridge, Boston College, Boston University, and New Bedford, hoping like hell our fans would figure out where to find us—and Sterge's creditors would not.

Even the newspapers lost our trail for a while. PR man Marty Bauman ran out of money for postage and couldn't send his releases. Our phones were shut down so often no sports editor could reach him.

Still, two or three thousand people managed to find us each week and the team kept a sense of humor. "Easy to see why we are Minutemen," Wolfgang said. "One minute we play here. The next minute we are gone."

Serious looking men in short hair and white socks spent entire days in Sterge's office, attaching monitoring devices to telephones, inspecting files. These men made everyone nervous. The foreign players thought they were from immigration. Others figured they were narcs. They were the Feds all right, but they were more concerned with funny deals than anything else.

The SEC had actually been watching Sterge for a year. In May 1975 he and five others were charged with fraud on a $12 million stock deal and for selling stock in oil and gas companies that Sterge controlled, then diverted the profits to their own personal use to the tune of nearly $650,000. Some of the money was alleged to have gone into financing the Boston Minutemen.

"Dirty money, clean money—bah," said Wolfgang. "If Sterge pays me, I don't care if he robs old ladies."

Eusebio was less sanguine. "Sterge screw me good," he growled, and hired another attorney to protect his interests. According to Eusebio, someone from Sterge's office gave him a paper to sign, telling him it was an immigration form. "I no read English, I trust him, I sign," he said. "Big mistake."

The big mistake was that Eusebio had actually signed a contract giving the Minutemen the option to retain him in 1976 for the same salary he was paid in 1975. But no one told Eusebio. So when a squabble developed over his playing for Club Football in Monterrey, Mexico, for their September 1975 season, Eusebio was forced to give back $10,000 of his pay before Sterge would release him.

Money became a pressing problem for all of us. General Manager Casey Frankiewicz was the guy we dealt with. Ask him for 50 cents for round-trip subway fare to a clinic, and he'd say "When I was in Poland, we lived a week on fifty cents." Ask him to pay you for giving a clinic and he'd vanish with a migraine.

Sterge did all he could to economize. He discontinued laundry service, so we had to wash our uniforms at home. He said he had forgotten to pay Harvard for a practice field, so we worked out on a small patch of grass by the Charles River. One day, I decided I'd had it. I showed up for practice in sneakers and a windbreaker, and just stood around while everyone else did pushups.

"What's with you?" Hubert asked.

"Simple," I told him. "I'm not going to work up a sweat today because I don't have money for the laundromat."

Payday started looking like the Crash of '29. Our checks bounced so often that we climbed over one another to get to the bank first. Our games were on Friday nights, so every Friday afternoon we met at the office at 4. And if we didn't get paid before the game, we'd park our cars to block Sterge's Rolls Royce, trapping him until he produced a wad of bills from which he'd grudgingly peel off tens and twenties, all the time bemoaning his fate. "Listen," he told me one night as he handed me half my pay. "Do me a favor, Shep. I got the hot dog concession for tonight's game. Buy a couple for your pregame meal."

Since we couldn't afford much else, Wolfgang and I occasionally did. "Two hot dogs, extra sauerkraut," I muttered one night, angry because we no longer had locker-room facilities and had to dress at home.

"Sure, Shep," the counterman said.

I looked up. Sterge. Sterge, the team owner, was in there selling hot dogs. Wolfgang laughed, then looked worried. I had the same thought. We dashed to the parking lot to check on Sterge's Rolls Royce. Sure enough, Colado had remembered to block it in with his battered van. The back seat of Sterge's car was piled high with hot dog rolls.

Later that evening, he finished paying us out of the hot dog money.

"How do you like that?" he said, beaming. "We pulled in more at the concession than we did at the gate." Now I understood why he scheduled our games for 5 P.M. Saturday night. It was five hours past lunch, and just in time for supper.

Because we changed fields so often, Sterge had to rent a set of portable goalposts that we trucked with us. The referee would check them before each game to be sure they were the proper distance apart. As soon as he turned around, I'd move them closer together, about 6″ on each side. I enjoyed the intrigue. The trick was remembering to move the posts back to normal at the end of the first half, maybe even stretching them a foot or so—to give our forwards a nicer target when we changed sides.

On the road, our problems became embarrassing. We arrived in Washington on one trip to find that our buses had been cancelled for nonpayment. We piled into cabs and rode to the hotel. Three hours later, there was still no call for dinner. We all met in the lobby where Hubert was dickering with the manager. He had used our meal money to pay for the cabs and now we couldn't eat.

"Me want plane ticket," Colado was screaming in the lobby. "You get me plane ticket to Lisbon, get me hell out this place."

A couple of weeks later, things really got ugly. Agents turned up at the Cosmos gate to garnishee Boston's share of the receipts. Still, we were all set to suit up when a phone call informed Hubert that the Minutemen were no longer insured against injuries. Someone had discovered the premiums had not been paid for a year.

"I can't let them play," Hubert shouted into the phone to NASL Commissioner Phil Woosnam. "These men have families. One injury could ruin their lives." We sat in the locker room wondering if we should bother to get dressed. With an hour to go, I called my father for legal advice. He told me not to play and I told the others.

"No way," we said to Hubert. "We're not going out there without insurance." Finally, Woosnam came through with a temporary arrangement. We finished dressing and took the field. Not until later did we discover that the game would have been played even without us. As a precautionary measure, the league had flown in another team, the Minnesota Kicks, who would have taken our place against the Cosmos. Another thing we didn't find out until later was that we actually did play uninsured.

After that incident, we should have walked out. Deep down, we all knew the end was near, but no one wanted to believe it. "It was like keeping together a bad marriage," Hubert told me later. "Instinctively, you know you should call it quits. But somehow, you're too caught up in relationships to admit it."

Our apartment became tactical headquarters for half the team as nightly we discussed how to get away from the Minutemen. Like besieged war lords, we'd sit around the table. Messing, Eusebio, Geoff Davies, Wolfgang, Colado and a Rand McNally map of North America.

The strategy was crude to say the least. One guy would decide where he wanted to play, another would call the coach of that team, and in his smoothest agent tones, make his client's interest known.

"Uh, I talk for Eusebio," Colado said. "He want go Toronno. Uh. Toronto."

His hand over the phone, Colado would motion to Eusebio.

"Coma dise?"

Whenever coaches had the simple faith or courtesy to return a call, whichever player answered would bargain for the player involved. "Nooo, Geoff Davies isn't in at the moment. But I think . . . why yes, he is considering Chicago."

Experience dictated that Eusebio should fill the role of village elder, weighing any offer critically from his chair at the head of the table. His advice was always "More money."

"Pffft," he'd make a withering sound with his lips at a low offer. "With this, you cannot get shoeshine. You must have more."

Eusebio's English was still lacking, but he was as conversant with U.S. currency as the chairman of the Federal Reserve Board. One night, fuming over Sterge's rubber paychecks, Eusebio came up with a way to recoup our losses.

"I see in paper, is much crime in Boston," he said. "Many thefts of cars. We still have rental cars. We sell them."

Though we were no longer getting reimbursed for gas or mileage, most of us did have leased cars and vans. There was no way Sterge could take them from us. Commuting to all those different stadiums required the tenacity of a rally driver.

"Maybe we steal John Sterge cars," Eusebio said. "Sell them quick quick, make a few bucks. Whatchu say?"

We were angry enough to consider it, but reason got the better of us. A small fleet of cars stolen from the same rental agency might be a touch suspicious.

We never told him, but Hubert knew we were all looking to get out. Later, he actually helped players get jobs elsewhere, staying on Sterge's sinking ship until the last player either drifted away or floated a loan. But while he was still trying to win games, thinning his roster was the last thing he wanted to encourage.

My break came when Bob Rigby, the Cosmos goalkeeper, broke his collarbone in a game against Washington. I got a phone call from Arden's brother Bobby at 3 A.M.

"It's all over the papers here," he told me. "They're looking for another goalkeeper. Why not come home?"

I hesitated a moment. I hated to go back to the same people who had treated me so badly the year before. Once, Hubert had stopped me from mailing the Cosmos a letter with my stats and a little "Fuck you" tacked at the end. Becoming the league's leading goalkeeper after warming their bench had been sweet indeed. No, there was no doubt about it, I wanted them to want me back. I wanted to come back into the Big Apple riding high.

"Call Gordon for me," I told Bobby. "Tell him I'm interested." But the next morning I called him myself, even though it might have been illegal by league rules. Bobby had called back to say the Cosmos were desperate to have someone in goal for a game later that week. There was no time to lose.

"I want to come back," I told Gordon on the phone. He laughed.

"I'd be delighted," he said. "But Clive has his eye on some English fellow. Come down and take a physical. We'll talk about it."

The following morning, I went to see Hubert.

"Trade me," I asked, my eyes on the ground. He reacted as though I had slapped him.

"Never, no way," he screamed. "I gotta fucking 7 and 3 record, only half a team. No money. And now you want to leave me with nobody good in goal? No. No way."

"Hubert, it's my future we're talking about."

"What about those guys still here? Don't they deserve a decent future? You want them to look like bums?" Some of the edge had gone out of his voice. He paced his living room for a couple of minutes, muttering in German. Finally, he turned and faced me.

"All right. Of course, you should go. We should all go. But understand my position. Once I trade you . . ." He threw his arms out toward the ceiling. "Once I let you go, I am opening the dam. It will start, what do you call it—a gang reaction?"

"Chain reaction," I said, and I knew he was right. Wolfgang had said he'd go as soon as I did. So had Colado, Davies and Simoes. And they kept their word. Wolfgang would go to Toronto, Colado to Rochester, Davies to Chicago, Simoes to San Jose, all on the strength of those absurd phone calls and Hubert's cooperation.

As I got ready to leave for my physical in New York, Arden sat in the bedroom, red-eyed, not speaking. We had stayed up all night talking about the move, and she was adamant.

"How could you?" she said. "After the way they treated you, how can you go back? Don't you have any pride?"

I explained there was pride in vindication, pride in returning in triumph, even pride in putting food on the table. "I don't care about money," Arden sobbed. She cared about her friends, her job, her home, all the things the wife of a transient athlete finds she can't have after it's too late. No football, baseball or soccer player ever proposed to his wife with the words "Marry me and I'll give you nothing."

It turned 8 A.M., then 9. Arden knew the airline schedule and was deliberately causing me to miss successive shuttles to New York. I stalked around the apartment, helpless, trotting in and out of the bathroom with wet washcloths for her eyes: What about the furniture we just ordered for our apartment? What about *her* job as a rental agent? What about human relationships? "I don't mind living out of suitcases," Arden sobbed, "but there is no such thing as drip-dry friends. We're so happy here. Why does it have to end?"

Gordon couldn't have been nicer. After my physical we met at the Roy Rogers restaurant near Hofstra, where the Cosmos were working out. He didn't want Kurt Kuykendall, his reserve goalie, to see me and get upset. There Gordon offered me the job. "Will you sign?" he asked.

"I have to talk to my lawyer," I said and called my father. All three of us then drove into the Cosmos office to talk to Clive Toye.

"I know you've heard a lot about the Cosmos huge salaries," Clive said. "But I want you to know those reports are greatly exaggerated except for Pele and Chinaglia. We're prepared to pay you right in the middle of the scale. $16,000."

"No way," I said, with my most blasé laugh. My father had coached me well. I'd been making just $10,000 in Boston, but I was going to squeeze the Warner moneybag for all I could.

"I want $40,000," I told him. It was Clive's turn to laugh. After an hour, we settled on $22,000 plus a $3000 signing bonus and a stipulation that the

Cosmos would reimburse me for all unpaid wages from Boston.

Before signing, I called Hubert in Boston. He sounded low. Seems there was this cash flow problem, and the Minutemen hadn't been able to board their scheduled flight to Portland. The airlines were no longer willing to extend Sterge's credit.

"Okay," Hubert sighed. "Tonight, I sell my goalkeeper."

I hung up and signed the contract. Traded again, this time for an airplane ticket.

7

COMING HOME

"Ahhh. My friend who likes to pull the pants. Welcome." Beaming innocently, which is the only way he knows, Pele greeted me in the dressing room at Yankee Stadium on June 30, 1976.

The first game of my second career with the Cosmos was due to begin in 20 minutes and already my nerves were shot. My shuttle flight from Boston arrived thirty minutes late, the taxi driver charged combat pay to motor through the South Bronx and rush hour traffic chewed up my last measure of calm.

At least Pele remembered me. He motioned to a locker near his, the ultimate in good neighbor policy. Bob Rigby, his arm in a sling, gave me half a hug and even the elegant George Chinaglia offered a manicured hand. The tension began draining away.

On the end of a bench, reserve goalie Kurt Kuykendall was sitting head in hands. He was holding a Bible. Here was one guy certainly not glad to see me. Kurt had been sent into the game after Riggs busted his collarbone and immediately allowed an easy goal. He made more mistakes the following game and, as if that wasn't enough, injured both legs. I was taking over the starting spot; he was looking oblivion right in the face.

I sat down beside him and began the whole rap. "It's a hard business, Kurt . . . don't let it get you down . . . you'll be back." I had to say something. He looked up at me, eyes full of tears, and muttered something about finding strength in the Lord. I couldn't compete with that kind of counseling.

"God be with you," Kurt said as I got up to take the field. I felt like crying myself.

Yankee Stadium, $100 million later, looked nothing like the blue and white wedding cake I remembered as a kid. The famous facade that rimmed the roof was gone, mainly because there no longer was a roof. The monuments to Ruth and Gehrig were now enclosed in some sort of crypt between the bullpens in center field. I felt a vague sense of dislocation, as if a symbol of my youth had been stolen while I was out of town. I wanted to sit with my father in one of those hard green wooden seats always obscured by a pillar. I wanted to hear Mel Allen's voice again.

Instead, the voice of the P.A. announcer echoed through the vast stadium. "Starting in goal for the New York Cosmos . . . Number One . . . Shep Messing." My thoughts are a tangle of pride and nervousness as I wave to the 22,000 spectators huddled against the chilly wind and rain and race toward the center of the field. The announcer rolls on through the names of my new/old teammates and one by one they jog into line and toward the crowd. The call comes for "Number Nine, Giorgio Chinaglia," and the stands rumble with applause; but they're holding something back. The moment I've been waiting for, but still can't believe, comes at last: "Number Ten, Pele." The familiar chant

"Pay-lay, Pay-lay, Pay-lay" comes ringing down and I find myself joining in, although not loud enough to be heard by my teammates.

I played that game on adrenalin. It was against the Rochester Lancers, a mediocre team that had trouble moving the ball past midfield, but once they did, the shots came in fusillades. I played out of my mind while the computerized scoreboard flashed SHEP . . . SHEP . . . SHEP with every save. We beat Rochester 2–0, my first Cosmos shutout, and in the locker room I scampered over to have my picture taken with Pele, feeling like a rookie and a fan.

The fatigue didn't hit until I slumped in my seat on the last shuttle to Boston. Arden met me at the airport at 3 A.M., but when I started to describe the game she cut me off.

"I don't want to know anything," she said. "I don't want to hear scores, details, Pele, nothing. Let's just treat it like a 9 to 5 job. I want to forget soccer when you're here in Boston."

I played the first part of the season in this domestic pressure cooker, commuting after every home game. During the week I practiced with the Minutemen, Hubert was as dedicated as ever to make me a better goalie even though I now played for the opposition. It was Macy's sending their hired help to Gimbel's for training. It was also the most unselfish gesture I've ever seen from a front office man in sports.

Commuting was actually more difficult on Arden than on me. I got a charge out of being flown in for games like some high-priced English import. And for the first time ever, I was free from the daily routines of drills and windsprints. I even saved some money. I couldn't be fined for being late to practice when I was 200 miles away.

I began to appreciate things, decided I wanted

a steady role with the Cosmos glittering production, so I took off on a hot streak, playing some of the best soccer of my life. "New Cosmos Have Old Look" the papers said, playing up the return of the prodigal son for more than it was worth.

It took a few weeks to adjust to the splendor of my surroundings. For my first Cosmos practice, I pulled on a pair of grey, cut-off sweatpants and an old black sweatshirt, the official Boston training outfit. Guys doubled over in laughter when I appeared on the field. They were wearing snappy green sweatsuits with their names embroidered across the shoulders. Once back in the locker room, I committed an unspeakable gaucherie. Accustomed to the barnyard ambience of the Boston facilities, I spit a bit of tobacco on the floor. The brown stain spread across the Dupont 401. Who knew from a carpet in a locker room? That night, I bought a brass spitoon.

Beyond the cosmetic, the Cosmos paid careful attention to such important details as getting a qualified trainer and using the best doctors. We were looked after by the orthopedic team at Lenox Hill Hospital—the same group that regularly overhauled Joe Namath's million dollar knees. In Boston, our medical treatment had consisted of B-12 vitamin shots injected before games.

Some NASL franchises were infamous for their perilous health programs. On those teams, guys would drive miles to clinics before going to their own trainers. One West Coast trainer with a reputation for handing out uppers pulled a little prank on the entire team. In a fit of pique over a lost argument, he spiked a whole drum of Gatorade with what was thought to be high grade THC, a potent hallucinogen. These guys had a bizarre practice, running in dizzy, drug-crazed circles. Needless to say, that trainer is no longer in the league.

Two weeks after I joined the Cosmos we played the Washington Diplomats, the team that had put Riggs out of action. The guilty party was Paul Cannell, one of the dirtiest players in the league. There are always a few of these cheap shot artists, identified by their particular skill. Selris Figaro who used to play for Miami specialized in the butt. He'd go up for a header against a guy and using the side of his head, butt him square in the forehead. Figaro would come away unscathed, his opponent with a headful of stitches. Then there were the screaming eagles, players like Minnesota's Peter Short or Toronto's John Coyne who'd come in spikes high, shrieking ethnic insults. More often than not the dumb bastard would hit his mark and take one of us out for a game or two. Other guys are just plain scary. Rochester had a huge African player, George Lamptey, with tribal markings on his cheek and a hatchet for a left foot. He approached opposing forwards like a Zulu warrior at battle pitch.

Goalkeepers seem to attract these hit men who like a piece of a goalie's nose or any other part of him. Gordon Banks, the legendary English keeper, has no knuckle in the little finger of his left hand. Says he just looked down one day and the knuckle was gone.

As Riggs' replacement, it was my duty to avenge his injury—a point of honor among goalies, almost a blood oath. So I felt like a crusader when the Washington and New York papers quoted Cannell as saying he wasn't at all repentent for injuring Riggs. Given the chance, Cannell said he'd do it again.

"I hope this turkey tries something on me," I told Riggs before the Washington game. "Even if he doesn't, I promise he'll remember me." I was almost looking forward to it. I've always enjoyed the sensation of hitting people. It just feels good to dominate the goal and knock hell out of whoever comes into your area. I've played with a broken ankle, ribs, nose and back. I'm not bragging, but my body is less important to me than my pride.

Against Cannell, I knew I'd have to assert myself early and let him know I wasn't a duck in his shooting gallery. Two minutes into the game the opportunity came when I deflected a shot and Cannell headed straight for the rebound—and me. I threw myself on the ball, coming up just in time to ram my knee under his chin. I heard his teeth click together from the impact. "Next time," he swore, "I'll bust your ass."

A goalie's most effective weapons are his knees and elbows—his hands are occupied with the ball and his feet are working to maintain balance; but on the way up from a save, a well-placed knee or elbow can be a fine deterrent.

As Cannell struggled back upfield, I caught a wink from Pele. No one understands the latent brutality of soccer better than he. For most of his 22-year career, Pele has been the prime target of the sport's bounty hunters, those outclassed defenders determined to neutralize him at any cost. I've seen him kicked, tripped and stomped on. Some fouls are disguised as tackles. Others are flagrant assaults. But few are ever called by timid NASL referees. As much as I admire the man's audacious talent, I am in awe of his durability and patience. If I was Pele, I'd either be in a wheelchair or behind bars right now. Yet in two years I have seen him retaliate only once and that was in the Cosmos first game of the 1976 season. With less than a minute remaining, he angrily hurled himself at the legs of Miami fullback Ralph Wright who for 89 minutes had mistaken Pele for the ball. It was an ugly, dangerous foul that delighted me immensely. Pele was human after all.

Five minutes later I get another chance at Cannell, an elbow to the solar plexus. "Pffft." Too stubborn to go down, he stumbled off doubled over. For the rest of the game, Cannell didn't come near me. We won 2–0, another shutout. Afterwards, I heard Gordon tell a reporter, "I always had faith in Shep. I knew once he decided whether he wanted to eat glass or play soccer, he'd be a fine goalkeeper." That was the final thaw between Gordon and me. Later, when I learned that he was almost solely responsible for my return to the Cosmos—Clive Toye and the Warner brass had wanted an Englishman, not an American—I vowed to work like a galley slave to prove that Gordon had made the right choice. I'd be the best damn goalie in the league.

I haven't said much about goalies. It's a peculiar position, one that can take a player from martyr to hero with the single fickle bounce of a ball. In 1907, an Englishman wrote, "there are thousands of players who consider themselves goalkeepers, but you must remember that there are thousands upon thousands of men who consider themselves poets. Just as there are poets and poets, so there are goalkeepers and goalkeepers."

Not only are there goalkeepers, but there are goalkeeper's goalkeepers. True, we all belong to the same fraternity: We dress somewhat differently; we practice alone, repeating strange, punishing drills; we trade names of good plastic surgeons; we wear our scars the way Oxford men wear their college scarves; and we shake hands with each other before a game, but not with anybody else on the enemy team.

All these things we hold in common. Still, there are those who have a keener intuition, a seeming mystical anticipation of where the shot will go. And these same few usually possess the supreme wiles and body feints that seduce an opponent into sending the ball exactly where the goalie wants it to be.

The greatest I ever saw was Gordon Banks. He was so good he made the most incredible save look like a simple reflex action. I first saw him on the big screen at Madison Square Garden when he played on England's 1970 World Cup team, and I was in awe. I had admired other athletes, like Mantle and Mays and Ali, but this was different. Gordon Banks was a soccer player. Indeed, Gordon Banks was a goalkeeper.

He was everything I'd dreamed of being. He was in total command of his goal; and the sheer force of his confidence could paralyze an opposing forward. That magical afternoon, Banks showed me it was possible to achieve the impossible.

The luck of the draw had matched England against Brazil in an early game and the Brazilians were on the attack from the opening whistle. With 11 minutes gone, their brilliant winger Jairzinho broke free on the right, darted to the end line and centered perfectly to Pele. This was also the first time I had seen Pele. There he was, outjumping the entire English defense and heading the ball powerfully toward the inside of the far post. "Goal!" I shouted, leaping to my feet along with the rest of the Garden. "Goal!" Pele signaled, bounding into his famous salute. Then something unbelievable happened. Just as I've seen myself doing in dreams, Banks launched across the entire width of the cage and with one outstretched hand managed to flick the ball over the bar. For a split second there was stunned silence, as if we had all been tricked by some new cinematic device. Then the realization struck and a tremendous roar rocked the Garden.

To this day, I've never seen anything approach that play.

The Ft. Lauderdale Strikers got Banks by default after a car crash deprived him of the sight in his right eye at the height of his career and he retired from the English first division. Despite his handicap, he's one of the best keepers in the league; though deprived of that vital depth perception, I don't know how he manages. It must be like looking at a flat photograph until a ball comes flying into your face.

To some extent, however, his problem is visible. The hands that used to clamp down like a steel vise will bobble the ball or just punch it away. He might be a split second off here, a step behind there. Still, the formidable instincts come through. If he can't see a shot until it comes screaming down on him, experience tells him where it will come and when, and he can hurl his body in its path.

"I have to read the game better now," he told me as we walked off the field in Florida. "I have to make snap judgments by taking a quick look about, turning my head to see whether I can cover myself should the ball get passed to my blind side. My teammates are a help, of course. They know I may not be able to see a striker off to one side and they'll go after him themselves, or give me a yell. Still, I think they have confidence in my being able to compensate."

Compensate he has. He played every minute of the 1977 season, had nine shutouts, and was voted the league's MVP. Not bad for a 37-year-old goalkeeper who's half blind.

I am from the first bumper crop of American goalies. It made sense that the American sports system would produce a lot of us because American kids know how to use their hands. We are weaned on catching baseballs, footballs, and basketballs. Put a ten-year-old in goal and he'll pick up the rudiments of the position in a week; already high school goalies are being drafted by professional teams. It takes a lot longer to learn to control a ball with your feet.

At the same time I was coming up, other American goalies were making their reputations. Bob Rigby, Seattle's Tony Chursky—he's Canadian but that's close enough—and two fellow New Yorkers, Arnold Mausser and Alan Mayer, all had NASL contracts.

Most of us were good athletes before taking up soccer. I had my wrestling and pole vaulting; Alan Mayer was the #1 tennis player and a starting guard on the basketball team at Islip High School in Long Island, where he played against guys like Mitch Kupchak and Foots Walker, both NBA pros.

In the beginning, Riggs was the fastest rising star among us. He had it all: blond curls, blue eyes, straight teeth and incredibly quick hands. If the team owners ever conjured up a vision of the all-American prototype, it would have been Riggs. He was born to be on a Wheaties box. Back in 1973, while the rest of us were still dreaming about a one line mention, Riggs made the cover of *Sports Illustrated* as goalie for the champion Philadelphia Atoms. Stardom, such as it was, hit him prematurely, before the sport or Bobby was old enough to put it in perspective.

He seemed to think he had to forge a lifestyle to match the way he threw himself around in goal. A night out with Riggs could sideline you for a week. Not given to doing anything halfway, Riggs trained like a madman when he was invited to compete in ABC's Superstars. Trying to be the best in every event, he once spent four solid months just working with weights. Another winter he took up ski racing and tore down killer mountainsides at heart stopping speeds. None of this helped his soccer. Don't get me wrong. Riggs is still a good keeper. But if he had channeled all that energy into one sport, he could have been the best.

The rest of us American goalies have run into problems of a different sort. Despite winning records, despite being better than many foreign goalies in the league, we get traded or sold with depressing regularity. I had been released by the Cosmos. Mausser was inexplicably dumped by Tampa Bay. He was playing incredibly well at the time, accumulating a string of shutouts and a goals against average far better than Paul Hammond's, the keeper he replaced when Hammond went back to his English club in the Third Division. It wasn't enough that Arnie was the NASL's all-star goalie, voted the league's best North American player, starred on the U.S. national team. No, as soon as Tampa Bay coach Eddie Firmani learned he could get Hammond back for the 1977 season, he peddled Arnie to the Vancouver Whitecaps. "Paul has more professional experience," he said.

Arnie and the Rowdies parted bitterly. Just before the trade, he had won a $10,000 award as the American MVP of the league. The Rowdies, mostly foreign, hurriedly called a meeting.

"What for?" Arnie asked.

"Why, to divide up your prize money, of course," one of the English players said. "It's the way we do it back home." Arnie had had just about enough of the great English traditions. After all, he was on his way out, dumped like garbage. He walked to the front of the locker room to address the team.

"Divide this," he said, thrusting his middle finger in the air. Then he left for good.

Goalkeepers are also touchy on matters of style, an intensely personal thing. I've been criticized for everything from being "weak in the air" (a favorite accusation of those overdosed on watching English goalkeepers save high cross after high cross after high . . .) to being too flamboyant. So have Mausser and Rigby. "What the hell does it matter if you stand on your head," Riggs said, "if you come up with the damn ball."

I couldn't agree more. You have to go with what works. Style is in the eye of the beholder. For some, goalkeeping is a momentary dance, like the iridescent leap of a salmon. It's reflective, instinctive. You stand for what seems like forever, peering from the depths of the cage into the action. Then, suddenly, the ball, small as an insect, grows larger, larger, buzzing toward you until the exact second arrives. You know just when. For an instant, you're soaring, high above the turbulence, no horizon lines beyond the curve of the oncoming ball. Seeing a stop action photo, I'm always amazed at the balletic poses I strike at that instant.

Other keepers, like Arnie Mausser, prefer a more positional, textbook approach. Less acrobatic, more firmly anchored to the ground, his body turns constantly to follow the play like a radar scanner, picking up a feint here, a move there. Carefully, with slide rule precision, his steps across the goalmouth mirror the wider path of the ball outside. When it comes, only minor adjustments are needed to meet the ball's flight path—to search and destroy.

Naturally, you adjust your style to your opponent. The long high balls of the English require leaping and catching; the same high shot from a South American player dips and spins crazily, and your only hope is to punch it away. Whatever works, you try.

It didn't take me long to know my fellow Cosmos since I had played with many of them before. We were close, with just minor hints of the ego clashes that would split our locker room the following year. The front office meddling had not yet begun and, left to ourselves, we behaved reasonably civilized. Some of us even became friends.

It's quirky the way close ties develop on a team. Such obvious factors as nationality can draw players together, but in general, friendships evolve around similar attitudes. I fell in with the "dangerous" guys. At least that's what Gordon called them. The most dangerous stunt we ever pulled was leaving pop tops around to pollute the environment.

The first guy to share curfew fines with me was Smitty, the street kid who read poetry. His ginger bread and eggbeater hair make him look like an overgrown leprechaun, but he has the eyes of a highwayman, a Billy the Kid. The first time I met Smitty, we were on opposing teams and he tried to detach my head. His virtues as a defender are springy legs and the physical toughness to contest the league's most dangerous forwards, but he is wont to foul. When airborne, Smitty likes to use his elbows like garden spades. Nothing juices him more than a defensive lapse. "You know I hate a guy to beat me, man," he'd say. "Somehow if I'm not into the game and a guy gets around me, I get mad as hell and I'm ready to play."

We became partners and roommates when I joined the Cosmos, Dirty Harry and Dennis the Menace. Our rooms were disgusting, so foul in fact that we'd tip the chambermaids ten bucks on arrival to just open the door and throw in fresh towels every day. Don't get me wrong. We weren't into wholesale destruction. We weren't rock stars building bonfires in hotel beds. We specialized in creative mischief, like winging grapefruit sections out the window and maikng freeform sculptures out of day old French toast.

Smitty fell in love on every road trip, disappearing for one or two days. I'd find a phone number written in soap on the bathroom mirror, or a little lacy something under the bed. Sometimes, I couldn't get in the room at all. Smitty and I had a system. If he wished to pass the night undisturbed, he'd leave a ketchup bottle outside the door and I'd move in with Werner Roth. Once he kept me out of the room for three days running.

"What are you, Superman?" I called to Smitty when I saw him at practice. "I need my goddamn razor." He was mystified.

"Where the hell have you been?" he asked, then slapped his forehead. He'd forgotten to bring in the ketchup bottle and room service was so slow that nobody had picked it up.

One clear, sunny day in San Jose, we were alone on the practice field. You could hear the dewy grass squeak under your rubber soles. Smitty and I were kicking a ball back and forth, enjoying the grace of a perfect afternoon.

"I love it," he said.

"Love what?"

Smitty smiled and kicked the ball.

"The thud. I just love the thud, the ball flying away. I don't need the stadium, I don't need the people, not any of it."

I knew he wasn't kidding. We have impassioned arguments on the subject. Sports are business, I'll tell him, you're nothing but a hired gun. They're fun, he'll say. They were fun *once*, I answer. And so it goes. I love the sport, but I'm a realist. Smitty still thinks the only game an athlete has to play is on the field.

"There has to be some way to separate the fun from the bullshit factor," he insisted. He claims the bullshit—a term used to describe anything that threatens to infringe on his pleasure—hangs over him like a foul cloud. Bullshit is practice, curfews, dress codes.

"I gotta find a way through it," he said. "Somewhere there has to be a bullshit free zone. And I'm just the guy to find it."

"Rubbish," said Chinaglia. "Soccer is a business and you're in a buyer's market. You are the commodity. You don't play by the market rules, goodbye."

George and I have a lot in common. We both loathe training rules and receive constant criticism for our styles. George is graceless, I am wild. We became close friends.

"Fuck 'em," George said. "We get the job done. I score goals, you stop them. Nobody says we have to be ballerinas."

Somehow, George and Smitty and I always ended up in the back of the bus. The first time the four of us went out together we made our plans in the back seat, jouncing along to our hotel in Tampa.

"Gotta get out," George blurted. "Can't stay in that bloody hotel, gotta get out." He needed a bar, a jukebox and a pool table, in no particular order.

"Hey George," I said, "that's $250 if I get caught. I can't afford it."

"No problem," he said. "How many guys here?" With Smitty, Werner and me, it was four.

"Fine," George said. "Four guys, one thousand dollars. I'll cover it." He pulled out a silver money clip and counted off $1000. "We get caught, I pay for us all." Later that night I learned that George was a shrewd gambler. He had stayed in the hotel once before and knew the perfect escape route. We never got caught.

George throws dollars around like they're lira. His background is classic rags to riches. Born in

Italy, he grew up in Cardiff, Wales, where his father opened a small restaurant. George left school at 15, playing soccer by the day, slinging pasta and washing dishes at night.

"Those were hard times," George mused one day. "I wanted to be a good student, a good soccer player and a good son all at once. I was getting home from work at 3 A.M., getting up for school at 7, falling asleep in class. I was going nowhere. Soccer was my only way out."

Four years later, he returned to his native Italy and joined Lazio, a third division team. Almost singlehanded, he took the club from abject mediocrity to the Italian championship in 1974. Along the way, the man became obscured by the myths that grew about him.

There were countless stories told of George when he joined the Cosmos, and they all seemed to be about different men. The guy is so unpredictable, so impossible to figure, the Italians coined a word for it—*chinagliata*. He wavers between impish and menacing, charming and crude. There is Chinaglia the Fiery who gave his World Cup coach half the peace sign before 100 million TV viewers and earned more assassination threats than Yassir Arafat. There is Chinaglia the Diety, worshipped in Rome alone, by a fan club of 21,000. These disconsolate 21,000 threatened to throw themselves in front of the plane carrying their hero aloft rather than see him go to the Cosmos. Chinaglia the Schemer got out of that by slipping onto a private jet to Paris a full 16 hours before his scheduled Alitalia flight. The enraged fans heaped garbage on the Lazio team during practice. Finally, there is George the Benevolent Dictator, who hired and fired ruthlessly in the days when he made Lazio a champion but took pains to institute a bonus system for the groundskeepers and charwomen.

"Chinaglia does not forget the little man," he told me. When the Cosmos toured Europe during the spring of '77, he peeled off two $100 bills and handed them to our Italian bus driver. "You see Shep, Chinaglia takes care of his own," he said. The driver kissed his hand and cried. As we came into Rome by train, thousands of loyal Chinaglia fans nearly threw themselves on the rails, strewing the tracks with poppies and carnations that were crushed into blood red pulp by the train. It was scary. They were glass-eyed, fanatical, chanting "Giorgio's song," trying to touch the lapels of his sportcoat. Women came up with babies for him to kiss, all named Giorgio.

"I get it," I thought. "He's a shrewd business-man in America, and here, he's Chinaglia the Working Man."

Wrong again. That theory dissolved when George invited me to the classiest disco in Rome. It's called Jackie O's, aptly named for the style of its clientele. Only the rich and the connected passed through the blinding chrome door to the inner sanctum.

"Signor Chinaglia's guest? But of course." I was swept to the back, to George's corner. There I watched the creme de la Continent brush cheeks and dance to American music on spike-heeled pumps. Givenchy, Dr. Aldo Gucci, Raquel Welch, Sophia Loren, the air was heady with expensive cologne and the pungent aroma of stilleto-thin cigars. Then all stopped dancing, as even the most blasé edged toward the halo of exploding flashbulbs at the door. Chinaglia.

"What do you think of my little night spot?" he asked grinning. A waiter slid a velvet upholstered chair beneath him while a valet crawling under the table slipped off his shoes and scurried away to polish them. An inclination of George's head and a tray of cigarettes appeared. My rum and coke vanished, replaced with champagne. For George, an entire bottle of Chivas Regal on a silver stand. I reached for my wallet and George grabbed my arm.

"No. No money here. Chinaglia tries to pay, but he cannot. Everyone wants to buy me food, drinks. Once a year, maybe, I settle my bill. Is $10,000 maybe. But many times, a wealthy admirer pays it for me. Is an honor, he tells me—so—" George shrugged, rolling his eyes, "what can I do? If it gives them pleasure, I let them pay."

So this is what it means to be a big time soccer star. "How the hell did it get this way?" I asked.

"A man stays small because he thinks small," George said. "I could have stayed in Lazio, been a nobody on a nothing team. Not Chinaglia. Me and my coach built Lazio, invested our hearts and wallets in it. I could have stayed in Italy. Two teams wanted to buy me for 2½ million dollars. But what do I need their money? My wife is an American, our children will be American, so will I. I will be an American businessman."

He started outlining his New Jersey real estate deals, the endorsement contracts he was negotiating. Though I'd later learn the Cosmos paid only $240,000 for George and not $800,000 as the press reported, he would still be a rich American when he stood with all the Mexican weavers and Shanghai cooks to take the citizenship oath.

"I got plans," he told me that night in Rome. "Big plans for me, for the Cosmos, for American soccer. Maybe even for you."

Whatever they were, George's plans had to wait for the completion of the 1976 season. Statistically, it had been a good year for him, 19 goals in 19 games including an incredible five goal outburst in our final game that earned him the NASL scoring crown. In fact, only one player in the league had a better season. Pele. Pele was the NASL's Most

Valuable Player in 1976. He was also the NASL's meal ticket. His presence set attendance records wherever we went. In Chicago, Pele and the Cosmos drew 28,000. One week later, 3500 showed up to watch Chicago play Rochester. George knew that had he scored 100 goals he would still have taken a back seat to Pele. Every now and again, his frustrations erupted.

After one awful game in San Jose, Gordon came down on all of us during a team meeting, but singled out George for not running as hard as he should.

"Keeeeenalya. I am Keeeenalya." George stood up bellowing. "And if I am Giorgio Keeenalya, I play *my* way."

He stomped out of the locker room and left the stadium. It killed me. So many times I've felt like doing the same thing, but there was no way I could get away with it. Only Keeeenalya.

You can learn a lot about a person from what they keep in their locker. George's locker looks as thought it's cared for by a valet. On one hook there is a blue, black and white velour robe. He even has handmade slippers. George is the only guy in the league who can get away with padding around the shower in goddamn slippers. The top shelf of his locker has an array of tonics and balms with European names and astronomical prices. From another hook hangs a shiny chrome hairdryer. Assorted necessities include a bottle of Chivas, one crystal glass, cigarettes, a Dunhill lighter and, of course, an ashtray. George Chinaglia does not crush butts with handmade slippers.

Pele's locker looks as if nobody lives there. He has rows of brand new shoes neatly arranged beneath plastic-covered uniforms. The Cosmos have to order his #10 shirts by the gross. Fans, players, team owners, children, everyone requests the shirt off his back after a game. He always comes back to the locker room barechested.

Once inside that steamy womb, once the pressures of the game had abated, Pele was a little kid. He would sneak up behind you in the shower and pinch you, or hide under a pile of towels to jump out and say "boo." Then he'd giggle and run off. He was fast, too, always getting away before you could retaliate.

On the road, his presence made for an atmosphere that was half carnival, half cloak and dagger. Everywhere we went, flashbulbs and security guards, the number of his hotel room so secret, even we didn't know where he was. Ask Professor Mazzei, Pele's close friend and advisor, and he'd say, "Oh, try 301." Go to 301, and there'd be two schoolteachers from Duluth. And even if you got lucky and found the right room, you still had to get past Pedro, Pele's bodyguard. Pedro is Cuban, a veteran of the Bay of Pigs. Pedro is also built: wide shoulders, narrow hips, biceps like eggplants. I was always on good terms with Pedro. I enjoyed watching him fend off the legions of female admirers who would somehow turn up outside Pele's room in laundry carts, offering towels and other favors. Pedro was never rough with the ladies, relying on Latin charm to get the message across.

One surefire method of finding Pele was to go down to the hotel shop and cruise the sunglass display. Pele loves sunglasses, must have had 60 pairs. He and the Professor would be standing there, Pele twirling the rack, unable to decide on the chartreuse horn rims or the Captain Video polarized space shield. Sunglasses were about all he ever seemed to buy. Ordinarily, he'd just look around, picking things up, putting them down. "I like to see what people buy," he told me, flipping through a rack of polyester leisure suits. His clothes are all custom made: pastel suits with wide lapels and french-cuffed shirts, matching sweaters and slacks and lots of leather. Pele loves fur and leather. "They last long time," he told me.

Coming from such a poor background, Pele has a working man's regard for money and the security it provides. The only times I've ever seen him lecturing younger players the conversation concerned money. Especially when he was about to retire in 1977, Pele would wax serious at odd moments on the road.

"Hey, Gary, you come here a minute, please?" He walked over and put his arm around Gary Etherington, an 18-year-old American rookie who had just returned from a shopping spree in Los Angeles. He had bags full of T-shirts, books, records, and souvenirs with "Hollywood—Home of the Stars" stenciled across them.

Pele looked into the bundle like a father poking through his son's schoolbag. "Listen," he told Gary, "you are very young, and you are good player. You will be in this city many, many times more. Save your money. In this game, you are old man very soon."

There was an avuncular warmth about Pele that always made rookies feel at ease. Once after a scrimmage, Bobby Rohrbaugh, a first year forward out of Dayton University, came running up to me in the locker room. "Did you hear him out there today?"

"Hear who?" I asked.

"Pele," he said. "He called my name. My God, he knows me!"

July melted into August. It was alternately muggy and blistering in New York. At the end of a workout, my jersey felt like it weighed ten pounds. After Arden closed up the Boston apartment in August and came down to New York, I began working out daily with the Cosmos. This hint of permanence did a lot for our morale. I didn't even mind practice—much.

As the playoffs drew near, tension built. "Running, running. Is all the time in America this running." Nelsi Morais, our Brazilian fullback, stood on the practice field dripping with sweat. He had taken off as much clothing as he could without getting arrested. Just then someone grabbed my elbow and pulled me into the entrance tunnel behind a pile of tarps. Pele.

"You are lazy like me, eh Shep?" he asked. I nodded, grinning. I think Pele hated Gordon's sprint drills almost as much as I did. We stayed there as long as we could, and from that day on, shared schemes to get out of running. I'd develop sudden muscle pulls and Pele would help me off the field and into the locker room.

At 35, Pele was obviously husbanding his energy for the games that counted. I loved watching the grace and precision of his moves, his economy of emotion. No muscle moved without a sense of purpose. He had a wondrous season in 1976, the unmatchable skills refusing to stop flowing after all these years. His 18 assists shattered an NASL record. His bicycle kick against Miami is still engraved on my mind: the ball coming across the goalmouth, Pele suspended in the air, his thick body reclining as it might in a beach chair. Then, suddenly, the legs slash the air, scissorlike, the right one pointing up, higher still until the instep meets the ball at the top of its arc, driving it over his outstretched body, straight and unstoppable, into the net. For the first time in my career, I said to hell with concentration and sprinted half the field to where Pele was sitting on the ground beneath a tangle of green jerseys. I was so happy I thought I was going to cry. In one blinding flash, he had revealed to Americans the beauty of the game he so desperately wanted them to embrace. It was a small miracle.

Function rather than aesthetics was George's concern. He played soccer the way he played poker, stone-faced and silent, until he put the ball in the net and went into his triumphant boogie. Dropping to his knees, he'd make the sign of the cross, then leap up and shimmy to midfield, fists clenched, face raised in a beatific smile. George danced a lot that season and we waltzed into the playoffs with a record of 16–8, second best in the league.

Only one dark cloud hung over our championship hopes. During the last month Keith Eddy, our British sweeper-back and captain, had been in constant agony from a groin pull. Bit by bit, the muscle kept tearing from the bone. The last few regular season games he could barely walk. He was forced to sit out the first contest against Washington; but after we won 2–0, and had to play Tampa Bay, he insisted he could get through one more game. I was relieved. Nothing could do more for my confidence than to have Keith there to direct traffic in front of the goal. He had been my mainstay all season, repulsing attacks like a craggy boulder resisting the surf. Before a shootout, the NASL tiebreaker where players on each team challenge the opposing goalkeeper one-on-one, I'd talk to Keith about how to set up against the different attackers.

"Steady on, Shep," he'd tell me. "Forget about the rest of the team. You and I will hold them off." Together, I knew we could; he was the only field player who thought like a goalkeeper. Against Tampa, I'd need him more than ever. Poor scheduling would pit the NASL's two best teams against each other in the Eastern Division playoffs. The

Rowdies were the defending champs and the only team in the league with a better record than ours. Coach Eddie Firmani had drilled and hammered his heavily English team into a well-balanced, cohesive unit that relied on long balls and leather lungs. We dribbled to a different drummer. "Our game is like music," said Ramon Mifflin. "It is short passes, always moving, tick-tock, tick-tock, tick-tock, goal."

Neither style had proved superior. The Rowdies had beaten us 5–1 in early June; we had avenged the defeat 5–4 a month later on two goals by Pele.

But none of that mattered now as I watched Keith limp off the plane in Tampa. I couldn't believe he was actually going to go through with it. "You're fuckin' crazy," I said. "You want to be an invalid the rest of your life?"

"Doctor told me I can't do any further damage by playing," Keith said. "He tells me it's just a question of how much pain I can stand."

I'm not squeamish. I've taken my licks. But I have never seen anything like the ordeal Keith went through before that Tampa game.

Sitting on the training table naked, beside an arsenal of hypodermic needles, he squeezed a washcloth in one hand as the doctor inserted the first needle into the tender skin of his thigh. His face a mask of pain, Keith waited a moment for the novocaine to take effect and then ran his hand over the area. "No good, doc," he said. "I can still feel it."

The process was repeated a second and third time. I was standing there for moral support, but by the fifth needle realized I wasn't doing anyone any good. By then I was as pale as Keith.

From the stands, Keith probably looked in top form, heading balls away from the goal mouth, launching offensive sorties with long passes along the flanks. Only those who got a close look at his face had an inkling of the agony the man was going through. It was horrible. And to make matters worse, we played badly. The Tampa Bay forwards led by the flamboyant Rodney Marsh were going through our midfield as if it were a rumor, so Keith and I were under heavy fire the entire game. Late in the second half, Marsh came in alone on me and curved the ball into the net. 3–1, Tampa. We knew it was over. Gordon signalled Keith to come out. Dirty, socks bloodied from a nasty cut above his knee, he hobbled off, head down. I've only seen a face like that in combat footage: the look of a man in final, utter defeat. Though he tried to come back in 1977, Keith's career really ended when he left that field in Tampa. For the Cosmos, the season ended 10 minutes later.

Next day I picked up the local paper and read: "We could have the first dynasty in American soccer. I'd rather have the good, steady players I've got; I don't want to have to deal with a Pele or a Chinaglia."

The words belonged to Eddie Firmani.

8

THE
CHAMPIONSHIP
SEASON

Our championship team was a promising blend of raw talent and scarred veterans, the material from which dynasties arise. It was also a seething brew of half English and half South American, a cauldron of mistrust and misunderstanding, the stuff from which world wars are born.

The dribble-through-their legs South Americans sneered at the English, calling them "crazy bulls." The run-until-you-drop English were disgusted with the South Americans, labeling them "the laziest bloody bunch in the game."

All this malevolence bubbled to the surface at training camp and it seemed to those of us not so ideologically involved that only one man had the grace and the stature to unite the Cosmos into a team. For the first 43 days of camp we endured, awaiting the arrival of Pele, who was delayed by business commitments.

When he finally showed up, we gasped. He was 36 and looked it. He was out of shape.

Pele said he had worked out nearly every day with Santos, his old team in Brazil, but there was little evidence. "Maybe he thinks training is lying on the beach," said George, dripping with sweat and sarcasm after Pele's first practice on March 30. George could afford to criticize. In our five preseason games, the Cosmos had scored eight goals and he had seven of them. "Until he gets in shape, he's just another player I'll have to carry," George said.

We opened against Las Vegas, and if the Cosmos had been a stage show, we'd have closed that night. We stunk. Our defense in front of the goal was desperate. For some reason, I was having trouble hanging onto the ball. More than once, Werner had to bail me out when a bobbled ball rolled perilously close to Las Vegas forwards swarming the penalty area. Finally, I let in a stupid one. I made my move too quicky, feinting to the left, and the guy read my intent, drilling the ball into the opposite corner.

"Why didn't I got to law school?" I screamed. Nobody laughed. Nobody was listening. All eyes were trained midfield, on Pele, rubberneckers glued to the scene of an accident. If George was having an off game, Pele was a disaster, missing George's passes, misdirecting his own, beaten easily by astonished Las Vegas forwards. One of them was Wolfgang Suhnholz, my old Minuteman crony.

As Wolfgang and I untangled in the goalmouth, he grabbed my arm. "Who's the old guy wearing Pele's shirt?" he asked.

Eusebio, who had been passed on to Las Vegas in the Boston dispersals, still possessed that redoubtable shot and that equally remarkable durability on and off the field. In the second half, he took a hard tackle and crumpled to the ground, having torn whatever ligaments were left in his right leg. I ran over to help the trainers lift him onto a stretcher. The pain was so intense that tears streamed down his cheeks.

"Ay, Shep," he croaked. "Where you gamble tonight? I meet you at Caesar's Palace. Crap tables, okay?"

That crack was the highlight of the game for me. The rest was an eternity of botched signals and sloppy play. We lost 1–0.

Walking off the field, Wolfgang came up to me shaking his head. "When people think of soccer, they think of Pele. I hate to see the legend tarnished. Tonight I think it was," he said.

That same evening, with some of the other players, Wolfgang and I went to a jazz club where I sat nursing a rum and coke, thinking of Willie Mays, a childhood hero. I remember seeing him stumble around the outfield at Shea Stadium, hanging on too long. The guy just didn't know when to quit. I didn't want Pele to go out that way, but now I was afraid he might.

Lifting my eyes, I saw him through the smoke. Everyone was gathered around the bandstand and the dance floor, but Pele was standing alone, hidden by the shadow of a column. He was gently tapping one foot to the music, his eyes flickering over the scene. I got up and walked over to him.

"Have a drink, relax," I said, knowing he'd decline both suggestions. Pele doesn't drink; nor can he relax in public.

"No, you come with me," he said. "We talk." We rode the elevator to his room where a checkerboard was set up on one of the tables. He motioned to a chair and we started to play. He was unusually quiet, almost withdrawn.

"Forget the game today," I told him. "We all played lousy."

He looked at me and smiled. "No, I am not bothered by my game today," he said. "I wonder instead about soccer here. I wonder if I fail in my mission, to bring soccer to the American people. To do this, we must have a championship. This team must be the best. The Cosmos must win. Every team I ever play on, it is the same way. If the team is no good, they will say is because Pele is no good."

I started to protest. He held up his hand. "No, is true. And is okay. I make a reputation, I must work to keep it. Only now I am afraid. Maybe I have made a mistake. And when I leave, people will only remember Pele to say he is an old man."

While I marvelled at the enormity of his burden, the grace with which he carried it, Pele double-jumped me. He giggled.

"So now—I finish you good." In a moment, the brooding man disappeared and the child returned. Of all the lowdown tricks, getting serious so I'd forget the game. Pele had been perfectly sincere, but he was also playing with me. What a master, what a competitor he was.

We were travelling with a new reserve goalie, Erol Yasin, a Turk. Later, I learned that he was signed on direct orders from the Erteguns, also Turks. Yas was a friendly, hardworking guy and as members of the net fraternity, we got along well. Though he played behind me, he helped me in any way he could, warming me up, working with me in practice. Still, the threat of replacement hung over my head. When we got to our next stop, Hawaii, I was sick with the flu, but I concealed it from Gordon, running off the practice field to heave out of his sight.

As Gordon gave his pre-game talk, I sat in the corner removing the brand name identification from a pair of soccer shoes. My supply of Pumas, the brand I endorse, had vanished in an airport mixup and it would violate my contract to trot onto the field wearing a competitor's shoe. Suddenly, the razor slipped and sank deep into the fleshy part of my right hand. In no time, I'd managed to cover everything with blood. Gordon turned ghastly white as the trainer scurried around for ice.

"Take it easy," Gordon said. "I'll put Yasin in."

Over my bloodless body, I thought. "No need," I told him. "I'm fine." I bound the hand in gauze and stuffed a glove over it.

"See," I said, wiggling the hand. "Complete mobility."

Reluctantly, Gordon let me play. And in spite of the flu and the bad hand, I had a good game. Everyone played better and we won 2-1. Afterwards, the glove had to be cut away with surgical shears.

We won our home opener 2-0 against Rochester, but then lost two straight shootouts, including a 3-2 disaster against St. Louis where I let in an easy goal. Afterward, the locker room was frigid. Bradley said we should have won by three goals. Pele said it was one of the worst games of his life. George said the team needed a shakeup. "Everyone," he said, looking in the general direction of Pele.

Before the next game, the shakeup came. Gordon called me into the hall just before we were to take the field against Connecticut. "I'm starting Yasin," he said.

"What? I know I've lost two shootouts but . . ."

"That's not the reason," Gordon said. "You've played well. But I haven't seen Yasin, and I want to give him a chance." Next he called Smitty out and told him that Nelsi Morais would have his spot. Naturally, we took it like professionals, sulking in our hotel room, refusing to suit up for the game.

"What the hell?" Smitty said. "Let's get fined, then let's get traded." So we dressed and sat on the bench, silently rooting for Connecticut whenever Erol or Nelsi came near the ball. It wasn't enough. The Cosmos won 3–2.

Back in New York, Smitty stayed furious. When the traveling list for the Chicago game was posted, he grabbed a can of foot spray and obliterated our names from the list.

"You fucking crazy?" I yelled, scribbling my name back on the board. Smitty didn't hear me. He was already tearing through his locker like an enraged pack rat. Sneakers, jocks, torn shirts flew through the air as he stuffed a laundry bag. Gordon, standing at the back of the room observing it all, was unimpressed.

"You're suspended," he said, and walked off to conduct practice. I assumed he meant both of us, so Smitty and I left the stadium for a nearby topless joint. We spent hours discussing our future, although the subject seemed worth about 10 minutes.

"I never felt happier," Smitty said, scowling into his beer. "I'm a free man. Right?"

"Free to do what?" I asked. "Wait tables? Sling hash?" I wove my way home, bracing to tell Arden the news. As soon as I got there, Keith Eddy called to say that only Smitty had been suspended. I was still on the traveling squad for Chicago. Relieved, I called Gordon.

"I want to be traded," I told him.

"We'll talk in Chicago," he said.

"I won't be jerked around," I said.

"See me in Chicago."

Once we arrived, Gordon and I talked for hours. Haltingly, he explained the situation. He had been playing me against the wishes of the Erteguns. Putting me in goal in the opener had nearly cost him his job.

Suddenly, a lot of things fell into place. Before

most games, I'd seen a Warners vice president, Rafael de la Sierra, hand a folded piece of paper to Gordon. There were rumors that it was the starting lineup, as decided by the front office. It must be true. If the Erteguns had their way, Gordon was coach in name only. And playing me instead of Erol was open defiance.

"I did it because I felt I was right to start you," he said. "Now I'm asking you to bear with this for a couple more games. I can't make a change now."

"If it looks bad, will you trade me?" I asked him. I wasn't going to spend the year on the bench behind a goalie who wasn't as good as me, not if I had any bargaining power.

"Just say the word."

"Fair enough," I said, and we shook hands. I rose to leave. Looking back over my shoulder, I saw him staring out the window of the hotel coffee shop. Decency in corporate affairs makes for a very lonely lifestyle.

I kept as quite as I could about the situation, but finally let a remark slip in a magazine article: something about being benched for not having the right passport. The day after the story appeared, Gordon called me into his office. He was trying to appear stern, but laughter broke through.

"Nesuhi Ertegun has called me ten times already," he said. "He's livid. You better call him."

I reached Nesuhi that night. As usual, I stood tall.

"Listen, Nesuhi, let me explain. It was a casual remark, out of context you know, and . . ."

"It's great," he said, stopping me cold. "Yes," he purred. "I've been thinking about it and I've decided that any publicity we can get is great. But I must see you before I leave on business at the end of the week."

I agreed, but it was Ahmet who appeared in the

locker room two days later. He pulled me from the bathroom to the office to the training room looking for a place to talk in private. We found a small cubbyhole in the hall.

"Listen, Ahmet . . ." I started my apology again.

"Forget it," he said. "Just remember, we can't have that kind of talk to the press in the future. We're all together, a family. Let's make sure to keep it in the family in the future, okay? Remember, one hand washes the other."

Relieved, I shook his hand and went off to practice. The next day I received a $5000 raise.

Yas played four games in a row, but had the decency to be miserable. He knew the situation. He stopped playing cards with us, quit running around with George, Smitty and me. I tried to make him more comfortable by warming him up, wishing him good luck. Maybe I put a whammy on him, because he didn't play well. Finally, after he let in two bad goals against Chicago and we lost 3–2, Gordon told me I'd be starting against Tampa.

Good thing. Tampa had been my personal deadline, the last game I'd watch from the bench before asking to be traded. It was to be on national television from Tampa and it was the debut of Franz Beckenbauer. After skulking around European airports and hotel lobbies for the better part of a year, Clive Toye had finally bagged his prize. Franz arrived early in the week, bringing with him half the working press of Western Europe. Werner taped interviews in German for British TV. I taped interviews in English for German TV. Pele said Franz was the greatest. Franz said Pele was the greatest, but I was so happy about returning to the starting lineup nothing else mattered. Trailed by a planeload of photographers, the greatest assemblage of soccer talent ever to traverse the North American continent left for Tampa.

We got handled. Our forwards played like strangers, which they were, and Tampa's "Murderer's Row" offense, the explosive force of their 1976 championship, cut through our defense. Franz played sweeper back like a soldier lost behind enemy lines, wandering aimlessly around the field.

Late in the game I took a spike in my right eyelid as I dove for the ball. I was stunned, unaware I was hurt. When I stood up to look around, I couldn't see. Figuring I had grass in my eye, I blinked, and blinked again. My whole face grew warm and I saw Franz running toward me with a look of horror. My eye was bleeding badly. I wanted to stay in, but every time trainer Jeff Snedeker wiped the cut, the eye filled again.

Even worse, we had fouled on the play and the Rowdies were to have a penalty kick, a lousy situation to leave for my replacement. Going off the field, I apologized to Erol and told him where I thought Rodney Marsh might put his shot. No use. As the ambulance doors closed, I heard the cheer. The Rowdies won, 4–2, with Franz coming back to score our final goal, drilling a rebound of his own shot from 20 yards.

Two days later at practice we heard the whir of a helicopter hovering over Giant Stadium. It touched down and Warners chairman Steve Ross entered the stadium through the tunnel. "This is it," said Smitty, rubbing his hands together like a witch from Macbeth. "He's gonna boot Bradley the hell out, I just know it."

I was thinking the same thing, without glee. In any professional sport, a coach's future is as solid as his won-lost record, and the Cosmos weren't doing much to fatten Gordon's chances. Our 5–5 record was mediocre, considering our talent; horrendous, considering our payroll.

There was one problem with Gordon. He was, quite simply, too decent. He hated to hurt anybody's feelings. Every once in a while, a coach has to kick ass, but Gordon couldn't. When George began to drop hints that his good friend Eddie Firmani would soon arrive from Tampa to rescue the team, some of the players stopped listening to Gordon. When Ross materialized like a thundercloud from on high, it looked like the end.

So you can imagine the shock when Ross started yelling at us. Smitty's grin disappeared quickly. In loud but measured tones, Ross told us that Warners would not be taken advantage of, that complacency would not be tolerated, that no job on the Cosmos was safe. His glance took in the whole team. "You'll love it in Rochester," I said to Franz.

Morale promptly sank to a new low and bickering increased. "Can you believe the head cases on this team?" Werner said at practice. The Cosmos were harder to follow than a ten-year soap opera, packed with petty jealousies, rife with warring egos, occasionally pausing for commercial interruptions from front office directives. Gordon was under pressure from the Erteguns to play Yasin, the Erteguns were under pressure from the press to play me, Pele was disgusted with the team and George was disgusted with Pele. He felt Pele kept him from scoring goals by not coming up with the right passes and crowding him in front of the goal.

Caught in the middle was Bradley, the beleaguered peacemaker, who shuttled between camps trying to pacify everyone, ultimately satisfying no one. On the field, our problem was coherence, the contradictory styles. The Latin players loved the languid pace of the South American game with its artistic passing and dazzling footwork. Gordon was crazy for the fast-paced long ball English game.

He had been raised in an era when ball-handling and subtlety were considered useless ornaments. His was a game that taxed players' lungs, not their skills.

"Everybody's pissed off about something but nobody's talking to anybody," Werner said. "I wish to hell I knew what to do." What he did was call a team meeting. It was more like an encounter session, primal scream therapy. This was the first time I heard Pele say "fuck." I think he did it to shock us, to let everyone know how upset he was, especially with George.

"You shoot from no fuckin' angle," he said, standing, facing George. "Why not put a few goals in from direct front."

"I am Chinaglia!" George leapt to his feet, shouting. "If I shoot from someplace, it is because Chinaglia can score from that place."

"Forget having a trainer," Smitty said on the way out. "What this team needs is a fuckin' shrink."

On the ensuing road trip to Ft. Lauderdale, all was slightly more peaceful. I bought the morning paper and headed for the coffee shop. Players dotted the restaurant, a few sitting together, most reading the sports section of their papers and not understanding a word. As I cracked mine open, a small item caught my eye. With his team in second place, and following a recent victory over the supposedly invincible Cosmos, Eddie Firmani had resigned as coach of Tampa, citing personal reasons. No one could find him for comment.

Weird, I thought. One of those man bites dog stories. I'd heard of coaches stealing away from teams with dismal records, but Firmani's expansion club was the success story of the league. Ah well, this sport was getting crazier by the minute. I forgot about it, for the time being.

Two weeks later, on June 13, the first head rolled off the corporate chopping block. The Cosmos called a press conference to announce, with regret, the resignation of Clive Toye as president. "This is the sickest day in the history of American soccer," Gordon muttered. Publicly, the matter was handled with high diplomacy on both sides. Clive would stay on as a paid consultant, maintaining a stiff upper lip in the best British tradition. Ahmet Ertegun would take time from his record business to step in as president. Despite Clive's diplomatic comments to the press, it didn't take a Harvard degree to know he seethed.

I bumped into him a few days later, after an incredible event at the Meadowlands. For a Sunday afternoon game against Tampa Bay, 62,394 people —the most ever for a soccer game in the United States—had shown up. This was nearly double the attendance of the last home game. Driving to the stadium, I thought I saw a mirage, lines of people snaking around the concrete walkways waiting to buy tickets. It took me half an hour to park. Juiced by the crowd, still playing for our jobs, we gave them a good show: three goals by Pele and a 3–1 win. In the locker room, Pele was so happy he even hugged George. "Today, it was like Brazil," he said. "When I went to the bench I was crying, not for my three goals but for all the people, for what is happening to American soccer. This is the biggest souvenir I ever get in United States, this crowd. This is the best present. This is why I come here."

I was heading for the post-game party when I spotted Clive. He was looking vacantly out over the emptying stadium, a father who had just given his favorite daughter away. He had conceived the Cosmos dream, raised it, nurtured it against all odds, and now it was gone, swept away on the French-cuffed arm of a big corporation.

"It's a shame," I said, startling him. "I just want to tell you I'm sorry about what happened. We won't forget what you did for us, none of us will."

He thanked me, a tight smile on his face. I asked him why it had happened, but he just shook his head.

"They're bastards," he said through his teeth. "I can't say any more but they're bloody bastards."

Once Clive left, Gordon changed, as though he knew that as part of Toye's old guard his days were numbered. He was somber and quiet, a man at his own wake. Between Gordon and George hardly any words were exchanged. George was playing badly; yet he complained bitterly that Pele and Bradley's coaching were holding him back. Gordon countered by telling a reporter that George was uncoachable and couldn't play fourth-division English soccer.

"Sure I'm uncoachable, because I know soccer better than the coaches here," George said. "Is that, how you say, 'presumptuous'? Well, it's true. I believe in soccer as team sport, but no one asks my opinion, so what am I supposed to do, huh? Sad to say but I don't feel a part of this team. I'm playing maybe thirty percent of what I can play. America hasn't seen the real Chinaglia. Soon I must do something. Is coming time to say something."

Ominous words from a player, an employee. But George wasn't the only one taking oblique jabs at Gordon's capabilities. Smitty had something to say, too. But his approach was more direct. An hour before a home game against Los Angeles, Gordon chalked the starting lineup on the blackboard. He was well into his pregame talk when Smitty started pacing up and down. I didn't like the smile on his face. The corners of his mouth kept turning up and down and the effect was no less than demonic. Werner whispered that Smitty's name had not been in the lineup.

"Omigod," I said, expecting the worst. Smitty kept pacing; it was like watching the fuse burn down on a stick of dynamite.

"Gordon, excuse me, Gordon." It was Smitty, in a strangely polite tone.

"Yes?"

He walked to the blackboard as if about to ask a question on tactics. Then he was kicking the blackboard, spitting at it. "That's what I think of your fucking coaching," he screamed. "It's a fucking joke, you English bastard." He challenged Gordon to a fight right there. Tightlipped, arms folded, Gordon stood his ground.

"Are you through?" Gordon asked quietly. Smitty lunged forward, kicked the blackboard again and stomped off cursing. The foreign players were stunned. Pele's mouth dropped open in astonishment. Franz was fighting to suppress a smile. The Englishmen weren't amused at all. "If this was England," said Terry Garbett, "Smith would never play soccer again."

Calmly, Gordon resumed the meeting and I slipped away to check on Smitty. When I got to the locker area, he was already gone, tearing off to his car half dressed. I did run into George, who was just getting back into his street clothes.

"What's going on?" I asked.

"Gordon benched me," he said.

"So you're quitting?"

"Never," he said. "Giorgio Chinaglia does not sit on the bench. I have a problem with my back, see? So I am going to rest it."

"Aren't you pissed off? What's going to happen?"

I was incredulous that he should take such an affront to his considerable ego so lightly.

"Look," he said, explaining the facts of life to a dumb kid. "I could play today if I wanted. I just call Steve Ross. But if this is what Gordon wants to do, it's his decision. I guarantee though, this will never happen again."

In other words, Gordon was digging his own grave. We won without George, 5–2, with Pele getting another hat trick; and the next day took off for the west coast. I was without a roommate since Smitty had been suspended, perhaps permanently. "While I'm coach," Gordon had told reporters, "Bob Smith will never appear in a Cosmos uniform again."

Unwittingly, he had set up a showdown. Just after we arrived in Vancouver, Gordon got a phone call informing him that Smitty had been fined $1000 and reinstated. In fact, he would be on the first flight out in the morning. Gordon went to Professor Mazzei, Pele's advisor, and asked him to take over the team. He was going back to New York. Mazzei conferred with Pele, and it was agreed that if Smitty came, Pele and Mazzei would also return to New York.

That was all Warners had to hear. They would never cross Pele, even to pressure Gordon. Smitty stayed in New York and we got our asses kicked 5–3. I had a particularly sterling game, allowing three goals in the first five minutes, maybe because I scarcely cared at that point. As we flew on to L.A., I was in a deep depression, knowing full well that the Erteguns had a perfect reason to put Erol back in. By the end of the season I'd need a lobotomy.

Gordon was now more resolute than ever to coach the team his way, and he started me in L.A. Returning home, he said he'd played me in direct

opposition to the Ertegun's wishes. "Not for senti-
mental reasons," he said, "but to help us win
games."

I appreciated his confidence, but knew his job
was on the line. And as I had hurt my knee slightly against L.A., I tried to give him an excuse to
placate the Erteguns.

"Just put me on the injured list," I told him,
"and play Erol."

"Absolutely not." He was being more stubborn
than I. "If your knee is all right, you play on Sunday."

All that week I limped in practice. I finally told
Gordon I couldn't play. Erol started against San
Jose and we won 3–0, giving us a 12–8 record with
a firm hold on first place.

Gordon got the sack the next day. Rather, he
resigned, much like Clive. Officially he was given
some nebulous title at one of those unctuous press
conferences where the word "fired" is strictly forbidden.

When we got the news that morning at the
stadium, it was painfully silent. In the middle of
the locker room, Pele was standing, facing front.
On a humid July morning, he was trembling. Tears
ran down his cheeks as he struggled for the right
words. "I hope," he said, "I hope that from now
on things will be different. I hope players now go to
the coach with problems, not over his head. Not
behind his back."

"He deserves an Academy Award," George
mumbled to no one in particular. Most eyes had
turned on George when Pele spoke because George
was thought to have orchestrated the whole plot.
After all, the new coach standing with an arm
draped over Gordon's shoulder was George's personal friend, the same coach who had mysteriously

resigned from Tampa a few weeks before. The new coach was Eddie Firmani.

Firmani took the job after a number of curious coincidences. George had gone to Tampa and trained with Eddie before reporting to Cosmos camp. And two days before he resigned from Tampa, Eddie had flown to New Jersey, watching a bit of the Cosmos exhibition game against George's former team Lazio. Then Eddie met with his old friend Vito Bavaro, who owns an Italian pastry shop in New Jersey and is, coincidentally, a good friend of George's. I found all this out after Eddie had come to the Cosmos, though he insisted it had nothing to do with his getting the job. Later on, Tampa would level charges of tampering against the Cosmos. But that first morning in the locker room, the acrimony had already surfaced.

When the meeting was dismissed, most of us walked around like survivors of a blitz, shocked.

"Who are you going to fire now, Giorgio?" Keith Eddy asked bitterly.

Most of us felt we really hadn't done Gordon justice. Our talent was greater than we'd shown. Most of us were ashamed when Gordon was fired. "You know," said Werner, "when Gordon said 'I just want to thank you guys for all you've done' I didn't know whether to laugh or cry. All we did for the guy was get him canned."

"Never in 15 years of playing do I see anything like this," said Franz. "I come to America and in three weeks I see a president fired, I see a fight in the locker room, I see a coach fired, I see Pele cry." He shook his head, then, apprehensively, shook the hand that Firmani extended. The new coach was making the rounds, shaking hands, saying hello. The reactions were telling. The Englishmen barely spoke to him, still loyal to Bradley. George was grinning hugely, rid of his nemesis at last. Firmani didn't even approach Pele.

From then on, George was a man transformed. He was still having problems scoring, but he was confident that Firmani would help him. The first team practice was devoted to passing drills, giving George the ball in front of the goal. Pele, on the other hand, was treated worse than a rookie.

"You're off free kicks," Firmani told him. "I don't want you taking any more. George will take them, or Franz. I want you there for rebounds." He motioned to a spot 10 yards behind where free kicks are taken. None of the other players could believe it. Pele had always taken free kicks, mainly because he had the most accurate shot in the world. Now Eddie was humiliating him, shoving him yards away from the action, even making him do extra wind sprints in practice.

"You're too damn slow," he'd bark at Pele. "Ten more sprints." Pele took it silently, trotting out to his assigned tasks obediently. His face, though, was etched with anger at this graceless man who felt a compulsion to humiliate him. For the rest of us, it was just embarrassing. We were outraged at the shoddy treatment of the man who had made our league, even Firmani's job, possible. But we were powerless to do anything. I was talking to Erol about it when a commotion started at midfield.

"Idiot!" Steve Hunt was screaming at George who had just blown one of his passes. They tried to connect again, and once more George misplayed the ball.

"Stupid!" Hunt yelling again. And all at once George nailed him in the jaw with a right. Steve staggered back stunned as others rushed over to keep them apart.

The following game against Connecticut Steve walked off the field when he thought Eddie was replacing him with rookie Gary Etherington. The press made much of both incidents, all but calling Hunt a demented egomaniac because that's how it looked from the outside. But those of us who knew his situation could understand.

Steve had been a reserve player for Aston Villa in England and knew that he would have to give it the old stiff upper lip treatment for a couple of seasons before making the first team. So when Charlie Aitkin, one of our fullbacks, recommended him to Gordon, Steve jumped at the chance to play in the United States. He was 20, newly married and agog at the opportunity to play alongside Pele.

At first, New York frightened him and the non-English players on the Cosmos discomforted him. He and his wife were so homesick that she returned to England for all of June. The incident with George was the result of frustration at watching the Latin American players dance with the ball while he was running relay races up and down the field. A week later, in characteristic fashion, George ran over to hug Steve after he scored a couple of goals, and eventually got him a contract with Pony, the shoe Chinaglia endorses.

The walkoff was a misunderstanding. Steve was hurt by the condemnation that followed in the newspapers, the booing from the stands. He and Eddie had gotten signals crossed on who was to mark the Bicentennials' fullback and when he looked to the sideline, he saw Gary Etherington warming up. Firmani nodded and Steve assumed this meant he was being replaced. The next day, a headline read: "Hunt Storms Off the Field, Never to Be Seen Again."

"What a pile of rubbish," Steve said. "I was in the stadium bar after the game but nobody bothered to check. If it happened again, I'd do it again. I'm not saying I'm perfect."

No, none of us is. Trouble is we're human and react naturally, something team owners don't always allow for. Put that many languages, egos and styles on the field and you're bound to have friction. If you throw a drum of gasoline into a fire, you should expect it to explode.

By mid July, we were in mid-season limbo, a state that comes on like a yawn. The freshness of the early season has worn off; the pressures of the end of the season haven't quite begun and days on the road become coffee shop conformity: formica counters, early American wallpaper, cocktail lounges with nautical motifs. An athlete can develop a pretty warped view of things. To pass time, we invented little games that ordinarily wouldn't entertain a three-year-old.

"I bet you, Shep," Pele said one afternoon in Seattle. "I bet you I spend more time in airplanes than you spend on the field your whole time in soccer."

"Let's see," I began. "Four years, four months a year . . . You counting practice time?"

Pele sat on the edge of the hotel bed, scratching away on a note pad, figuring air time from Tokyo to Zambia, Caracas to Munich. Then he tossed the paid in the air.

"You fish?" he asked.

"Sure," I answered. I decided not to explain that I was best at stalking Chicken of the Sea with my can opener. In New York, the only people who fish are the police, dredging the East River for bodies.

Seattle has real fish, not ugly carp that live on industrial wastes and old shoes. Pele's bodyguard Pedro found a secluded dock where Pele and I spent a lazy afternoon sitting on warm planks, dangling our feet over the water, absorbing the peace and quiet. For the first time in weeks Pele was relaxed, leaning against a piling, his eyes closed as he inhaled the salt air.

On the way back, he talked of returning to the beaches in Brazil, of fishing, of his farm. "I will be glad when this season is over," he confessed. "It has been very hard for me this year. I am happy to see soccer grow. But I am sad, too. So much politics, so many people hurt." I turned to look at him. Behind the ubiquitous sunglasses, his expression was difficult to gauge. He sounded tired, ready to quit.

"Pele is the heart of this team," Franz had said a few days before over a beer. "Once he goes—how can a team play without its heart?" I might have grieved away all the relaxing effects of that afternoon over such a thought, but then Pele changed the tempo. As we drove into the hotel parking lot, he was singing at the top of his lungs. Some crazy carnival song, he said, about a big fish and a bright, happy beach.

Eddie's second game was almost my undoing. It was against Rochester and it started well enough. We got there on Wednesday and with Franz and George, I made the rounds of the local TV and radio talk shows and luncheons, hyping the game. I'm good at that, love talking about soccer and trading jibes with the local media on how I'm going to shut out their team. We devoted three days to that and practice. Eddie didn't arrive until two hours before the game on Friday night.

I was tying my shoes when he came into the locker room.

"You're not playing," he said abruptly.

"What?"

"Sorry I couldn't tell you before. I'm playing Yasin." With that he strode off to talk to George. I looked around and sure enough, there was Erol suited up and into his pregame exercises. Somehow he had known early that he'd be called on. I felt like I'd been played for a fool, running around doing all the Cosmos PR chores as though I'd be in goal, practicing, psyching myself up. All to sit on the bench like a chump.

I hardly watched the game. Sitting on the bench proved more lively, if unsettling. I heard from several rookies that Eddie had spent much of his first game cursing Pele and Franz from the sideline. It was apparent in training that he didn't care for them—perhaps he felt they were a threat to his authority. Whatever was bugging him, he let it all out during that game.

"Look at that bastard, he's playing like an amateur!" This about Pele. And for Franz: "He's out of position again, fucking hell, they call this man a professional?"

This was his method of working with two of the best players in the world, certainly the two best on his team, which tells a lot about the guy.

When the game ended in a tie, I noticed Erol motioning to his neck and shaking his head. I couldn't believe it. He was asking to be taken out. If he was injured, it was certainly slight; and he was violating a very strong point of honor among goalkeepers. Even if you are in considerable pain, you try to play the shootout or the penalty shot, rather than dump your burden on the next man.

"Get in there," Eddie said; and like a thundercloud, I took my place in the goal. I was angry and I did well, stopping three out of five shots. Unfortunately, our forwards only made one score at the other end and we lost, 2–1.

It was all too much. I ran into the bathroom, locked myself in a stall and cried for five minutes. This afforded some release, but later that night I was still tense and depressed. After a few drinks in the cocktail lounge, I was ready to talk about it. Spotting Eddie at a corner table, I walked over.

"Look," I said quietly. "You're new. You don't know me, and I don't know you. You do whatever you think is right, but it will have to be without me. I'm tired of being jerked around and I'm finished playing soccer."

I felt a hand on my shoulder and, suddenly, George was leading me outside.

"I know how you feel," he said. "Just take it easy. This is only a temporary thing, believe me. When we play at home on Sunday, you'll be in goal, you have my word."

My head may have been a bit muddled, but the message was clear. Eddie, too, had been pressured to play Yasin and the day's game had been his token gesture in that direction. He'd simply handled it badly.

The following day, as we walked to the baggage claim area in La Guardia, I overtook Eddie. "Listen," I told him. "Forget about last night. I had a few drinks, I was feeling frustrated. I'm sorry about what I said, and of course I want to stay on."

He nodded and managed a half smile. "Fine," he said, "I'm glad you came to me."

Eddie's the first to admit that talking to players is not his strong point as a coach. He just can't communicate. Even during practice he prefers to suit up to demonstrate a play rather than struggle for a means to explain it.

Werner, as team captain, had to go to him for information on meal money, practice times and hotel arrangements. Things became increasingly difficult. Eddie rarely showed up until several hours before an away game, leaving Professor Mazzei and George to run practice between games. If a player had a problem, personal or professional, Eddie was

219

unavailable; he'd be off "scouting a player" or simply "on business."

"I never thought it would come to this," Tony Field said on a bus ride from the airport. "We didn't realize how good we had it when Gordon was coach."

George was laughing. Eddie was a close friend, and he was aware of his communication problems. "Why do you think they called him the *tacchino freddo* when he played in Italy?" George said. "It means cold turkey."

The nickname certainly fit. In his days as a player in Italy, Eddie was a high scorer, much like George. But because he was loathe to embrace his teammates or display any emotion after scoring, the Italians called him freddo, cold. Soon after, they added a noun that described his style of play. Firmani ran and scored holding his arms dangling close to his body, giving him the configuration of a turkey. *Tacchino freddo.*

By the third week in July we were 13 and 10. Not great, but better than most of the teams in our division. We had a hot streak of sorts going at home with six straight wins. It was the road trips that kept our record so close to .500. But the NASL team rankings go by points scored as well as games won, and a spot in the playoffs was now a distinct possibility for our high scoring team. We were becoming more cohesive, and whatever his failings as a human being, Eddie was a fine tactician. Some of his changes seemed to help. When the Cosmos signed Carlos Alberto, a former teammate of Pele at Santos, Eddie gave him the sweeper position and moved Franz to midfield. Franz took the news well, though he seemed uncomfortable at first. After all, he had taken the sweeper position and made it an art form at Bayern Munich.

Putting Smitty back in the lineup was an even gutsier move because it signaled an attack by the press. Just the week before Smitty had grabbed a Rochester reporter by the neck and slammed him against the lockers for a stupid remark. So when Phil Mushnick showed up at practice after criticizing Smitty in the New York *Post*, he was a marked man.

"Morning, Smitty."

Smack. A ball slammed into the wall inches from Phil's head. And another, and another. Smitty kept catching the rebound, slinging it back.

"Come on, you fuck," Smitty growled. "I'm taking pot shots at you just like you do at me."

Sensing that trying to reason was suicidal, Phil slid along the wall and out of the locker room.

I couldn't share Smitty's dislike of Mushnick. If it hadn't been for Phil, I'd probably be in Harvard Law School pursuing torts. From the start Phil believed I was the better goalkeeper and he wasn't afraid to write it. Apart from the complimentary things he said about me, I like a guy with a sense of humor. After Erol had a few bad games, Phil wrote that when he appeared at Beckenbauer's signing, Erol went to shake Franz' hand and missed.

Of course the press has its share of dolts, who ask stupid questions. But the beat reporters, the regulars, generally know when and what to ask. Lawrie Mifflin of the New York *Daily News* has the tightest deadline. She gives me 15 minutes to towel off and then appears like clockwork. Lawrie is like a sister to me. When she was barred from the locker room early in the season on grounds of modesty, I went on strike and refused to speak to any reporters. The English players were horrified at a lady in the locker room. "You can always hide in the shower or wear a towel," I told them. Finally she was allowed in. From that day, South African Jomo Sono set world records for putting on his pants.

Paul Gardner, a transplanted Englishman who's been writing about the game in this country for the past ten years, was another special person. I don't agree with everything he says. In fact, I agree with very little of it, but all the players respect his knowledge. Even George admits, "He's the only guy who knows what he's talking about." I'm not sure George felt that way after Gardner wrote a piece critical of him. The next time he ran into Paul, George smiled and said, "Don't spit on the plate you eat from." In Italy, journalists are exposed to methods of persuasion. Lest you think this involves cement overcoats and wire neckties, rest assured the means are as civilized as gold watches and fur coats.

Our fortunes took a decisive turn that last week in July in a home game against the Washington Diplomats. In that one game, our level of play rose from acceptable to outstanding. True, Washington was a basement team. True, we were helped along by the support of a home crowd of 35,000. But there was something different about George that day. He was scoring goals. He was even helping other people score goals.

He played like a reincarnation of his former self. Eddie had given him more room to maneuver, moving Steve Hunt upfield, setting Pele a few paces back. The area in front of the goal became George's stage and the performer came out. He always did have a knack for reacting well to pressure situations, and with just three regular season games left, the squeeze was on to get into the playoffs. George thrived on the burden, scoring three goals on gift-wrapped passes from Hunt and Tony Field as we slaughtered Washington 8–2. How can you take a team seriously that calls itself the Dips?

After that romp and another one over Connecticut, we were hardly prepared for the brawl that constituted our last away game—also against Washington. By then we had clinched a playoff spot and knowing the Dips were not loath to plunge into their bags of dirty tricks, Eddie kept Franz, George and me out of the lineup. Pele, always aware of his impact, agreed to play anyway. He didn't want to disappoint the Washington fans who were coming to see his last appearance in their city. So, in front of the second largest soccer crowd in that city's history, 31,000, the mighty Dips set out to avenge their loss by kicking and stomping every New York player they could catch. The result was brutal, with three players ejected. At one point, Tony Field slipped and a Washington player, taking advantage of the fall, dug his spikes into Tony's back. Pele's reaction was swift and surprising. He decked the guy. The final score was 2–1 Dips.

We ended regular season play with a 16 and 11 record, George racking up five goals and two assists in the last six games. The only better record in our division belonged to the Ft. Lauderdale Strikers, another in the continuing series of NASL Cinderella expansion teams.

In the first round of playoffs, we had to dispense with Tampa. Remembering our last humiliation by the Rowdies on national TV, we were anxious and tense. Only Eddie and George were confident enough to predict we'd go on all the way. The rest of us fell into an eerie state of suspended animation. Everything outside soccer became peripheral. The playoffs always affect me that way. Once the championship becomes more than the abstract concept it is in June or July, it becomes an obsession. The trophy explodes into cosmic significance.

"There's too much riding on this," Smitty said to me in the locker room. "The pressure is incredible. A lot of contracts are up this season. If we don't win, we're gone."

There it was. The ultimate threat, unspoken but always present. Blow it in the clutch when any mistake is excruciatingly visible and you are gone. Every step, every shot counts. It's a nerve jangling, joyless experience. For Smitty, it was almost unbearable.

"I bust my ass for 15 years to improve my game," he said, "and I have to put up with all this bullshit. I used to be an idealist about this game but . . ." He jerked his head toward the other side of the locker room where most of the team was suiting up for practice. "Money means too much in there. This is not a tight team, and I'll tell you, if we play a team in the playoffs where the guys really care about each other, we'll get our asses kicked."

I couldn't quarrel. The Cosmos had over $8 million worth of world class talent, but we were bankrupt when it came to team spirit. There was just one hope for us, one man to pull it all together and that was Pele. Here was a man who had spent 22 years in professional sports and managed to find Smitty's bullshit-free zone, at least some of the time. "Let's do it for Pele," became the rallying cry. On the strength of that sentiment, we pushed ahead.

Pele knew his role. And in that first playoff game he responded with his best performance of the season. A mob of 57,828 screamed approval as he put in two beautiful goals. George added another and we won, 3–0. Four days later, we played Ft. Lauderdale at home.

Attendance had been astounding during the second half of the regular season, but before the Ft. Lauderdale game, soccermania reached fever pitch.

The Cosmos offices turned into a madhouse of jangling phones and ticket lines snaking through hallways. People claiming to be second and third cousins of Franz and George drove the ticket sellers crazy. Everyone on the team saw his circle of friends expand overnight. One morning at 2 A.M., I got a phone call from a former Wheatley High classmate. I hadn't heard from him in ten years. He needed a pair.

That muggy Sunday night, August 14, the craziness peaked. Five minutes before game time, Warner and I stood in the tunnel, listening to the crowd. It was like being inside a giant conch shell, hearing the roar swell in waves. The announcer began reciting the starting lineup.

"In goal, wearing Number One for the Cosmos, Shep Messing!" As I ran out onto the field, a strange sensation began at my neck and ended in my shoes. Thousands of hands were massaging me, patting me, carrying me across the Astroturf. For a second, all the traumas of the season seemed worth the price. Having 77,691 people cheering does strange things to you, especially when you're the only one on the field.

77,691. A sellout. The largest crowd ever to watch a soccer game in North America. The number 77,691 was ten feet high on the computerized scoreboard as the announcer continued. "Werner Roth, Bobby Smith . . ." Smitty came bounding over to me, his eyes narrow slits of pure enjoyment. "Listen to that," he screamed over the din. "All these people and the first three names they announce are fucking *Americans!*"

"Hey, check that out," Werner nudged me and pointed over to the sidelines. There, dressed in a white see-through shirt, white pants and sandals was artist Leroy Neiman. He had spread a blanket just off the synthetic surface and sat tugging the cork from a bottle of wine. Beside him, a young woman in matching white pants, a green tank top and a straw hat watched with interest.

"Now you know we're big time," Smitty cracked. "He's the guy who paints posters for Burger King."

I felt sorry for Ft. Lauderdale. The crowd must have intimidated them. How else could the great Gordon Banks give up eight goals? The Strikers defense was powerless against a supercharged attack by Pele, Steve Hunt and Franz. George had three goals. We played near perfect soccer. Players communicated, passes connected, plays unfolded. In front of the goal, Carlos Alberto turned back challenges as though he were swatting away flies. It seemed so easy, so effortless, when we played like a team.

The real battle was in the locker room after the game. It looked like the lounge of a glittery East Side disco, crammed with the beautiful, the famous, the connected. I signed shorts, shirts, arms and programs; and talked to journalists from all over the world. Naked, I watched the passing parade. You couldn't buy a towel down there; little executive offspring were carrying them off as souvenirs along with anything else that wasn't bolted to the tiles.

I was drying off with an old shirt when Warners executive Jay Emmett tapped me on the shoulder.

"Shep, meet Dr. Kissinger. Dr. Kissinger, this is Shep Messing, our goalie. He tells me he went to a lecture of yours when you were teaching at Harvard."

Henry Kissinger extended his hand, smiling.

"So? How did you find my speech?"

Figuring you should tell the truth to former cabinet members, I confessed I had fallen asleep. Kissinger laughed and continued along to the whirlpool room in search of Franz. He was quickly replaced by the familiar faces of Robert Redford and Mick Jagger appearing through the steam and bedlam. Ahmet and Nesuhi Ertegun, the Turkish stargazers, posed for endless photographs alongside their high rolling friends, corralling occasional undressed players to give the shots some authenticity. Noticeably absent was Steve Ross, who is not as publicity conscious as the rest. Late in the season he started coming to the locker room before games, just to shoot the breeze and wish us luck. The postgame festivities he left to others.

After such a heady start to the playoffs, our second game against Ft. Lauderdale was sobering. On their home turf they were transformed. Despite a driving rain they played with the brilliance that had made them the best in the division. We were stunned at the difference and it showed. With just six minutes to go, our opponents leading 2–1, into the breach stepped George Chinaglia.

A long high ball plummeted into the Strikers' penalty area. Smitty ran and positioned himself beneath it, then headed it toward the goal. A desperate race ensued between goalie Banks and George. With surprising speed, George steamed ahead and flicked the ball over Banks, then ran a tight semicircle around him to ram the ball into the net.

I wanted to hug him and I wanted to kill him. Thanks to him, we were still in it, but a tie meant a shootout. And a shootout meant it was all up to me.

I started pacing in the goal, calling up mentally the names of the Ft. Lauderdale forwards, trying to remember which had the better left foot and which the better right. Thoughts blurred. I called for a pair of dry gloves. I started getting nervous, when behind me I heard a reassuring voice.

227

"Steady on, lad, we'll wrap it up, no trouble." It was Keith Eddy. Although on the permanently disabled list from that groin injury, he was still traveling with us, still very much the competitor. Just as we had when he was still playing fullback, we went over strategy in the five minutes before the shootout began. This was all I needed to settle myself.

I couldn't have dreamed up such a situation. The playoffs, a tie, and just me out there pitted against five point-blank shots. In the other goal, a goddamn legend. Gordon Banks must have thought he was back in that 1970 World Cup game against Pele, so incredible were some of his saves in regulation time. But he proved mortal in the shootout. Steve Hunt and Jomo Sono drilled the first two shots by him while I blocked the Strikers' attempts, putting us up 2–0. All of a sudden, Pele rushed toward me from the bench barefoot, waving his arms.

"You did it, you did it," he yelled.

"Hold on, we haven't finished," I reminded him.

"I know. I have confidence," he said. "We will win."

Close behind Pele, came Eddie Firmani. He was screaming, "We won, we won."

I had to laugh. Pele couldn't contain himself and Eddie couldn't count.

"No," I told him, holding up five fingers. They have three more shots. We only have two goals. See?" I bent my fingers down one by one. "One, two, three . . ."

"Oh yes, of course." Red faced, Eddie trotted back to the bench.

Banks stopped the next Cosmos shot, tipping the ball over the crossbar. Now the Tampa forward, David Proctor, took his place in front of me, standing nervously behind the ball. He took a few steps back and cocked his leg, feinting a bit to the left.

I sensed the ruse and dove the other way, just deflecting the ball with an outstretched hand. We still led 2–0; one more goal would clinch it. Terry Garbett got it, faking Banks to his knees and chipping in the winner. We went wild. The Cosmos bench emptied and I was borne aloft, light as air, across the field on my teammates' shoulders.

The playoffs were simple after that: a sweep of the Rochester Lancers and the dramatic 2–1 win over Seattle in the Soccerbowl in Portland. The victory over Ft. Lauderdale under the most intense pressure had fused us together into a team, one that was destined to stay together only long enough to win the championship. Then the 1977 Cosmos, for those last few months the finest soccer team ever assembled in North America, came apart.

Warners had arranged to extend Pele's long goodbye into a world tour climaxed by a farewell game with his old Santos team in early October back in New York. It should have been a carefree month with the pressure behind us and a string of friendly exhibition games ahead. That's what it should have been, but it was not. The championship was just a momentary lull in the madness. Like a bunch of rowdy schoolboys who had scrubbed and smiled for their class picture, the Cosmos fell to scrapping once again. Our disagreements took on a cosmopolitan flair, tantrums in Tokyo, bickering in Brazil. It was Divorce, International Style. Once the tour and the farewell game were over, most of us would never play together again.

Arden made the trip to Japan; Pele brought Rose, and a number of other players also took their wives along. It was expensive, but most of us felt this was a global party we wanted to share with our families. And it was the end of our time with Pele. Everyone was prepared for a low-key affair, with a lot of sightseeing and shopping between

games and practice. There was no pressure for
starting positions since all of us, including Erol
and I, were playing alternate games.

"I won't have this kind of thing!" Eddie bellowed
vehemently so that the tips of his ears reddened.
As soon as we got to Tokyo, he had called a meeting in the hotel; he was furious about something.

"No wives," he said. "I'm coach and I say no
wives."

"But Eddie," I replied. "They're already here."

"No wives. Not while you're playing soccer."

Even Pele was annoyed. "We come all the way
to Japan," he said, "just for exhibitions, and we
can't stay with our wives?"

We did the logical thing and ignored Eddie's
dictum. Besides, his pettiness was quickly lost in
the hysteria surrounding our visit. When we appeared at Osaka Stadium, there were 27,000 people
in the stands. For a practice.

"It is their last chance to see Pele," our guide
explained. "He is very much revered here." We
were amazed, gaping like the tourists we were,
taking pictures with newly purchased cameras. It
made for an amusing shot, a huge battery of Japanese news photographers, aiming their lenses at
our lenses.

Feeling that all those people deserved to see
more than ball drills, Eddie set up a scrimmage
between a Pele Cosmos team and a Beckenbauer
Cosmos team, with some Japanese youth players
to fill out the ranks. When one of them scored a
goal, Pele ran up and shook his hand. A tremendous "oooh" escaped from the crowd. To acknowl-
edge this honor, the boy bowed in return.

Outside the stadium, and boarding the bus,
hordes of kids surrounded us, pressing on us bits of
paper, shirts and hats to sign. One guy followed us

for miles on his motorcycle before Rildo got Pele's autograph for him and handed it out the window during a red light.

The game itself was tumultuous. We played the Japanese All-Star team in front of a 72,000 standing room only crowd. If the Japanese are supposed to be a reserved lot, you'd never have known it that night. Every time Pele touched the ball, the roar was deafening, broken up every minute or so by the chant, "Pele, Pele, Pele." All during our tour, that one word sufficed as an international language. Of course we all knew of the adulation, but I couldn't help being stunned by the sheer force of it in this strange country halfway around the world.

Stranger still was our visit to Red China. Can you imagine what it's like to play soccer in front of 80,000 people, and not hear a sound except your own voices yelling to each other on the field. Later, a guide explained that there were periodic announcements over the public address system instructing, "We must have silence" or "A goal has been scored, you may applaud." The tour was an incredible education for us all. And once again, we owed it to one man: Pele.

While we were safely behind the Great Wall of China, the Cosmos office was under siege back in New York. Something the executives described as "faulty bookkeeping" had caused Pele's farewell game to be oversold. Irate fans turned up in droves at the Warner Communications building. Mail orders, it seems, had been accepted since early spring and checks were cashed. Three weeks before the game, Warners discovered that for a capacity of 77,000, they had sold 100,000 seats, give or take a few thousand. The office of the New York Attorney General was investigating this as a case of ticket fraud, and extra security guards had been retained after one Cosmos official received a threat on his life.

Arden went to the offices to pick up our tickets and came away shocked, having seen one of the scariest mob scenes of her life. "There were people in there crying their eyes out," she told me. "Others were refusing to budge. One woman was talking about chaining herself to the doorway . . ."

Only by massive refunding did the Cosmos avert retaliation from the outraged and the desperate. "Pele tickets," as people were calling them, were the hottest item in town. Rumor had it that unscrupulous ticket agents were getting $100 a pair. It was into this bedlam that we returned, to play out the final scenario.

The week before his farewell game on October 1, we had a few light practices at Giant Stadium. On Thursday afternoon, Pele gave me a ride back to the city. We sat in the rear of his limousine and talked.

"It's been an amazing experience," I told him. "You can't know what you've done for me, for all of us. But as you leave, I have mixed feelings about the game."

"What do you mean?" he asked. "You don't like playing soccer?" He grinned, and there was just the slightest tinge of mischief in his voice.

"Come on," I said. "You know what I mean. It's been lousy, all this craziness on the team, and the politics. It's all bullshit like Smitty says. I don't know if I want to play anymore. Maybe this will be my last year, too."

"No, no, no," he shook his head. "I know you love the game. I watch you. I can see, soccer is good for you. I know, it is hard, all this other thing. It makes a player sad, and very tired."

"How did you do it?" I asked him. "You've been in it for 22 years. You can't tell me the bullshit hasn't gotten to you. How do you stay happy?"

Again, the thousand-year-old smile. "Is very simple thing," he said. "First you must be a good person. You must be able to look in the mirror, no matter what, and be happy with the man you see. Then, you must remember the beautiful game. Never, never let it become business to you. Stay as a child who loves the game. Let the other men have the business, worry for the money, the tickets. You play. Rise on top of everything else, remember when it all finish, is still a game. If you love it, if you are happy with Shep, it will be okay."

The limousine slid out of the Lincoln tunnel, and into the neon glare of Manhattan. We rode in silence as Aziz, Pele's driver, negotiated the midtown traffic. When he dropped me off, Pele clasped both my hands. "You will see," he told me, smiling. "I know you will see."

I didn't want Saturday to come. But it did, all too quickly, and I found myself standing in the locker room before the game, part of a tight circle gathered around Pele. Werner had just given him a plaque, with all our names on it, and these words: "To Pele, the soccer player, and Edson do Nascimento, the man. Thank you."

A small thing. But he thanked us, and then produced a little red box of his own.

"I have a present for all of you, too," he said. "You have all made a dream come true for me. Always, I carry you in my heart." He walked around the circle, talking to each of us, and into each hand, he pressed a small silver medal, engraved with our name, and a likeness of him. When we took the field, I was almost glad it was raining. For tears were running down my face.

I stood in the team lineup just off the center of the field which was ringed with scores of wide-eyed kids from local youth teams. Though it was pouring, 75,000 people filled the stands. I looked over at the TV monitor on the sideline a few feet away, and saw some familiar faces as the camera panned the sheltered VIP section.

"Oh God," Smitty moaned. "I see Diane Keaton up there. Think she'll come to the locker room later?"

My laugh was swallowed up by the roar as Pele came running from the tunnel at the far end. The chant rumbled up one last time "PELE, PELE, PELE." He made a slow circle around the field, stepping sideways as he often did so that everyone could see his face. Against the dark sky, the flash bulbs looked like unremitting lightning. Then the tributes began.

Dressed all in black, Muhammed Ali strode up to the podium, said a few words, and did an amazing thing. The Greatest hugged Pele and cried. I took a few steps forward, disbelieving. Next, the small, balding man who was the inspiration for all this—Pele's father—Dondhino.

I remember thinking how strange it was, seeing these two men from the poorest back streets of Brazil, embracing on this bright synthetic carpet. The TV lamps created a dazzle around them as they were reflected by the rain. It was like an aura, almost spooky. My reverie was broken when Pele leaned out of the glare to pick up a little girl.

He had taken it all with characteristic grace, maintained a smiling composure until it came to the children. They scuttled up in their baggy soccer shorts, shivering against the chilly October rain, to hand him gardenias, chrysanthemums. He spoke haltingly, choked up, fumbling for the right English.

"I want to thank you all, every single one of you," he said. "I want to take this opportunity to ask you to pay attention to the young of the world, the children, the kids. We need them too much . . ."

Tears were beginning to fill his eyes. I turned my face up into the rain.

"Love is more important than what we can take in life," he continued. "Everything pass. Please say with me, three times. LOVE . . . LOVE . . . LOVE."

Seventy-five thousand vocies formed the words that hung, reverberating, beneath the rain clouds. For a minute, Giant Stadium was filled until the sound dissolved, gently, like a rainbow falling away. I knew that if soccer gave me nothing else, I had been a part of this moment, and maybe that would be enough.

The game itself was an afterthought. Warners had set it up for Pele to play the first half with the Cosmos, the second with Santos. I agreed to split the game with Erol and had my choice which half to play. I opted for the first and the honor of playing with Pele for his last 45 minutes in a Cosmos uniform. Looking back, it was a mistake.

With 2 minutes 34 seconds left in the first half, the Cosmos were awarded a free kick from about 30 yards out. There was no question who would take it. The right foot lashed into the ball with such force that it carried the left foot with it and Pele ended up with both feet off the ground. The ball crashed into the back of the net just as Ernani, the Santos goalie, was starting his full-length dive. For Pele, it was the 1281st goal of his career. It was also the last. Pele would not score in the second half against Erol but he would have against me. The way I pictured it, Pele would come in alone on my goal with seconds remaining and hit a weak dribbler right at me. I'd wait until the ball was inches from the goal line, and then do what I always wanted to do when I played against Pele in Boston. I'd bow and let the ball roll into the net as time ran out. It didn't happen that way, of course. You're only allowed one such fairy tale a season and we had used up our quota winning the championship. Reality intruded and the Cosmos defeated Santos 2–1.

When the final whistle blew, Pele pulled off his shirt and handed it to his first coach, an old man named Valdemir De Brito. He took a final victory lap, miniature flags of Brazil and the United States held aloft in each hand, shouts of "Pele, Pele" cascading over him. Barechested, crying but smiling, he came running toward us. I looked at Erol, and without exchanging a word, we lifted Pele onto our shoulders and carried him triumphantly off the field.

9

"WELCOME TO SHOW BIZ"

December 15, 1977. As expected, my new Cosmos contract arrived in the mail. I eagerly tore open the envelope, like a kid on Christmas morning, and flipped through the pages to the bottom line.

$24,200.

I couldn't believe it. It wasn't even the minimum standard increase given to all players in the NASL, what they'd have to pay a third string reserve. Since they were no longer offering the $3000 apartment allowance I received in 1977 and overlooked my midseason raise of $5000, it actually amounted to a substantial cut.

I thought about that shootout in Ft. Lauderdale. I thought about the championship. I thought about the millions the Cosmos were still spending on foreign stars. I thought about the praise, the promises, the executive arms slapping my back.

I thought it stunk.

A month passed without a new offer. I was officially a free agent, the first in NASL history. To protect myself, I spoke to a few other teams. Two offered to double the Cosmos salary. Still, I had faith. I wanted to stay with the Cosmos. I wanted to stay home.

"Sure, we want you," Ahmet Ertegun told me. "There will always be a place for you here as far as I'm concerned. The only problem is Eddie. He's not sure you're the kind of player he wants."

Translation: Start shopping, sucker.

The deck was stacked. A fool could tell that, but I didn't want to believe it. My father and I kept negotiating with anyone the Warner front office made available. We bargained in good faith, they bargained to buy time and a new goalie. We met with Cosmos Vice President Rafael de la Sierra and General Manager Mike Martin.

"We'll give you $30,000, tops," Rafael told me. "On one condition." That condition was astounding. Eddie Firmani insisted on a behavior clause in the contract to insure that I wouldn't give the team any bad publicity by talking to the press. One "unsuitable remark" and I'd be "terminated." They wanted to buy the U.S. Constitution, at least the first amendment, for $5000, but I refused.

"Maybe they'd toss in $5000 more if I cut out my tongue," I said to my father. Later that week, Ahmet called to sweeten the offer by another $5000.

"No behavior clause?" I asked him.

"I can't guarantee that," he said. "Nor can I promise you that Eddie won't trade you as soon as you report to camp. It's all up to him."

I put in a flurry of calls to Eddie. He was out scouting, away on business, never in. Finally, I reached him and we met in his office. No problem, he assured me. Certainly, something would be worked out, and soon. He walked me to the door, his arm around my shoulder.

"I'll be in touch shortly," he said.

I never heard from him again. I only heard rumors. Eddie was in England looking for other goalies. Eddie was in Poland looking for some guy named Tomaszewski. Eddie was in Rochester, trying to sign Jack Brand. Eddie hates my guts. Some of these rumors reached the media. On February 1, sportscaster Dick Schaap invited me on his evening broadcast on NBC and gave this opening monologue:

In recent years, New York has lost a lot of gifted athletes. Tarkenton left, Namath, Seaver, Rod Gilbert and each time one of these athletes left I was saddened. . . . but I wasn't really angry. But now I'm angry because there's a report that the New York Cosmos are going to trade Shep Messing. Now outside of Pele and maybe Beckenbauer for his ability, no one has done more for Cosmos soccer than Shep Messing. Every time I was out there you would see Shep standing outside the stadium signing autographs. Shep was always available. He has done everything he could to make the game a success in New York and now that the game seems to be a success and was going to pay off, it looks like the Cosmos want to get rid of him and I think this is an outrage.

Schapp stopped and looked hard into the camera.

I think that all the people that have enjoyed his play, for whom he has signed autographs, to whom he had spoken, should do something about it. Write the Cosmos, call the Cosmos and keep them busy talking so that they can't trade Shep Messing.

The following morning, Ahmet Ertegun ordered the Cosmos switchboard shut down, forbidding the operators to accept any calls.

Wednesday morning, February 20, 1978. I popped awake to the shrill sound of a shriek from the kitchen. Arden came bounding up the stairs, flung open the *New York Times* across my bed. The headline said: COSMOS GET BRAND, STAR GOALIE. I rubbed my eyes and red on. "Coach Eddie Firmani, a man of many surprises, found another goalkeeper this morning. His name is Jack Brand and he is apparently destined to replace Shep Messing, who is definitely out of the plans of the North American Soccer League champions."

I crumpled the paper into a huge ball and threw it across the room. Arden looked shellshocked. Tears were starting in the corners of her eyes.

"Couldn't they have been more human?" she asked.

"Hey, come on," I said, reaching for her hand. "You know what it's all about. Welcome to show biz."

Five days later, I sold myself to the highest bidder. On February 27, I signed a contract to play goal for the Oakland Stompers. It was a new team, a new life, and a new salary record for an American player in the NASL. The night before signing, I scratched out a statement.

It went like this:

I love being an American, and I love playing soccer. Until recently, the two didn't fit together very well. But things have changed. Playing with the Cosmos, I had the privilege to see new standards set in the NASL. Playing with the Cosmos, I had the privilege to know

Pele and Beckenbauer and Chinaglia and Alberto. All of it has been a great education and a great experience. Something new, special and still fragile is being born, and though some people may inadvertently stunt its growth, I'm confident American soccer will grow and flourish.

I never read the statement. I didn't have time. After a few hurried phone calls from the press, I caught a flight for Oakland. Arden and I had to find a new place to live again. I watched the snowy New York airport dissolve beneath me, as the DC-10 banked, and headed west, into the sun.

Epilogue

"You're gonna love California," I said, speaking to my flight bag at San Francisco's International Airport. The stewardess gave me a careful look as she swung open the door. She couldn't and probably didn't want to know I was talking to Eddie and Ahmet, new members of my garter snake empire. They had come through the security X-ray unscathed and undetected—I think some states view airborne snakes as potential hijack weapons—survived the crumbs of airplane food I tossed to them, and now they were thrashing happily in their vented pillowcase as a violent rainstorm soaked me and my baggage. They just love wet weather. Not so for my iguana, Sam. Iguanas get grouchy about lying around in damp wood shavings. As we got out of baggage claim, Sam scurried about in his little cardboard traveling box.

Snakes, iguana, and luggage in hand, I was led by one suspicious chauffeur to a waiting limousine and off we sped to a chartered yacht in San Francisco Bay. On board I was to meet the press and answer questions as we skimmed elegantly beneath the Golden Gate Bridge. I had to hand it to Dick Berg, Oakland's general manager. He knew how to promote. Unfortunately, he didn't know how to forecast. It was raining so hard we couldn't take the boat out, so the press conference was held beneath the poopdeck. I huddled miserably as the questions began:

"Chomp any good glass?"

"Did you know The City has great nude beaches?"

I groaned inwardly. Glass-eating. *Viva*. I thought I'd left my iron-jawed narcissistic image behind two years ago. Nobody in New York asked those questions anymore. Guess the media stage coach hadn't reached the west coast. And I *had* created the monster. I smiled and endured.

"Was that really all you in *Viva*?" someone asked."

"Naw," I said. "It was my face superimposed on O. J. Simpson's body."

The boat was pitching. I was getting mediasick. Mercifully, the session ended after an hour. Berg handed me the keys to a yellow Lincoln Continental and I found my way to a large local hotel, my home until I found an apartment for Arden and me.

Inside the flight bag, the snakes were getting restless. I let them out in the bathtub for a little R&R, changed clothes and went off to the next round, a photo session at Mum's, the disco owned by Gene Washington of the San Francisco 49ers. I danced. I shook hands. I smiled. I had a rum and coke. Maybe three. Wirephotos across the nation labeled it a "training session." At 2 a.m.—5 a.m. New York time—I managed to slip away.

I was hungry and disoriented. I headed the Lincoln down a California highway and turned into the first place that looked remotely like home; a Jack in the Box. That grinning plastic face looked mighty friendly amidst the instant taco stands and bean curd health food joints. I picked up a burger and fries, like I'd done so many times on Long Island and sighed. Out of reflex, I swung the wheel left. All these places are built the same, right?

Wrong. There was the screech of pained metal, a jolt, an eerie floating feeling. I looked out the window. I was aloft. The huge car was suspended atop a 2 ft. high concrete island. They didn't have *those* in Long Island. Thunk. The transmission dropped out. Cool as could be, I picked the french fries off my velvet pants and eased out the side door. I left the car as it was, bobbing like some ghostly chrome galleon, and caught a cab. What the hell. Leon Spinks is not a great driver, either.

When I got back to the hotel, I hurried into the bathroom to tell my snakes the bad news. I had left their brunch, fat moths and wet worms, back at the Jack in the Box. I stopped short. No snakes. I spent the day looking for them. Nothing. By dinnertime, I decided I'd better inform management. They were not pleased. By late evening, service to my room had become spotty. Towels were shoved under the door. Food was passed to me on the run.

The story got out to the press and the hotel had a flood of cancellations. I felt terrible. That night I went on TV and swore that I had caught the snakes. I lied. For all I know, they're still nestled happily in some chambermaid's bucket. After a month or so, the manager informed me that the hotel was again able to rent what was judiciously referred to as "The Messing Suite."

This out of the way, it was on to serious business. Before I left New York, Reggie Jackson of the Yankees had warned me that I'd probably make more banquets than saves my first weeks in the Bay Area. No kidding. I gave speeches to women's auxiliaries, clinics to kids, kisses to Dolly Parton. I had my shirt off with Dolly (she didn't reciprocate), put all my clothes on when I modeled with

Cheryl Tiegs for a woman's magazine. I told her she was the reason I subscribe to *Sports Illustrated*.

I lost my mustache on a poker bet, drawing to fill a three-card flush, and looked obscenely clean for my first month in town. When I wasn't signing or posing, I wrote a weekly soccer column. Boy, this writing is easy money. I even hosted a daily TV show, *AM San Francisco*, for a week. I knew I had a name when it appeared as 41 across in a newspaper crossword puzzle. It was obvious I had a face from the ten billboards scattered across town. They advertised the Stompers but half the advertisement was me. I nearly got in a dozen accidents making U-turns on busy roads so I could see myself a second time.

When I had a free minute I met my teammates, a marvelously motley collection of six Yugoslavs, five Germans, four Americans, two Englishmen and one representative each from South Africa, Nigeria, Poland, and Israel. We tried to talk to one another. It was early Cosmos communications, all grunts and hand signals. I was honored by their voting me captain, but a little worried. Did that mean I had to make curfew?

After our first practice, I posed with four raggedy sheep, Berg's concept of me as the ShepHerd. I found an apartment right on the bay and thankfully, Arden arrived. She brought a pair of replacement snakes, and the club provided a replacement Lincoln. I got stopped three times for speeding. Once, the cop stuck his head in the car and peered at me.

"Hey," he yelled back to his partner. "This is the wiseass I just read about in *Sports Illustrated*."

I smiled. I oozed charm.

"Wait'll I tell my wife," he said, handing me the ticket.

Three weeks after my arrival, most people in the

Bay area knew my face. They had little choice.
Television, newspapers and Berg's billboards had
seen to that. Everyone knew who I was. Trouble
was, they had no idea of what I did. The sport of
soccer had become incidental to the thrill of publicity. As the home opener against the San Jose
Earthquakes approached, the promotional drum
beat louder until it became a circus parade. Berg
wanted me to make my debut astride a huge
stomping elephant. Get the symbolism? I declined.
Sheep is one thing, but I never did think of soccer
as a circus.

That last week before the April 2 opener, I
settled down and trained. It suddenly dawned on
me that those billboards inviting the multitudes to
"Come Join Shep" were promising some unspecified
wonder. On a lesser scale, I began to experience
something of what Pele must have felt when the
hope of American soccer was pinned to his jersey.
Pele had the poise of three World Cups behind him,
but this great American hope could very well fall
on his ass.

On opening day I was nervous. Very nervous.
The front office had cast me as the savior. They
were making it clear that if I didn't walk on water,
the whole PR campaign—maybe the franchise—
would sink like a stone. I stood in the tunnel, sweating, until the announcer called my name. For a
moment, it was as though I were back in Giant
Stadium. The record crowd of 32,104 made as much
noise as 77,000 Cosmos fans. There were bedsheet
banners, posters of my face bobbing in the stands.
I threw myself at a few balls to get loose.

Mercifully, the whistle blew. The action began,
what there was of it. Near the end of the second
half, I had made six saves, nothing spectacular, and
the game was a lackluster scoreless tie. The crowd
was drowsing, when suddenly, near disaster:

Quakes striker Ilija Mitic was fouled inside the box and the referee signaled a penalty.

I had to think fast. A 37 year old veteran of international play, Mitic had never missed a penalty shot in his 20 year career. And he was the all-time leading scorer in the NASL. I ran up to the referee and sank to my knees.

"No. No Penalty shot. Please. That was no foul."

The crowd was screaming. The rest of the Stompers were laughing. The ref pulled a yellow card. The crowd screamed louder. I bent my head to his shoe tops.

"Pulllleeeeeeeeze." I beseeched him, wringing my hands.

"Please get up, Shep," he was muttering through the side of his mouth. "Enough. Please. Don't embarrass me like this."

"Okay," I said. I turned to defender Lee Atack and said, "We got this sucker in the bag." Then I trotted obediently back to the goal.

Mitic stepped up to the spot. Twelve yards never seemed so scant a distance. He ran at the ball, feinted to his right and hammered it left. I lunged. I'd read him correctly. As my arms closed around the ball, the crowd roared my name, old 41 across.

The rest of regulation was anticlimactic, a tie. Then, a shootout. I stopped four shots. Their goalie stopped three. The Oakland Stompers had their first victory 1-0.

The next day, the headline said it all:

SHEP'S SAVES SWALLOW EARTHQUAKES.

Opening day turned out to be the high point of our season. We were game enough but we suffered from the chronic ills that seem to plague any new NASL team: too many languages and too many styles. I got along well with coach Mirko Stojanovic, a former star goalkeeper who spent hours with me working on technique. I actually got better. But so far as uniting a team, Mirko had no chance. Every week or ten days, management was throwing a new Middle European at him. German midfielder Charlie Mrosko got off the plane in New York and said his only words of English: "I vant Studio 54." Atack, who once gave shooting instructions to a sideline photographer while awaiting a corner kick ("Get my good side") joined my all-time all-star crazies team.

I unintentionally inspired the team to grow long hair, beards and mustaches, but my captaincy didn't seem to inspire the defense and my goals-against average soared. "It could be worse. You could be back at Hofstra," Arden suggested brightly. "Think of yourself as a pioneer in the soccer wilderness." I did. I felt like a wagon train surrounded by Sioux. Still, I had few regrets about leaving New York. I didn't miss the politicians and rock stars in the locker room. By July, I wasn't even paying attention to how the Cosmos were doing, except to note who was in goal. What would have thrown me into a rage before only made me laugh now: Firmani was starting Yasin, my backup last year, after misinforming the world that he had hired "the best goalkeeper in North America," in Jack Brand. I felt sorry for Jack, having to deal with all that front office meddling. Still, I felt detached. The Cosmos were a migraine headache that had gone away.

Meanwhile, I threw my spare time into that exotic American experience, the California life. Ah, California. Land of the tuned in and blissed out. I opened another button on my shirt. I rapped with Earl the Jacuzzi salesman. I "got behind getting loose," as they say, but did not come unglued. No trips to the psychic supermarket to get rolfed, est-ed, TM'ed or primal screamed. Instead, I took up fishing. My mantra was "I got one."

Pele used to fish on road trips every chance he got. Once, I remember him hauling in a 3 foot sand shark through a motel window on the waterfront in Seattle. He looked ten years younger when he was that relaxed. I searched for my laugh lines in the mirror, saw none, and headed for a sporting goods store.

I bought a cheap pole, some cheap lures, and strolled down to the dock near our expensive apartment. My companions were affable winos who spent their nights beneath the pilings and their days baiting hooks and pulling on Ripple. We got along fine. They taught me to fish and anytime I caught one, they ate it.

I began to realize how relaxed, almost serene, my life had become. I was 3,000 miles away from the glitterati of New York. At first, I couldn't identify the strange feeling that was coming over me. Suddenly, I had it. The odd feeling could only be contentment. Maybe it wasn't chic, but it felt good. Oh, I still got a rise out of breaking curfew, but . . . could it be?

I think I was growing up.

In May, Stojanovic was suddenly fired and the *New York Times* wrote of his replacement, "Shep Messing has finally found a coach he likes." I had to agree. I was given the job along with Charlie Mrosko and Johnny Moore. Yes, indeed, Shep Messing, coach. Seemed like a great idea. I was delighted with my new position, inasmuch as it included the authority to set curfew, until the first practice rolled around. To begin with, I had to show up. It was a scene from my worst nightmare. I was the guy watching the clock to see that everyone reported on time. Worse, once they all arrived, I had to figure out what to do with them. Even more horrible, I had to do it with them. Calisthenics.

Drills. Windsprints. I was turning the wheel on my own torture rack.

Finally, we three player-coaches, as the program listed us, hit on a great idea: we would, once and for all, test that hoary dictum that discipline was the foundation for winning. We played one game with stringent controls, the next with cheerful anarchy. I am pleased to report the following results: after a regimen of strict curfew, grueling practice and clean living, we lost. With controls removed, we won. The quality of goals scored seemed in direct proportion to the number of beers consumed.

Following this notable experiment, I was ready to run a franchise. Tragically, I never got the chance. The Stompers hired a new coach, Ken Bracewell. I was not to be the Vince Lombardi of the NASL. As fate would have it, Bracewell was English. Nice, but English. For what seemed the thousandth time in my career, I watched the determined British style of soccer in collision with the rest of the world. Bracewell favored long balls and hard running; his players wanted to dribble and dance. He did not have time for a Berlitz course in Yugoslav and they didn't have time to translate team meetings. On the field, we were getting our asses kicked.

In the midst of all this, I came upon a great diversion: literature. The hardback edition of this book was published, and in each city we visited, I tried to make the promotional rounds—TV, department stores, radio. It was hectic but I enjoyed it until we got to Detroit.

Fitting, that in the Motor City I would leave my mouth running. I was in high gear during a morning talk show and I made a few imprudent comments about Detroit coach Ken Furphy, who had briefly coached the Cosmos. By game time, a local reporter had shaped my remarks into a vicious attack, as reporters needing a feature for their early editions are wont to do. So there was a little shoving match between Furphy and me before the game. And a little incident during the game when Keith Furphy, the son of the coach and a forward for the Express, tackled me and tore off my shorts. And there was another little piece of business after the game, which, incidentally, we won 4-3 in overtime.

It started innocently enough. I was posing nicely on the sidelines with a crippled kid whom I had met on the morning talk show and invited to the game. That's when I heard a torrent of obscenities. This was not nice. I left the kid with his mother and walked over to investigate. This was not smart. A half-dozen drunken bozos started screaming impolite things about me and my mother. Then they climbed over the low fence and started doing impolite things to me with their fists. The whole day ended on a novel note. We were all led away in handcuffs. After 15 minutes in custody, I was paroled to the showers.

Late in August, the team was getting more desperate and the billboards were getting more specific. "Watch Shep Messing Face His Former Teammates" was the latest promo, and everyone seemed determined to make the Stompers vs. the Cosmos into Armageddon. I was just as determined to keep it low key. It was a sure thing they'd blow us out, so why call attention to it? Besides, I had no quarrel with the guys on the team, just with the management. Oh, it would be weird to have Chinaglia thundering down upon me, odd to be on the receiving end of a Beckenbauer torpedo, but pro athletes are more flexible than most people think. Lord knows, I've had to be.

The Cosmos were on a western road trip. The night before our game, I caught up with Werner in San Jose. I spent half an hour trying to sell him on the wonders of the west coast.

"Play for us," I said, hardly a practical consideration. The Oakland owners had not entrusted me with their checkbook. But I couldn't think of many defenders I'd rather have between me and opposing forwards. Nor would I have minded giving a job to the greatest sweeper back ever, a guy who had to play out of position for the Cosmos. "Shep, you are lucky you left New York," said Franz Beckenbauer, entering Werner's hotel room. "We are winning but we have many problems. I am very unhappy playing in midfield. All my life I play sweeper, for Bayern, for Germany, in World Cup. For Firmani, I have to play midfield. He says it is better for me. This is crazy. Maybe next year I find a team that needs a sweeper."

The day before the game my least favorite coach and I met face to face for the first time in six months. Cameramen at the press conference trained their lenses on our tight faces. Firmani was asked what he though of me and his ears turned a faint pink. George, ever at his elbow, nudged a response from him.

"I wish him all the best," was all Firmani said.

I also went into my Ferdinand the Bull act. I just sat and smelled the flowers. Reporters tried waving a few red flags, repeating Firmani's remarks about me, reminding me that Yasin, not Brand, had taken my place. I just smiled.

"I love all the sunshine," I told them. Later that night I had a very real triumph. So what if it was childish. I liked it. I was walking through the lobby of the Edgewater Hyatt with New York News reporter Lawrie Mifflin. It was about 12:30 a.m. and we were off to meet some friends for a drink. I spotted Firmani with Cosmos general manager Krikor Yepremian.

"Don't you have a curfew, Messing?" Yepremian asked.

"I'm the captain," I told him. "I set my own curfews."

Firmani just shook his head. I really enjoyed the next three beers.

I should have had 12. The way we played the next day, it wouldn't have made much difference. We were an 11 and 14 team with a desperate chance for a spot in the playoffs up against a team that had spent the season making a mockery of the rest of the league.

Two minutes into the game, our defense dissolved like one of those no-name paper towels. Chinaglia came barrelling down the middle, the ball one step ahead of him. My first thought was to yell "Hey, George, it's me, Shep, your old drinking buddy!" Instead, I greeted him with a flying body block just as he was about to decapitate me with a point blank shot. Not a minute later, he unloaded a rocket to the far corner that I jackknifed left to save. On the fifth shot of the blitz, I wasn't so lucky. Dennis Tueart lofted a perfect corner kick and George headed it just under the left post. 1-0. I was thinking double figures.

"Appreciated your note, Shep," George said as he trotted upfield. At the beginning of the season I'd written to my friend, "Dear George: Kick ass this year. I hope you score 30 goals."

Of course, I hadn't expected him to score them all against me. But it was no time for nostalgia. No sooner had I recovered from George's fusillade than my good friend Carlos Alberto, who usually scores about as often as every eclipse, sent a beautiful right footed drive under the cross bar. Then it was Tueart. At half time the Cosmos led 3-0.

"Sorry about your defense, Shep," George grinned as we headed for the locker room. "Sorry you don't have one."

The second half was no better. The Cosmos were awarded a free kick from 20 yards out. Up to the ball stepped Beckenbauer. Nice, considerate Franz. The night before he had presented me with a special pair of goalkeeper's gloves from his friend, German national team goalie Sepp Maier. Savvy, competitive Franz. His shot was in my face before the Stompers could even think about forming a defensive wall. 4-0. The gloves hadn't helped. What I needed was a suit of armor. George ended the carnage with a stinging low shot. 5-0. Just before the game ended we caught a bored Yasin in repose to make the final score 5-1. I staggered into the locker room with the discomforting knowledge that I'd helped George gain the lead in his scoring race with Mike Flanagan of the New England Tea Men. George now had 29. I didn't send any congratulatory notes.

Not long after that our season was done. The end came not with the rush of a championship, but with the tired hiss of air being let out of an old tire. We didn't make the playoffs. I was prepared for a painful autumn of reading newspaper accounts of the Cosmos thrilling championship exploits. I could be a beggar with my nose pressed to the window of a banquet. But before I could wallow in any self-pity, I received an invitation to participate in the ABC Superstars, in the Bahamas.

"Hey," I said to Arden. "They've heard of soccer."

"You may find it incredible," she said, "but some people do consider you a professional athlete."

Professional indeed. Few athletes could have acquitted themselves so nobly on the artificial turf of network sport. There I was, with the likes of Earnie Shavers, Maurice Lucas, Doug Collins and Jimmy Young. I trained assiduously on pina coladas. I bulked up on filet mignon. And when it was time I charged out to play . . .

Golf. Anything Bop Hope can do, including telling jokes, I can do better. I stepped up to the tee in the driving contest for the first of my five shots. It was so quiet you could hear a swizzle stick drop.

Whoosh. My first shot moved the breeze and nothing else. Whoosh on number two. Titters from the crowd. The third time I got a piece of it. The ball fell off the tee. Try number four yielded a stunning five-footer.

"I can't stand this," I screamed. "I gotta have NOISE."

The crowd obliged with whistles, stomps and cheers. Thwack. Fifty yards. Dead solid lousy.

"Thank God for swimming," I said to Arden that night. I reminded her of my teen-idol days posturing in the Speedo tanksuit. Between swimming and bowling, a sport at which I claim some expertise from my boyhood days hanging around the alleys of Long Island, I collected enough points for fifth place. And if you think I was bad at golf, you haven't lived until you've seen Jimmy Young, the boxer, break a bowling alley with a right hand loft. He bowled a 66 without ever putting his fingers in the holes.

I left for New York feeling fine. Being treated like a respectable professional athlete was wonderful after a career peppered with tobacco cans thrown at me from the stands. And once I arrived in Long Island, there was another offer waiting: indoor soccer.

It was an intriguing concept and a better place

to spend the winter than a pool hall. After negotiating a few weeks (just to keep my skills intact), I signed to play for the New York Arrows, the local franchise in the new Major Indoor Soccer League. It's a totally different game—literally played off the walls in a hockey size arena. It's faster, wilder and sheer hell for a goalie. I figured I'd love it. The Arrows' press release called me the "Joe Namath-Vitas Gerulaitis" of American soccer and in keeping with such uptown status, I was introduced at a press conference at the posh "21" restaurant.

As I stepped up to the mike, I remembered. This was the place they had brought Pele to sign that $4.7 million contract five years ago. My contract had a few less zeroes in it, but they were billing me as the figurehead for yet another new American spot.

"I feel like a pioneer again," I told the press. "I've been around professional soccer as long as any American player in the game today. But I don't mind trying something new."

I paused, and trotted out one of my favorite banquet anecdotes. "I remember Pele's last game," I said. "The Cosmos other goalie, Erol Yasin, and I took him on our shoulders afterwards, and both teams, some fans—everybody—did a victory lap around the field. We got to the end and were about to put him down when he nudged me, 'Pssst. Shep,' he said, 'one more time.' "

ABOUT THE AUTHORS

SHEP MESSING is a soccer player, a former goalie for the North American Soccer League champion New York Cosmos, now playing for the Oakland Stompers. He's a Harvard graduate and has done a nude centerfold in *Viva*, modeled for *Harper's Bizaar*, *Vogue* and other magazines, done ads for underwear in magazines and for the U.S. Tobacco Company on television, conducts soccer clinics in high schools and colleges, co-hosted A.M. San Francisco for a week and has a fan club.

DAVID HIRSHEY is a feature writer for the New York *Daily News*, coauthor of *Pele's New World* and contributing editor for *Soccer Express* magazine.

Hey There Sports Fan!

We have something just for _you!_